Ed.
your work on
earth will be
greatly enhanced
when your work
hand in hand with
the hand. Just
just relax and put
the control in his
hands. Giving. Hands
having. God bless.
Joe.

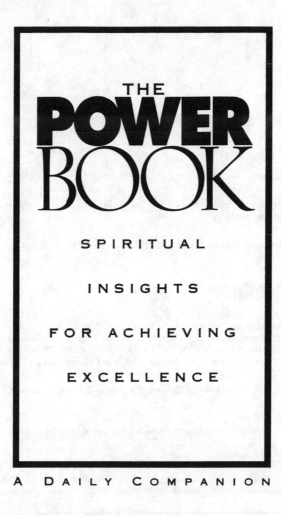

THE POWER BOOK

SPIRITUAL

INSIGHTS

FOR ACHIEVING

EXCELLENCE

A DAILY COMPANION

COMPILED BY
STEPHEN ARTERBURN

OLIVER
NELSON

THOMAS NELSON PUBLISHERS
Nashville • Atlanta • London • Vancouver

Published in Nashville, Tennessee, by Thomas Nelson, Inc., Publishers, and distributed in Canada by Word Communications, Ltd., Richmond, British Columbia.

Material from *Voice* magazine is used by permission.

Unless otherwise noted, Scripture quotations are from THE CONTEMPORARY ENGLISH VERSION. © 1991 by the American Bible Society. Used by permission. Scripture noted NKJV is from THE NEW KING JAMES VERSION. Copyright © 1979, 1980, 1982 Thomas Nelson, Inc., Publishers. Scripture noted KJV is from The King James Version of the Holy Bible. Scripture quotations marked NIV are taken from the HOLY BIBLE, NEW INTERNATIONAL VERSION ®. Copyright © 1973, 1978, 1984 by International Bible Society. Used by permission of Zondervan Publishing House. All rights reserved.

Library of Congress Cataloging-in-Publication Data

Arterburn, Stephen, 1953—
      The power book : spiritual insights for achieving excellence / compiled by Stephen Arterburn.
            p.   cm.
      Includes bibliographical references.
      ISBN 0-8407-9704-4 (cb)
      1. Businessmen—Prayer-books and devotions—English. 2. Devotional calendars. 3. —Success in business. 4. Success—Religious aspects—Christianity—Meditations. 5. Excellence—Religious aspects—Christianity—Meditations. I. Title.
BV4596.B8A77 1996
242′.2—dc20
                                                                                                                                    96–16779
                                                                                                                                    CIP

Printed in the United States of America

1 2 3 4 5 6 — 01 00 99 98 97 96

CONTENTS

ACKNOWLEDGMENTS AND DEDICATION

INTRODUCTION

CONTENTS

ACKNOWLEDGMENTS

My thanks to Rick Christian, who helped with the initial development of the project; Lela Gilbert, who worked tirelessly to turn an idea into reality; and Brian Hampton, whose editing made the material more powerful.

As always, I am very thankful for my relationship with Victor Oliver, who convinced Thomas Nelson that this material could change lives.

Last, my thanks to you for allowing me to be a part of your life and share God's power for successful living.

DEDICATION

To my nephew Chris, the oldest of four bright, loving, and very fun children. God has planted seeds of greatness within you, and they have been richly nourished by your father's and mother's love and dedication.

You are a bold example of the power one possesses when serving others as you have learned to serve. Please know that I am one of your biggest fans, watching from the sideline and cheering you on.

INTRODUCTION

The power of love. The power of positive values. The power of faith. These and other aspects of natural and supernatural power at work in people's lives have always fascinated me. When my life is filled with uncertainties and unanswered questions, my spirit is immediately lifted as others tell me about powerful interventions in their personal or professional lives.

In a similar sense, I've seen countless lives changed when men and women have turned to God for help with seemingly impossible difficulties. These individuals have received hope, direction, and wisdom.

Over the years I've collected stories of power that have been told first person, have been personally shared with me, or have been published. Some of these stories are about well-known men and women; others' names are not so familiar.

In the following pages I've put these uplifting reports together in a series of daily readings, with a weekly theme and an opportunity for weekend reflection. I hope that when you're feeling the most powerless, you'll remember that you can reach beyond yourself. With God's help, you will find the help you need. And I pray that you'll find it just when you need it most.

CHARLIE FAY
Vice President, A. G. Edwards Co.

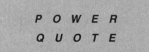

POWER BUILDER

POWER QUOTE

God's leadership in our lives puts the power of heaven to work in the midst of our earthly concerns.

SCRIPTURE

Proverbs 24:14

Wisdom is like honey for your life—if you find it, your future is bright.

A. G. EDWARDS COMPANY IS one of the largest investment banking firms in America. The company is more than one hundred years old. Charlie Fay's strong Christian faith has had a large impact on both his family life and his career.

After he saw his wife and a close friend healed from physical problems through prayer, Charlie's faith was dramatically deepened. He longed to take his faith into his workplace. He believed God was leading him to pray with every person who reported directly to him during an annual review.

He did that by talking about goals for the year and by saying, "You know we are so far from these goals that it would really take a miracle to reach them. Speaking of miracles. . . ." Then he shared some experiences about the power of God, and he asked if it would be all right to pray with the individual.

Charlie's view of power and success is insightful: "For me, success would be defined as having the love, joy, peace, power, and purpose of Jesus in my life. I can't define success in terms of dollars, or a certain position. . . . The key is to first recognize that Jesus is who He said He is. . . . Jesus must be Lord of your job. If He's not, it won't matter how much you've done, how much you've made, or how many people you manage, you will discover sooner or later that you are nowhere without Him."

POINTS TO PONDER

Executives at the top of their corporations are among the most powerful people in the business world. They hold thousands of lives within their sphere of influence, and they control millions of dollars with their decisions. "My kingdom doesn't belong to this world," Jesus said (John 18:36). No matter how powerful we become in the world's eyes, we are weak and needy spiritually, made strong only by an infusion of His Spirit and made wise only by His leadership.

POWER BUILDER

BEN BURTT

Filmmaker

Ben BURTT WAS THE genius behind the sounds in the *Star Wars* film series made by Lucasfilms. Academy Awards honored him for those films and for *Raiders of the Lost Ark, Indiana Jones and the Last Crusade,* and *E.T., The Extraterrestrial.*

As a college student, Ben learned from the world that "man is in control of life." Somehow Ben knew better, although at the time he didn't know much about God.

One day, while driving through a beautiful winter scene, Ben suddenly became aware that God was the source of every good thing in his life. Spontaneously, he asked Jesus to come into his heart and said, "Lord, You are running things, not me."

Ben enrolled in a graduate school program where he earned his master's degree in film. From there, his career began to soar. He went to work for Lucasfilms. Year after year he received accolades for his brilliant sound creations.

After winning his fourth Academy Award, he opened the car trunk, and the Oscar rolled out and shattered on the road. Ben picked up the pieces. God gently showed him that he had begun to worship a "golden idol." Humbled by the graphic parable, once again Ben Burtt relinquished his life to his Creator, acknowledging that power belonged to Him alone.

POWER QUOTE

Idols can be people, places, possessions, or positions—anything that robs God of His leadership role in our lives.

SCRIPTURE

Isaiah 30:22

You will treat your idols of silver and gold like garbage; you will throw them away.

POINTS TO PONDER

Most of us never intentionally search for an idol to worship—the process is far more subtle than that. We get involved in something we enjoy. It takes more and more of our time and attention. We hear applause for our efforts, and our identity gets tangled up in our success. The next thing we know, the true God begins to vanish from our consciousness. Our priorities have changed, and until He reminds us of His sovereignty, we continue in our idolatry, unaware that we have left our first love.

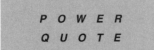

POWER BUILDER

WALTER ARTERBURN
Servant Leader

People have been seeking personal power since the snake first promised godhood in the Garden of Eden.

James 2:20 NKJV

Faith without works is dead.

MY FATHER WAS BORN into a family of hard workers who knew how to succeed. His mother worked in the cane fields making molasses, and I don't think she has stopped working yet—at ninety-five years of age! His father succeeded with a machine shop that fished broken drill bits out of oil wells during the oil boom in Texas. Dad owned Laundromats, dry cleaners, vending machines, beauty salons, and fast-food restaurants. While putting in his twenty years at Texas A & M University, he sold real estate in his spare time. One day, while completing a real estate contract for a couple, his glasses dropped down his nose, he fell to the floor, and he died of a massive heart attack. He died working, something he had been doing since he was a young boy.

My father didn't have a boss on this earth. He worked and lived for only One, and that was the One with all of the power of the universe. At his funeral, the preacher said, "In the life of Walter Arterburn, it doesn't matter if faith or works get you into heaven; he had so much of both." What money or power my father had, he placed in God's hands. He used it to help feed people living in one-room houses. He worked with prisoners who had contracted AIDS, and he took care of my brother when he contracted the deadly disease. My dad was a powerful servant who used what he had to share God's powerful love with others.

Earthly power can be very seductive because it seems to be under people's control. The power of God, on the other hand, is unmanageable. God is unimaginably great, and His will is beyond the scope of our minds. When we seek His power, we do so with the understanding that we must submit to His leadership. God is not under our control, but His mercy is everlasting, and His love provides everything we need.

POWER BUILDER

JACK DELONG

Businessman

WHEN A PSYCHIATRIST TOLD Jack DeLong that he was virtually beyond help due to alcoholism and mental illness, Jack wasn't surprised. His verbally abusive habits had wounded everyone around him. His family was in disarray. And his businesses had fallen into deep financial trouble following a change in tax laws.

Jack's wife began going to a Bible study, and before long she was praying regularly with a group of women. Jack was a prime target of their prayers. Jack's wife quietly said to her troubled husband, "Jesus has all the power."

Reluctantly, Jack began to search for some way to know the "powerful" God his wife kept talking about. Finally, after attending a Bible study for several months, Jack knelt and said, "Lord, I really messed up my life. I understand that Your Word says that You have all the power. So I am going to give everything over to You."

His family relationships began to be restored as Jack prayed with each of his children. His desire for alcohol was removed. His symptoms of schizophrenia vanished. He began to travel the world on lay missionary outreaches, during which God used him frequently to successfully pray for healing for people who were sick. Jack DeLong believes that his story is living proof that "when you see Him at work around the world, you realize that Jesus has all the power."

POINTS TO PONDER

The only thing that can prevent God's power from changing our lives is the power of our human will. He will influence us with His Spirit; He will encourage us through the words of other Christians; He will hear the prayers of our loved ones. But God will not take over the leadership of our lives unless we invite Him to. Once He does, we are amazed at His power and overwhelmed by His love.

POWER QUOTE

Have you asked God to take over the leadership of your life? If you haven't He is waiting for your invitation.

SCRIPTURE

Titus 2:14

He gave himself to rescue us from everything that is evil and to make our hearts pure. He wanted us to be his own people and to be eager to do right.

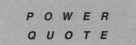

POWER BUILDER

ROBERT N. EDMISTON
Chairman and CEO, I. M. Group Ltd.

POWER QUOTE

When you wish somebody would share God's love with a person you know, you're most likely the one who is supposed to do it.

SCRIPTURE

Matthew 14:31

Jesus reached out his hand. He helped Peter up and said, "You surely don't have much faith. Why do you doubt?"

R OBERT N. EDMISTON IS a deeply committed Christian who believes that his power to operate a successful business comes from God. He writes, "An old boss of mine once said, it's not the length of experience that counts, it's the intensity. You can work 50 years filing papers and learn nothing, or you can work six months in an intense situation and learn a tremendous amount. I went through a very difficult situation at Jensen Cars. The company went bankrupt within nine months, and there I was, the financial controller. . . . My career was suddenly taking a downward dive. But God was able to snatch victory out of that, and it became my best learning experience.

"After the bankruptcy, I formed a little company called Jensen Parts and Service. From there, with 6,000 pounds [$10,000 US] we built a company in 17 years which was recently valued at something like $450 million.

"In business, there are many difficult decisions that have to be made. I endeavor to make each of these prayerfully. Jesus Christ is very much involved with both my life and my business. It is as if He were my senior partner."

Friday
Week

1

POINTS TO PONDER

God places godly people in high positions because He wants them to represent Him to others in similar positions. Each godly person has a light to shine and an area of darkness in which the light can be seen. As we look around, we are aware that no one else can speak to the people in our lives quite the way we can. God has placed us in power—in the earthly sense as we do our job and in the heavenly sense as we deliver our message.

TAKE A FEW MINUTES to record your ideas about what God's leadership means to you. What does He do? What responsibility do you have? Is He in a leadership role in your life today?

_____

_____

_____

_____

Weekend
Week

1

Lord,

You know how much I like to be in control.

You know it better than I do

because I try to hide it from myself.

But I want You to know

that You are the true Lord of my life.

When I get in the way, forgive me.

When I try to force my will on You,

don't let me.

When I resent Your authority and Your

strong, silent will,

help me to bow before You,

help me to worship You, love You,

and thank You for leading me like a Good Shepherd.

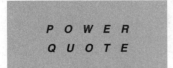

LOUIS PAPPAN
Restaurateur

POWER QUOTE

Generosity is an act of faith that says, "There is always more where that came from."

SCRIPTURE

Nehemiah 8:10 NKJV

Go your way, eat the fat, drink the sweet, and send portions to those for whom nothing is prepared. . . . The joy of the LORD is your strength.

Each year Louis Pappan hosts one of the world's largest picnics—he welcomes more than seven thousand older citizens to Pennsylvania. Participants travel from all over the East Coast to enjoy unlimited free food, medical checkups, entertainment, and contests in crafts, baking, and needlework. Employee volunteers from Pappan's thirty-six restaurants prepare the food, serve, and clean up.

Pappan also serves many nonprofit organizations as a board member, and he has raised as much as $400,000 for worthy causes. During the Gulf War, he served free meals to the children of American servicepeople. He supports local industries, and he sends a silver dollar to every baby born at the local hospital. Even a triple-bypass heart operation hasn't weakened his enthusiasm.

Twenty-year-old Pappan arrived in the United States in 1951 from Greece. He spoke no English and had less than $30 in his pocket. All he owned was in two battered suitcases. Today, he seems almost obsessed with gratitude and a desire to share the fruits of his success. He has touched tens of thousands of lives with his kindness. "Anyone can write a check," he says. "I'm only paying back what this country and its people did for me."

POINTS TO PONDER

What makes some people generous and others stingy? One explanation is gratitude. When we realize that the hand of God gave us the things we have, we aren't so inclined to greedily hoard them. Generosity assumes that there is an unlimited storehouse of blessings available to us, and that we can never exhaust it. Generosity is a practical way of saying, "Thank You!" It is our gift to Him and to the men and women who have shared with us, asking for nothing in return.

POWER BUILDER

FREDERICK RICHMOND

Industrialist

Frederick Richmond made his fortune in industry, and he always tried to share his wealth with less-fortunate people. He did so from a distance—usually by writing checks and mailing them. Then one night, his sense of generosity required him to become personally involved when he heard on the evening news that a forty-six-year-old father had been beaten to death by three hoodlums. The killers had made off with less than $0.50.

Frederick rushed out the door and drove directly to the man's house in Brooklyn. Unsure what he should say, he asked God to give him wisdom. He just knew that he had to get involved and offer help.

Frederick started a fund for the family, using the media to publicize their plight. The fund bought the widow and ten children a house, including an apartment to generate extra income, and provided an education for each child. Frederick Richmond's compassion and generosity powerfully changed the mother's and children's lives. And those traits deeply touched people who responded to their need.

Tuesday
Week
2

POWER QUOTE

We have been called to stretch out the hands of God to a lonely, needy world.

SCRIPTURE

Psalm 31:21

I will praise you, LORD, for showing great kindness when I was like a city under attack.

POINTS TO PONDER

A generous spirit is a wonderful attribute, but sometimes being generous requires an act of obedience. In Frederick Richmond's case, his obedience involved both his wealth and his willingness to inspire others to give. His compassion reflected the love of God to the heartbroken family he helped. Whether the gift is time or money, when we are stirred from within by an inner urge toward generosity, we have two choices: (1) we can choose to be generous, or (2) we can make excuses and refuse to get involved. If we are unwilling to give of ourselves, we often miss the greater blessing: "It is more blessed to give than to receive."

ELIZABETH FRY
Prison Reformer

SCRIPTURE

Hebrews 13:3

Remember the Lord's people who are in jail and be concerned for them.

ELIZABETH FRY FIRST VISITED the Newgate Prison infirmary in London in 1813. She recoiled in horror at the sight of such squalor. A few days later she returned to pray with the women prisoners and their children.

Mrs. Fry's courage in entering the prison was shocking to the guards—the women prisoners were reportedly more dangerous and hostile than the men. Elizabeth Fry was a Quaker and a quietly strong believer in God. She insisted upon entering the prison alone, which she did.

The mother of eight, she voiced her concern for the children's future. The women listened in rapt attention. Mrs. Fry went to work outside the walls of the prison and established a committee that provided a teacher. Soon a school was begun inside the prison with thirty children.

Elizabeth Fry's vision spread throughout England and on to Europe and as far away as Australia. Heads of state contacted her to organize similar schools. Mrs. Fry's love for downtrodden women and children launched a movement of prison reform. And through that movement, countless women and children have come to know Christ.

Wednesday
Week

2

POINTS TO PONDER

Generosity comes from our willingness to identify with less-fortunate people, whether they are in need because of unjust circumstances or because of their own failures. When we are willing to say, "There but for the grace of God go I," we are far more likely to be generous. As we face our weaknesses, we are more able to give wisely—not enabling others to continue to fail, but strengthening them so that they can eventually succeed.

POWER BUILDER

NICHOLAS GREEN

Organ Donor

NICHOLAS GREEN WAS SEVEN years old when his family took him to Italy for a holiday. Young as he was, the history of Rome captivated him. Then as the Green family was driving one night, robbers pulled the family off the road. Shots rang out. A bullet lodged in Nicholas's brain, and he never recovered consciousness.

The Green family was brokenhearted. The tragedy nearly overwhelmed them. They were far from home, family, and loved ones. But despite their grief, Nicholas's family had something to offer the people of Italy. Nicholas's life was gone, yet he was able to give life to others. In fact, while he was still on life support, his family made the decision to donate his organs to five desperately ill young Italians.

The country was stunned. News commentator Enzo Biagi wrote, "Although American values are often dismissed as naive by Italians, every once in a while we discover that your customs, your upbringing are not just talk, and that truly you believe in feelings." The power of the Green family's love for Italy was reflected in Nicholas's father's words upon receipt of a medal from Italy's president: "It would have been [Nicholas's] most prized possession."

Thursday
Week

2

POWER QUOTE

A generous spirit can be a profound statement of forgiveness and reconciliation.

SCRIPTURE

Matthew 5:7

God blesses those people who are merciful. They will be treated with mercy!

POINTS TO PONDER

Overcoming bitterness through forgiveness and generosity has the potential of healing everyone involved. And yet it is one of the most difficult acts we can perform. Although the entire nation of Italy had not robbed the Green family of a child, they could have chosen to generalize and hate. Instead, they chose to love. And in loving the five Italian organ recipients, they said, "We love you," to an entire country, including Nicholas's unrepentant murderers.

SAMUEL BOLLING WRIGHT
Philanthropist

POWER BUILDER

SAMUEL BOLLING WRIGHT WAS an expatriate American who relocated in Mexico near the turn of the twentieth century. Everything he touched seemed to turn to gold, even though he began his business by collecting and selling scrap metal. Within a few decades he owned and sold a $7 million steel mill.

But Samuel firmly believed in giving away half of every dollar earned. He was on his knees praying one night when someone knocked on his door.

"I need your help," Samuel's caller, Alejandro Guzman, said. He drove Samuel to some nearby slums where thirty men were sleeping on the floor. They were newly released from prison. He said, "They have no money, friends, or jobs. And there are many more like them. Their only alternative is to start stealing again. Will you help me help them?"

Ten years later, the buildings Samuel Wright had bought—a chapel, a dormitory, and training facilities—for Alejandro Guzman's men were entirely paid off. They became the Mexican headquarters of the Salvation Army.

When questioned about his generosity, Samuel said, "Why should I take any credit? Guzman's appearance at my door that night was an answer to my prayers. My mother taught me to help those who are less fortunate. . . . Aiding those people has brought me the inner happiness which is the secret of everything I've ever been lucky enough to accomplish."

POINTS TO PONDER

We should be aware of our motives when we give to others. Giving to manipulate, to influence, or to impress is not really generous. But if kindness to people who are poor amounts to lending to the Lord, we can certainly expect to receive what we invest—with interest. God will never overlook our generosity, even if at times those to whom we give do not fully appreciate it.

Lɪsᴛ SOME OCCASIONS WHEN you have acted generously.

_____

_____

Now write down some times when you probably should have been generous but weren't.

_____

_____

Weekend
Week

2

Lord,

there are times when I really want

to help others,

but I don't.

And there are times when I am generous

and wonder if I'm doing the right thing.

I need Your guidance, Lord.

Help me test my motives,

remove my selfishness, and

strengthen my faith in Your power

to take my talents

and use them to help others.

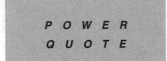

POWER BUILDER

SCRIPTURE

Psalm 27:1

You, LORD, are the light that keeps me safe. I am not afraid of anyone.

Monday
Week

3

WHEN QUEEN ELIZABETH II visited Nigeria in 1956, she laid a wreath at the gravestone of a Scotswoman, Mary Slessor. However, Mary did not go to Africa under the authority of the British Crown—she served a different King. The child of a violent alcoholic father and a devoutly Christian mother, she learned survival skills in the slums of Dundee, Scotland. As a young girl, Mary read her Bible faithfully. Because of her earthly father's violence, she was terrified of speaking in front of males. But she never doubted the unconditional love of her heavenly Father.

When she heard of Dr. David Livingstone's death in Africa, she was deeply moved by his plea for someone to carry out his work. In 1876, she sailed for West Africa. Many fears, the results of her traumatic childhood, haunted her. But one by one she overcame them, and she made herself a part of the African community. She cared for abandoned children, stood firm against abuses, and loved the African people wholeheartedly. When she was awarded the Maltese Cross, she kept it secret. After her death, believers sang "Praise God from Whom All Blessings Flow" in memory of Mary Slessor, who had found the power to overcome her nightmarish childhood and to reach out to other abused boys and girls.

POINTS TO PONDER

Instead of working through fear, we sometimes divert ourselves with activity or deny that we are afraid, even to ourselves. Faithful people are encouraged to fear God—in the sense of awe, respect, and obedience. But we are not to be afraid of anything or anyone else. Overcoming personal fears is a lifelong process. It is possible only in the knowledge that love is greater than fear and that God loves us deeply and dearly.

POWER BUILDER

EUGENIA PRICE
Writer

EUGENIA PRICE ENJOYED THE glamorous career of a successful radio writer. She had her own production company, and she was beginning to explore a lucrative future in television. Then she encountered Jesus Christ and accepted His offer of salvation. Through the friendship and guidance of a godly childhood friend, she was led out of a worldly and somewhat self-destructive existence.

Eugenia launched out in a different direction, landing a job as the host of a radio talk show called "Unshackled." The new opportunity delighted her, but some deep inner darkness troubled her. "I pushed myself doggedly through one 'Unshackled' script after another," she wrote. "I stood before hundreds of people telling them what Christ had done in my life. Night after night I forced myself to stand in pulpit after pulpit when I wanted to break and run for the nearest bar."

Eventually the truth became evident to Eugenia Price. Although she had genuinely received Jesus Christ into her life as Savior, her walk with Him had not been as godly as she thought. Pride in her own powers of persuasion had eclipsed His power. Struggling against the darkness, she tried to renounce her faith. Instead, she found Jesus "there in the room with me, waiting just outside my self-pity."

POWER QUOTE

Pretending we don't need help robs God of the opportunity to give us everything we need.

SCRIPTURE

Psalm 51:6

You want complete honesty.

POINTS TO PONDER

Too many believers have created a false self in order to appear godly. They hide their weaknesses behind an array of masks that reveal just enough failures to make them seem human. In fact, like most other human beings, they are struggling with disobedience and doubt.

Facing our hypocrisy can be a devastating experience. Like Eugenia Price, are we sometimes tempted to renounce our faith rather than reveal our true selves?

POWER BUILDER

POWER QUOTE

With God's help, we are responsible for our emotions—they are not supposed to control us.

SCRIPTURE

Psalm 34:4

I asked the LORD for help, and he saved me from all my fears.

Agoraphobia is an intense fear of being in public. Al Kasha had already fought his way through eating disorders, workaholism, drug abuse, and panic attacks when that phobia imprisoned him in his home.

At age seven, Al appeared on Broadway with Ethel Merman in *Annie Get Your Gun*. His brother Larry became a Tony Award winning theater producer, and Al's career was soon to be successful. He won his first Academy Award for writing the hit song "The Morning After." The award led to the worst panic attack he had ever experienced.

Al's battle with agoraphobia intensified, and he and his wife, Ceil, separated. In a rented apartment, Al popped Valiums and sat up all night, trying to figure out a way to get his life back together. He heard a television minister say that fear could be removed by having Jesus in one's life.

It was hard for Al to say the word *Jesus* because of his Jewish upbringing. But he finally got the word out and began to pray, then to weep, to confess his sins, and to beg God for reconciliation with his wife.

That night, deep in his heart, Al heard God speak these powerful words: "You are My son and I love you." His agoraphobia disappeared. He and his wife were reunited in faith. His new life of freedom from fear had begun.

POINTS TO PONDER

Sometimes inner panic intensifies even though careers are soaring, marriages are flourishing, and finances are multiplying. When we can no longer live with the agitation within our souls, we need help from outside ourselves. Like Al Kasha did, we need to speak the name Jesus aloud. He could calm the Sea of Galilee with a word; surely, He is able to calm the turbulence of our raging, stormy emotions.

POWER BUILDER

RUTH BELL GRAHAM
Wife, Mother, Author

"THE JOY OF THE LORD is your strength" is God's promise to His people (Neh. 8:10 NKJV). And few Christians have taken that promise more to heart than Ruth Bell Graham. Her colorful and very visible life has been interwoven with pain, loneliness, and difficulty. And yet she has chosen to cling to God's joy.

Although Ruth Bell's parents were hardworking missionaries, and her father was one of the finest surgeons of his time, the family came first. Ruth grew up in a home filled with music, laughter, and faith. As a young wife and mother, she longed to recapture the joy of that childhood household. But her beloved husband was called by God to minister all around the globe, and she and their five children rarely were able to travel with him.

She faced the children's growing pains with faith and courage, but not without an aching heart. Volumes of her beautiful poetry record times of despair along with overcoming hope and love.

Ruth Bell Graham continues to share her wit and wisdom. While her husband preaches to countless millions, Ruth reaches out, one by one, to individuals. Her body is weakened by degenerative arthritis, but her spirit is strong. Her smile is radiantly joyful with the joy of Christ whom she has made "her home, her purpose, her center, her confidant, and her vision."

POINTS TO PONDER

"The joy of the LORD" is an attribute we receive from heaven. It is both a gift and a choice. The Lord's joy doesn't provide constant happiness or shallow amusement. Rather, it is a deep awareness that we are His, and that eternal life is ours.

POWER QUOTE

Joy is not a natural high; it is a supernatural empowerment.

SCRIPTURE

Psalm 37:18

Those who obey the LORD are daily in his care, and what he has given them will be theirs forever.

DENNIS CONNOLLY

Prisoner

POWER BUILDER

POWER QUOTE

No matter how great our hurts or fears, they shrink in the presence of God's forgiving love.

SCRIPTURE

Proverbs 27:5

A truly good friend will openly correct you.

WHILE SERVING A LENGTHY prison sentence, Dennis Connolly began to sense, by reading the Bible and good literature, that he wanted more of God's love in his life. And he gradually began to see that his family needed to be reconciled.

Twelve years had passed since he had seen or heard from his mother, father, sister, or brother. Dennis said, "I prayed to God in the name of Jesus Christ that if it was His will to bring my family together, it would come about through Him."

First, he spoke on the phone to his mother, who told him his father had died. Next, he heard from his sister, who wrote him an angry letter, listing past offenses. Before long, the two brothers were communicating on a weekly basis. Then, the sister and mother went to visit Dennis.

Dennis said, "All my prayers to see my mother and sister were being answered. . . . When I reached out to her with open arms, she ran up, embraced me, and started to cry. I cried, too. Then I saw my mother crying and reached out to her without releasing my sister. We were all crying. . . . Why not? We were all witnessing the birth of a miracle . . . Love!"

POINTS TO PONDER

It is so much easier to walk away from a hurtful past than to confront the issues. And our hectic, transient culture makes it easy for us to start over far away from the people and places we have left behind. But we discover that we cannot remove the past from our hearts—it is there to stay. And the only hope for true peace with the past is to face it at its worst and, with God's help, to seek to forgive, to be forgiven, to make amends, and to be reconciled.

WHAT ARE THE EMOTIONS that you struggle with most in your life?

_____

_____

What steps could you take to overcome those difficult emotions and find peace with God and others?

_____

_____

Weekend

Week

3

Lord,

at times my soul rages like an angry sea

with fear, anger, disappointment,

and other feelings I can't even name.

I need You to help me

move beyond my feelings.

Calm the anger and rage

within me,

and bring peace to those around me

with Your wisdom, guidance, and love.

MARIA GRZANKA
Overcomer of Illiteracy

POWER QUOTE

God's unfathomable intelligence determines that the time is right—then He acts with lightning speed.

SCRIPTURE

Matthew 23:12

If you put yourself above others, you will be put down. But if you humble yourself, you will be honored.

MARIA GRZANKA WAS SEVEN years old when she began her lifelong struggle with literacy. Every day at school, she was ordered to stand and read. Terrified, Maria got up and hoped the words on the page would make sense. When they didn't, her teacher locked her in a closet.

One night when she was eleven, Maria dug a ditch in the backyard, climbed into it with her schoolbooks, and said, "Please, God, kill me or make a miracle! Make me able to read."

It seemed that God had not heard her prayer. Maria married and had children of her own. She became angry when her sons and daughters were unable to read; she secretly hoped they would teach her, but she realized they, too, were caught in a cycle of illiteracy.

Then a TV announcement made her aware of a local literacy program. She signed up with a volunteer tutor and began to study. Before long, her children joined her. Their grades improved, and Maria's self-esteem grew dramatically. She even found enough courage to go back to her old high school and speak to the students about the importance of reading. Sitting in the audience was Maria's proud daughter. Maria realized that the cycle of illiteracy had been broken, and that a thirty-year-old prayer had finally been answered.

Monday
Week

4

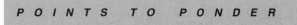

POINTS TO PONDER

We often speak to God during times of great emotion. Then when we don't experience immediate results, we assume He either didn't hear us or didn't care about us. We often fail to consider His view of our lives—His infinite perspective—and His refusal to become entrapped by our sense of the immediate. God is an eternal Being who operates on an eternal schedule. He heard Maria Grzanka's childhood prayer, and He answered it when it was the perfect moment to bless her—and her children.

POWER BUILDER

JACK FROST

Fisherman and Fisher of Men

Jack Frost grew up near the ocean in Florida, and he wanted to be a fisherman. By the time he was twenty-four, he had married and was making a good living by fishing. But fishing didn't satisfy Jack's deepest longings, and it certainly wasn't rewarding enough to distract him from his drug habit.

When Jack and his wife became Christians, they believed that God was leading them into full-time ministry with the Salvation Army so they could share their new life in Christ with others. The only thing stopping them was a seemingly insurmountable burden of debt.

"Lord," Jack prayed, "we have to pay the I.R.S., live for the next eight months, and come up with $12,000 for school by August. But I'm willing if You're willing."

Tuesday

Week

4

The next day, Jack went to sea. He put on the automatic pilot and feel asleep behind the wheel. When he woke up, he was directly over a remarkably fertile fishing area. Fishing the same waters for eight weeks, Jack caught seventy-five thousand pounds of fish and made $25,000. With the help of a $4,000 scholarship, Jack Frost and has wife went from fishing to being fishers of men with the Salvation Army.

POWER QUOTE

Nothing is impossible for God.

SCRIPTURE

Matthew 19:26

There are some things that people cannot do, but God can do anything.

POINTS TO PONDER

Sometimes we receive nearly immediate answers to our prayers, and the demonstration of God's power awes and amazes us. It's almost as if He answered the prayers before we asked Him. That is exactly what happened— He was waiting for us to come to an awareness of what He wanted.

RAY BARNETT

Founder, The African Children's Choir

POWER BUILDER

RAY BARNETT WENT THROUGH a personal and professional crisis early in his ministry. Born with dyslexia, Ray was ill-equipped to deal with the financial side of his work. He faced near bankruptcy, a situation aggravated by media reports implying that he was dishonest. He was heartsick.

Born in Northern Ireland, cared for by a foster family, Ray had never been able to locate his natural family. The unknown element in his life added to his emotional upheaval. From a seaside bench in Portstewart, the town of his birth, he prayed, "God, help me! If I'm on the right track with my life, I'd like to hear from You today."

Ray got in his car. On impulse, he headed toward Culmore Point where his mother was supposed to have lived. As Ray walked around there, a grizzled fisherman appeared. Ray asked, "Did you ever hear of the Barnetts?"

"Oh, yes!" the man said with a smile. The fisherman gave Ray names, addresses, and phone numbers for his birth mother, sister, and other relatives. Ray scribbled them down, barely having time to thank the man before he walked away.

Later on, Ray tried to locate someone in the community who knew the fisherman. How could he have known so many personal details? No one had seen or heard of such a man. He had apparently come in answer to Ray's desperate prayer. And he had brought with him the assurance that, yes, Ray was on the right track with his life.

POWER QUOTE

Angels are the messengers of God, sent to remind us of the good news that He loves us—no matter what.

SCRIPTURE

Psalm 91:11

God will command his angels to protect you wherever you go.

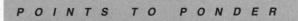

POINTS TO PONDER

When circumstances drive us to the end of ourselves, we are reduced to one question: God, are You there? By the time we reach that point, we are ready to listen, prepared to change, and willing to start over.

God is more than willing to provide necessary human solutions and practical answers. But He also sends mighty help to us through spiritual realities we cannot foresee or imagine.

POWER BUILDER

ANNIE BERNTSEN
Missionary

As A YOUNG MISSIONARY nurse to China, Annie Berntsen provided health care and hope to her patients. In fact, she was willing to sacrifice her life to confirm the truth of her beliefs to others.

One day, Annie and a Chinese colleague watched a procession move past them. "Take off your hats!" the two women were ordered. A group of men, carrying idols, explained that the women's straw hats would prevent the gods from sending rain to end the drought.

Annie straightened herself to her full six-foot height and said, "I cannot take off my hat as a salute to your idols . . . but my God can give you rain. Your idols cannot!"

Enraged by her words, the men threatened to kill the young women. Sister Annie, as she was known, stood her ground: "I promise you rain before midnight!"

At her mission, her elders severely reprimanded her. "If there's no rain, you'll pay with your life!" they told her in despair.

She replied that she believed God had called her to China and He would demonstrate His power. And she got on her knees and prayed. Just before midnight, Annie's door burst open. "It's raining, Sister Annie!" a missionary announced. "God has heard your prayer."

POWER QUOTE

When we are driven to intercede by God's Spirit, we cannot refuse to pray, and He cannot refuse to answer.

SCRIPTURE

1 Kings 18:44

After the seventh time the servant replied, "I see a small cloud coming this way. But it's no bigger than a fist."

POINTS TO PONDER

Would God answer a prayer like Annie's in today's world? First of all, He would consider our motives. Why are we challenging Him to prove His power? Are we trying to impress others with our spirituality? He will not honor that. Are we trying to play God by controlling circumstances that are beyond our sphere of influence? He will not relinquish His authority. But if God's Spirit compels us to pray that He will reveal Himself to others though His power, we can expect powerful results.

POWER BUILDER

POWER QUOTE

God hears the silent cry of your heart. Are you listening for the response of His still, small voice?

SCRIPTURE

Proverbs 9:10

Respect and obey the LORD!

This is the beginning of wisdom.

Billy Diamond devised daring escape feats and planned the "disappearance" of major buildings to enhance his career. But the only things that seemed to disappear were his money, his conscience, and his peace of mind.

Billy attempted suicide, but three days after taking a bottle of sleeping pills, he woke up, alive and amazed. Before swallowing the pills, he prayed, "Lord, this is my only way out. If You could just forgive me, if You could only get me out of my situation . . . I would perform my magic for the kingdom of God."

But it wasn't long before Billy forgot his promise. He headed for Hollywood, and his troubles followed him. Soon drugs and alcohol compounded his problems. He was on the verge of another suicide attempt when he remembered two things—his first attempt, when he promised God that he would use his talents for God's glory, and 1 John 1:9, which says that if we confess our sins, God will forgive and cleanse us.

Ultimately, Billy gave up his career goals. He entered a rehab program for his substance abuse, and he is now keeping his promise to serve God. He says, "Today I know beyond the shadow of a doubt that God wants me to use my talents for His glory. Why? Because He's changed my heart. I know there are no other gods before Him."

Friday
Week

4

POINTS TO PONDER

Sometimes we assume that God doesn't take our promises to Him seriously, so we pretend we never made them in the first place. Nonetheless, He listens to the smallest whisper of truth that can be heard in the midst of all our shouting—the tiny confession that we really want to do the right thing. It has been said, "Be careful what you pray for, or you'll get it." That is surely true when we pray for healing, for righteousness, or for eternal life.

W HAT DO YOU BELIEVE about challenging God in prayer? Jot down your thoughts on the subject.

_____

_____

Has God ever responded to your challenge? What happened?

_____

_____

Lord,

You are sovereign, and I am mortal.

You are powerful, and I am so limited.

I wait for You to act on my behalf,

even though Your timing seems intolerably slow,

and You seem to be ignoring my circumstances.

Give me patience, Lord, and help me understand Your timing.

I can't make it without Your help.

POWER BUILDER

RICHARD GONZALES
Real Estate Agent

Monday
Week

5

God's Word tells us the truth about Him, about ourselves, and about the way He does things.

SCRIPTURE

Numbers 23:19

God is no mere human! He doesn't tell lies or change his mind. God always keeps his promises.

RICHARD GONZALES HAS WON the Century 21 Centurion Award several times. To receive it, an agent has to close $150,000 in real estate commissions in one year. Clearly, Richard is a powerful achiever in his field, but lessons he learned early in life have given him a sense of God's power and the power of God's Word.

As a young man, Richard was caught up in what he describes as a "sin-sick, drug-oriented southern California lifestyle." He was finally confronted by his girlfriend Elva, who said, "This life is destroying us. Sure we have every luxury money could buy, but we are still miserable. I'm leaving!"

In his desperation, Richard turned to God for a new way to live. One day while trying to learn more about the Bible, he discovered Matthew 6:33: "But more than anything else, put God's work first and do what he wants. Then the other things will be yours as well." He felt led to take that Scripture as a promise. If he would focus on God, Elva would return. About a month after his conversion, she called, curious about his new faith. He insisted on taking her to church with him. During the service, she received Christ, too.

Richard Gonzales applies God's Word to his business as well as his personal life. His remarkable success speaks for itself. He has not been disappointed.

POINTS TO PONDER

God's Word is a living message to His people, literally "God-breathed." Those who read Scripture often recount the times when a particular message jumped off the page and spoke to their hearts.

Of course, He doesn't intend for us to use His Word like a collection of disconnected slogans that promise us everything we want. But when we sincerely seek to know God, the Scriptures provide clear guidance, warm comfort, and supernatural solutions.

POWER BUILDER

EDDIE KNOX

Politician

AS MAYOR OF CHARLOTTE, North Carolina, Eddie Knox kept a Bible on his desk at all times. He had grown up a Christian, and he sincerely tried to live as one. While a state senator, he worked to improve mental health care and the prison system. He attended Sunday school, and he sang with a gospel music witnessing group.

Tough decisions were part of Mayor Knox's job, and he soon learned that he couldn't please everyone. He sometimes flew off the handle instead of maintaining a reasonable attitude.

One day, Knox was appalled by a decision the city council made. He was infuriated, and he headed toward the council to set the individuals straight once and for all.

A devoutly Christian assistant caught Knox by the arm and said, "Listen, please." Then he stated a biblical passage that directly addressed the problem.

Peace returned to Knox in the nick of time. He confronted the council honestly but without hostility. He explained that he profoundly disagreed with their action, but he left it at that. God's Word had corrected his intentioned course and reminded him of his commitment.

POWER QUOTE

God's Word is powerful in our lives when we hear it, believe it, and obey it.

SCRIPTURE

Hebrews 4:12 NKJV

For the word of God is living and powerful.

POINTS TO PONDER

In a world that often speaks of personal empowerment, we may be tempted to take our personal power to the limit and force our point of view upon others. Our emotions may drive us toward behavior that goes against Christian virtues. A fellow believer brought the Word of God to Eddie Knox's attention, and it spoke to his heart, overcoming his natural reactions with its supernatural power. It will do the same for us when we devote ourselves to reading, studying, and memorizing it, wisely arming ourselves for the inevitable battles of life.

JAMES BRYAN SMITH
Seminary Student

POWER QUOTE

Head knowledge helps us understand, but only a humble heart can help us live a godly life.

SCRIPTURE

Hebrews 4:12

[The Word of God] discovers the desires and thoughts of our hearts.

As A SEMINARY STUDENT, James Bryan Smith went to a retreat at an Episcopal seminary. He was an eager student, having studied with world-class Bible teachers how to analyze biblical texts. James looked forward to meeting the monk who would assist him, but he was mildly disappointed with his new spiritual director. The monk had little to say; he told James to meditate on the story of the angel's annunciation of Christ's birth to Mary.

James quickly read and analyzed the passage. The next day, his exegesis did not impress the monk. He reassigned the passage and told James, "Read it with your heart, and not with your head."

James was bored and frustrated when he met his mentor again. The monk said, "You're trying too hard, Jim. You're trying to control God. . . . Read this passage again. . . . Open your Bible, read it slowly, listen to it, and reflect on it."

He was feeling defeated and at his wit's end. James's eyes fell upon Mary's words: "Let it be to me according to your word" (Luke 1:38 NKJV). He was challenged: "Could I—*will I*—say, 'Let it be to me'?" Could he relinquish the control? As he gave the power of Scripture back to God, James Bryan Smith found it descending from his head into his heart. He never studied Scripture again without listening as well as analyzing.

Wednesday
Week

5

POINTS TO PONDER

Knowledge and spirituality are two different things. Although understanding the Bible from an analytical point of view is helpful, God's spiritual power is unleashed in our lives only when we submit to His message. He has chosen to reveal Himself to humankind through His Word, and Bible study provides a firm foundation for knowing Him. But submission to God's power and authority activates true spiritual living.

POWER BUILDER

AUDREY WETHERELL JOHNSON

Bible Instructor

Thursday

Week

5

AUDREY WETHERELL JOHNSON WAS not interested in teaching American women. Her heart was in China. After fourteen years of service there, she had been driven out by Communist forces in 1950, and her heart was set on returning to continue her missionary work. But God had a different idea.

As a young Englishwoman, Audrey embraced agnosticism. And as she received an education in Europe, she began to doubt both the Bible and the faith. But personal unhappiness caused her to seek truth, and "suddenly God's mysterious revelation was given to me. I can only say with Paul, 'It pleased God to reveal His Son in me.'" Audrey's love for Christ led her to China.

Her health was not good when she returned to North America, and while she recuperated, she was asked to teach the Bible to a handful of women who already knew much about Scripture. As she sorrowfully envisioned teaching thousands of Chinese, the Lord gave her the verse, "For who has despised the day of small things?" (Zech. 4:10 NKJV).

At that moment, Bible Study Fellowship, a program for women across America, began. The program continues to use Miss Johnson's three key questions: (1) What does the passage say? (2) What did it mean to the people in the day it was written? and (3) What does it mean to me?

POWER QUOTE

God's Word provides us with objective truth—yesterday, today, and forever.

SCRIPTURE

Philippians 2:15–16

Try to shine as lights among the people of this world, as you hold firmly to the message that gives life.

POINTS TO PONDER

Studying holy Scriptures provides food for the spirit, just as eating healthy food provides nourishment for the body. Audrey Johnson's three key questions regarding Bible study guarantee a well-balanced diet for both groups and individuals.

BOBBY MAGUIRE
IRA Member

POWER BUILDER

POWER QUOTE

The Bible—from beginning to end—speaks of humankind's rebellion against God, and of God's forgiveness of humankind through Jesus Christ.

SCRIPTURE

John 17:17

Your word is the truth. So let this truth make them completely yours.

BOBBY MAGUIRE GREW UP Catholic in Northern Ireland. Even as a child, he hated the British Protestants who had, in his opinion, brought so much pain into his country. Once he was old enough, Bobby joined a junior branch of the IRA (Irish Republican Army). After involving himself in their activities, he was imprisoned for nine years.

Bobby participated with other inmates in the H Block protests. As punishment, the participants were locked up twenty-four hours a day, seven days a week. Their only clothing was a blanket; their only reading material was a Bible.

After thumbing through the Bible, Bobby went to Mass to ask the priest for materials to help him understand Scripture. The priest shook his head and said, "What you need is to open your heart to the Lord. Ask Him into your life, and He will open your eyes to His Word."

Bobby went back to his cell and did what the priest suggested. Suddenly, the Bible came to life before his eyes. He saw that Jesus was not just a man, but God Himself, filled with compassion for all people. Humbled, Bobby Maguire sought forgiveness. He gave up "the blanket" for a Bible study. He exchanged the power of human protest for the power of God.

Friday
Week

5

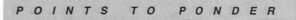

POINTS TO PONDER

The Bible is powerful when God's Spirit applies it to our hearts. Sometimes we read the same passage over and over again and find nothing of value there. Then all at once, either because we ask or because He seeks to enlighten us, the words are filled with meaning and power. The Bible was written by the Creator of the universe for all who will hear it.

Remember a time when God's Word spoke to your heart in a specific way. Write down the Scripture and how it affected your life.

_____

_____

Can you recall a passage of Scripture, perhaps a single verse, that has always been meaningful to you? Why?

_____

_____

_____

Weekend
Week

5

Lord,

Your Word is a lamp for my feet

and a light for my pathway.

Thank You for revealing Yourself to me

in the pages of Scripture.

Please open my heart and mind

to receive Your message to me,

and teach me the self-discipline I lack.

Cause me to make time to read, remember, and respond

to Your truth.

**POWER
BUILDER**

DIETRICH BONHOEFFER

Theologian

The only real peace we can
know lies in the heartfelt
declaration: "Not my will but
Thine be done."

SCRIPTURE

Revelation 12:11

They were willing to give up
their lives.

A CHRISTIAN DISSIDENT IN the midst of Nazism's insanity,
Dietrich Bonhoeffer grew weary of persecution by the Nazis and by his
Christian colleagues who had chosen to compromise with the Third
Reich's philosophy. After the infamous *Kristallnacht*, he was sick at heart,
and he set sail for America.

But Bonhoeffer was not at peace with his conscience. Setting aside
the threat of further struggle, he returned to Germany—sailing into, in all
likelihood, his own death. He believed that God had called him to be
involved in the reconstruction of Germany once the Nazis were defeated.
How could he participate in that process if he had not shared the trials of
the people?

Six years later one of the great theologians of the twentieth century
hung from a gallows at Flossenburg concentration camp. Before he died,
Bonhoeffer wrote, "Daring to do what is right, not what fancy may tell
you, valiantly grasping occasions, not cravenly doubting—freedom comes
only through deeds, not through thoughts taking wing. Faint not nor fear,
but go out to the storm and the action, trusting in God whose commandment you faithfully follow."

Monday
W e e k

6

POINTS TO PONDER

Our struggles with ourselves are often more dramatic than our confronta-
tions with others. We are designed and fashioned in the image of God.
And yet we are marred by the promise of the Eden fruit: "Ye shall be as
gods." On the one hand, we consciously desire to obey the will of God.
On the other, we are torn by our human will to create safety, power, and
pleasure for ourselves. Nothing short of submission to His higher calling
brings the powerful struggle to an end.

POWER BUILDER

RON MESSENGER

President and Chief Operating Officer,
Paracelsus Heathcare Corp.

THE JOB AS PRESIDENT and chief operating officer of Paracelsus Healthcare Corporation meant that Ron Messenger was in charge of one of the top seven health-care providers in the world. His family was doing well. His God-centered marriage to a woman he had loved since high school was without conflict.

Then in the 1980s, Ron began to experience symptoms of something most people laughingly call a midlife crisis. Ron was not amused. To his distress, he had to fight strange new cravings and an overwhelming dissatisfaction with all his blessings from God.

In the struggle between himself and his Creator, Ron Messenger asked, What is life really all about? Is there eternity? Do heaven and hell exist? He knew about physical health care, but he was about to learn God's way of dealing with his spiritual health.

He said, "God interceded in a powerful way to help heal me. . . . He wants us to be disciplined people—not only our bodies but our thoughts—directing our spiritual life in terms of getting back into the Bible, really trying to rely upon God as our source, our strength, and our direction. Nothing we have is ours. . . . We have to do for Him because of what He has given us."

Tuesday
Week

6

POWER QUOTE

God has promised to meet us in the midst of our greatest temptations.

SCRIPTURE

Revelation 12:11

Our people defeated Satan because of the blood of the Lamb and the message of God.

POINTS TO PONDER

Not only do we struggle with ourselves, but our contemporary culture warmly invites us to disregard the virtues that Christianity teaches and to pamper ourselves with pleasures. The word *sin* has been removed from the modern vocabulary. In our darkest hours of confusion and longing, we need to remind ourselves of God's principles and to cry out to Him for help. He has promised strength to keep us from falling, and forgiveness when we have failed to ask for strength.

POWER BUILDER

JACK ECKERD
Owner, Eckerd Drugstore Chain

Submission to God's authority provides hope, peace, and personal fulfillment.

SCRIPTURE

Psalm 1:6

The LORD protects everyone who follows him, but the wicked follow a road that leads to ruin.

JACK ECKERD WAS CONFRONTED by Charles Colson while working with him for prison reform in Florida. Colson looked the sixty-nine-year-old executive in the eye and said, "You businesspeople make all these tough decisions, but when it comes to something that will affect you for eternity, you keep sitting on the fence. When are you going to make up your mind?"

Eckerd had built two small drugstores into the nation's largest drugstore chain. To him, business was war, and competition sent his blood surging through his veins. The idea of submitting to God, giving up control, and loving the enemy wasn't particularly appealing.

Could he really give the credit for his success to God and submit to Him? Could he learn to love the competition he had always hated? Eventually, recalling Colson's challenge, Jack Eckerd got off the fence and gave his life to God.

He said, "I'm still competitive, whether on the tennis court or in the non-profit ventures I manage. And I still face the everyday struggle of giving control of my life to Christ. I've had to ask myself, 'Are you doing this because you think the Lord wants you to do it or because of vanity or ego?' Sometimes it's a tough call. But I know now that God is in charge of my life."

Wednesday
Week

6

POINTS TO PONDER

Releasing the control of our lives is essential to our relationship with God. It involves trusting an unseen Power with the things that matter the most to us. It means letting go of our own methods for success. And it requires submission to the divine will. This cosmic struggle ultimately determines the destiny of our souls. Are we willing to let God be God?

POWER BUILDER

HELEN ROSEVEARE
Medical Missionary

HELEN ROSEVEARE GRADUATED FROM Cambridge University with her medical degree in 1951. She was a strong-willed, self-sufficient Christian woman, who had once asked God's permission to serve Him as a medical missionary.

Her years in Africa were marked by both success and failure. Dr. Roseveare nearly single-handedly started a training hospital, and she taught the Congolese medicine. Although her desire was to spread the Christian gospel, her duties as a physician consumed her days. Her strengths were also her weaknesses—she had at times antagonized her fellow missionaries with her controlling personality, impatience, and willfulness.

During the war for independence between Congo and Belgium, she stood her ground. Eventually, she and her colleagues were captured by rebels. Dr. Roseveare was beaten and raped in the process, and she was held captive for five months. During that time, she shared the gospel with her fellow prisoners, and she comforted other women who also had been raped.

Dr. Roseveare's career was a continuous struggle between success and failure. But God met her in her most vulnerable, powerless condition and gave her the strength to carry on.

POWER QUOTE

When we declare ourselves powerless, God's unlimited power is unleashed.

SCRIPTURE

2 Corinthians 12:10

When I am weak, I am strong.

POINTS TO PONDER

One of the great Christian mysteries is God's extraordinary ability to use our weaknesses to His best advantage. While the world demands personal empowerment and offers countless ways of strengthening our bodies, minds, and wills, Christ insists upon being powerful in our lives in the very areas where we are weakest. He takes our inability to love and embraces unlovable people through us. He takes our failures and uses them, through us, to teach others His best lessons to us and to others.

POWER BUILDER

REGGIE WHITE
Professional Football Player

POWER QUOTE

The Christian life involves many battles, but Jesus Christ has already won the ultimate victory.

SCRIPTURE

Psalm 138:3

When I asked for your help, you answered.

REGGIE WHITE OFTEN SPEAKS at churches, schools, and youth group meetings. And he has been known as the "Minister of Defense" in the NFL, where he is an all-pro player.

He said, "Playing football for the Lord sounds like a contradiction to many people. . . . I'm aggressive on the gridiron because the sport is a reflection of my life. The Christian life is like that. In order to share Christ with someone, to take on the enemy and to overcome life's obstacles, you have to be aggressive. There is no room for wallflowers in God's army."

Reggie wanted to quit playing football early in his career. Other players were just as talented as he was. His first game with the United States Football League was less than auspicious. Yet despite his discouragement, he returned to practice: "I recalled the inspiration that Christian basketball players Julius Erving and Bobby Jones had been during my teen years. . . . My goal of being a role model for young people inspired me to tough it out."

Reggie's overwhelming presence on the gridiron is exceeded only by his powerful spiritual testimony off the field.

POINTS TO PONDER

Scripture frequently compares warfare with the life of God's people. Those who come to know God seeking only serenity and peace will be disappointed—Jesus made it abundantly clear that following Him would bring about struggle and difficulty. As Reggie White says, believers have enlisted in a spiritual army, and it isn't always a peacekeeping force. We have to ready ourselves for inevitable spiritual battles. God's power is available to us as we prepare ourselves with His Word, prayer, and obedience to His principles.

P OWERFUL PEOPLE OFTEN EXPERIENCE powerful struggles with God. Do you recall your most difficult encounter with Him? Write down your experience and the way it was resolved. What did you learn?

_____

_____

_____

_____

Weekend

Week

6

Lord,

You are sovereign and mighty,

more powerful than I can possibly imagine.

And yet, in some foolish way,

I think I can spar with You,

get my way, gain the advantage,

and pull my life's controls out of Your hands.

Lord, forgive my willfulness.

You know best, and You are able

to make the most of my limitations

as well as richly bless my strengths.

I'm letting go, Lord.

I trust You. I give myself to You.

I worship You. Your will be done.

DIETRICH BONHOEFFER

Theologian

POWER QUOTE

Obedience to God begins with an act of the will and is made complete by His empowerment.

SCRIPTURE

Psalm 139:12

But you see in the dark because daylight and dark are all the same to you.

DIETRICH BONHOEFFER WANTED TO see moral responsibility, unselfish concern for others, intellectual integrity, self-discipline, and personal commitment demonstrated in the Christian life. The rise of Nazism and the church's compromise of values in order to fit into Hitler's agenda appalled him and his family.

As the Nazis gained more ground in Germany, Bonhoeffer had to choose between a comfortable and politically correct church or a living relationship with the living Christ. The second choice was the only one he could conscionably make, but it meant loss of security, persecution and, potentially, death at the hands of the SS.

As the temptation to compromise increased, Bonhoeffer's commitment deepened. He was not concerned with the criticism of his brothers and sisters; he was concerned only with the approval of his Lord. His choice of spiritual power rather than political power ultimately cost him everything. Nonetheless, he preached from the depths of his heart: "When dark hours come, and when the darkest hour comes upon us, then let us hear the voice of Jesus Christ, which cried in our ears—victory is won."

POINTS TO PONDER

We know from Scripture that spiritual rebirth means that God has begun a new work within us, transforming us from the inside out by renewing our minds. Obedience requires us to do our best to obey Him and to cry out to God for help when the going gets rough. As in Dietrich Bonhoeffer's case, when the most difficult situation arises, our obedience will be complete because of our willingness to obey and God's willingness to assist us.

POWER BUILDER

A. C. GREEN

Professional Basketball Player

Where does Phoenix Suns star A. C. Green get the power to avoid the temptations that all too often overwhelm professional athletes? Green writes, "In order to walk a straight path, I follow a careful plan, including . . .

- Daily Bible reading and prayer. My first priority is spending time with Jesus. I rise early so I can read His Word and fellowship with Him.
- Maintaining close contact with my natural family and my spiritual family. When we go on the road, people are lifting me up in prayer.
- Speaking publicly about my faith. I love to talk about Jesus. Not only does it build up my faith and witness to others, it serves as a check on my actions.
- Remaining accountable to others. . . . It's necessary that I allow men to examine my spiritual life and stand beside me.

"Are you a man with the guts to stand for Jesus? Or will you be like those we see in our league, mouthing faith to the public while drinking and carousing in private? That is what Christ is all about. Developing men to be men. There's a big difference between being a man and being a male. You're born a male, but you have to choose to be a man."

Tuesday
Week

7

POWER QUOTE

Obedience to God requires determination, daring, discipline—and a deep longing to please Him.

SCRIPTURE

2 Timothy 2:15

Do your best to win God's approval as a worker who doesn't need to be ashamed and who teaches only the true message.

POINTS TO PONDER

Although the possibilities for moral failure in professional sports are formidable, we are all faced with similar choices. It is not enough to declare ourselves religious—our behavior needs to demonstrate our statements of faith. Jesus said, "If you love me, you will do as I command" (John 14:15). He was inspiring His people to become men and women who are being spiritually transformed into His likeness, imitating Him through love, not through obligation.

POWER BUILDER

POWER QUOTE

Put God first. Then come relationships, goals, and dreams. True fulfillment will follow.

SCRIPTURE

Deuteronomy 30:19–20

I am offering you this choice. Will you choose for the LORD to make you prosperous and give you a long life? Or will he put you under a curse and kill you? Choose life! Be completely faithful to the LORD your God, love him, and do whatever he tells you.

CHIUNE SUGIHARA WAS BORN on a day of new beginnings—January 1, 1900. As a boy, he cherished the dream of becoming the Japanese ambassador to Russia. By the 1930s, he was the ambassador to Lithuania, just a step away from Russia.

One morning, a huge throng of people gathered outside his home. They were Jews, who had made their way across treacherous terrain from Poland, desperately seeking his help. They wanted Japanese visas, which would enable them to flee Eastern Europe and the Gestapo.

Three times Sugihara wired Tokyo for permission to provide the visas; three times he was rejected. He had to choose between the fulfillment of his dream and people's lives. He chose to disobey orders. For twenty-eight days he wrote visas by hand, barely sleeping or eating. Recalled to Berlin, he was still writing visas and shoving them through the train windows into the hands of the refugees who ran alongside. Ultimately he saved six thousand lives.

Sugihara was not only a courageous Japanese; he was also a committed Christian. He spent his remaining days in Japan, humbly selling lightbulbs. When his story was finally told, his son was asked, "How did your father feel about his choice?" The young man replied, "My father's life was fulfilled. When God needed him to do the right thing, he was available to do it."

Wednesday
Week

7

POINTS TO PONDER

As we seek to obey God, one of our most powerful assets is a set of proper priorities. What comes first in our lives? Our world places great importance on personal goals, financial achievement, and powerful status because they claim to guarantee both security and self-satisfaction. As significant as these accomplishments may seem, however, we have to guard ourselves against allowing them to diminish our commitment to God and His righteousness.

POWER BUILDER

LANCE LAND
North Carolina Police Officer

LANCE LAND WAS MAKING a routine patrol one evening when he came across a car stalled on a railroad track. The frightened driver asked him to help her move the car. Her three-year-old son was still inside.

All at once the railroad signal bells warned of an approaching train. The bar swung down and landed atop the stalled car. Lance would have pushed the car with his patrol vehicle, but a line of cars had stopped in front of it because of a red light.

As the mother fumbled with the child's safety seat, Lance looked up to see the locomotive and its sixty-two cars thundering toward them. There was no way the train could stop.

Thursday
Week

7

Lance grabbed the front bumper of the car. He yelled, lifted, and pushed. The car moved only about three feet. By then the train was thirty feet away. With one last, desperate burst of energy, Lance moved the car another nine feet. The locomotive brushed against him as it passed.

How did Lance find enough power to lift the car? "It was adrenaline—and the good Lord," he explains.

POWER QUOTE

The way we live our lives today prepares us for the crises we may face tomorrow.

SCRIPTURE

Isaiah 64:3, 5

Your fearsome deeds have completely amazed us. . . . You help all who gladly obey and do what you want.

POINTS TO PONDER

Sometimes obedience is an ongoing process. But now and then it is an act of lightning-quick response. Instantaneous obedience might almost seem as if it was sheer reflex, as in the case of Lance Land. But a lifetime of commitment and courage had prepared him for his sudden reaction to danger. He could have given up in despair. But he responded to a higher call, and his personal power and the Higher Power that came from beyond himself overwhelmed the seemingly impossible odds.

POWER BUILDER

JOHN GRAHAM
M.D.

POWER QUOTE

It is up to us to obey God's guidance; it is up to Him to bring about the good works that our obedience makes possible.

SCRIPTURE

2 John 6

Love means that we do what God tells us.

DR. JOHN GRAHAM OF Shreveport, Louisiana, had a thriving ear, nose, and throat practice. One morning during his prayer time, a clear and startling message came into his mind and heart: "I am calling you to be a plastic surgeon."

Dr. Graham shared the unexpected challenge with his wife. Dr. Graham had everything going for him—professional respect, a lucrative practice, and a wonderful home and family. Yet when he told his godly wife what had happened, she said, "As far as I'm concerned, that was the Lord."

Dr. Graham returned to medical school and served a residency as a plastic surgeon. Eventually, he established a new practice.

One day he received a call that a four-year-old boy had lost his arm in a tractor accident. Dr. Graham prayed, "Lord, You have given me the training and experience for this operation. Now I submit myself to Your perfect will."

In surgery, the operating room staff held their breath to see if the color would return to the boy's arm once the main artery was reconnected. A faint pink blush brought a cheer to the room. The boy went home, his arm restored. And Dr. Graham had peace of mind, knowing his obedience to God's voice had made it possible for His power to rescue a child.

POINTS TO PONDER

A great challenge to obedience comes when we can't see any point in what we're being asked to do. As far as we're concerned, it makes no sense. God's guidance may take us in a different direction from what we expected. At first we may balk. But we are wise to seek the counsel of other godly people and to turn to His Word for confirmation of what we believe He said. When we have that assurance, only the task of obedience remains.

OBEDIENCE MAY INVOLVE AVOIDING temptation, heading in a new direction, or living up to the values you believe in. Can you list five times you have been required to obey God?

_____

_____

What did you learn from these five circumstances?

_____

Weekend
Week
7

Lord,

I want to be good,

but very often I fail.

I give in to temptations,

I take the easy way out,

I go after short-term gratification

and sacrifice long-term rewards.

Forgive my disobedience, Lord.

Continue to remake me

from the inside out

until I become like You,

obedient, faithful, and consistent.

KEN WALES

Film Producer

POWER QUOTE

Being committed to God's purposes means not giving up.

SCRIPTURE

Psalm 37:5

Let the LORD lead you and trust him to help.

*C*HRISTY WAS A MOVIE about a young girl who demonstrated sacrifice, humor, and compassion. But before the film was ever made, a story of sacrifice and faith took place behind the scenes.

Two decades earlier, Ken Wales read *Christy*, a best-selling book written by Catherine Marshall, and he dreamed of creating a feature film based on the book. Ken was both persistent and patient. The son of a pastor, he has a deep core of personal faith. And his commitment to the Christy project tested that faith to the extreme. Over the years, as he struggled to see his vision become reality, Ken mortgaged his home and exhausted his personal savings. He nearly gave up when he saw his investors devastated by the 1987 stock market collapse. All the while, he prayed for a miracle.

At last it came from CBS. The network agreed to air *Christy* as a movie of the week and to keep the spiritual centeredness of the script intact. Ken Wales, reflecting on his ultimate success, realizes that he kept the dream alive by faith. But only the power of God could bring it to reality.

Monday

Week

8

POINTS TO PONDER

Our commitment to God sometimes leads us to commit ourselves to people or projects. But when obstacles get in the way of our commitments, we may give up, assuming that our efforts are futile and we're locked into a no-win situation. Like Ken Wales, we may be called upon to give up a great deal on behalf of our commitment. It may cost us emotionally, financially, socially, and perhaps even physically. If our commitment is based on obedience to God, however, we must persevere to see it through. Faith promises that He—not we—will eventually bring it to pass.

POWER BUILDER

TSUI CHI HSII

Immigrant from China

W HEN THE U.S. MARINES left Tsingtao, China, in 1948, they left behind young Tsui Chi Hsii. The Americans called him Charlie Two-Shoes because that is the way his name sounded to them when he pronounced it.

Charlie had lived in the barracks and had learned to speak their language.

Charlie begged the marines to come back for him. They promised, with tears in their eyes, that they would.

Years passed, and Charlie was persecuted by the Communists, who claimed that his friendship with the U.S. Marines indicated disloyalty to the Maoist regime. He prayed, "I have no place to worship, but I know You are with me."

In 1979, Charlie got permission to write to America. But his address books had been burned for years, so he prayed that he could remember the addresses of his friends. He recalled three of them.

When the three marines received his letters, they immediately went to work to relocate Charlie and his family in America. They brought Charlie, his wife, and children to America in 1983. Today, the family operates a Chinese restaurant in Chapel Hill, North Carolina.

Tuesday
Week

8

POWER QUOTE

Commitments to friendship are gifts we give ourselves that last a lifetime.

SCRIPTURE

Psalm 31:23

The LORD protects the faithful.

POINTS TO PONDER

Apart from marriage, friendship is one of life's most lasting and rewarding commitments. It is based on more than promises—its deep connections have to do with mutual respect, common experiences, and love. In our highly fluid culture, friendships sometimes fall prey to the countless transitions of our lives. That is when commitment comes into play. And that's why stories like Charlie's touch our hearts—halfway around the world and a quarter century later, people loyally, lovingly kept friendship's commitment.

POWER BUILDER

ELIZABETH DOLE
President, American Red Cross

ELIZABETH HANFORD DOLE AND her husband, Robert Dole, have been called "the second most powerful couple in the country." But Mrs. Dole often speaks of a power that exceeds the political power she has gained. At a National Prayer Breakfast, she said, "Life is not just a few years to spend on self-indulgence and career advancement. It is a privilege, a responsibility, a stewardship to be lived according to a much higher calling—God's calling."

Elizabeth Dole began to respond to that calling as a young woman when she was drawn to the arena of politics. Her first federal job was deputy assistant secretary in the Department of Health, Education, and Welfare. Subsequently, she took on other positions, serving in every administration from the 1960s to the 1990s. She was secretary of transportation for President Ronald Reagan and secretary of labor for President George Bush.

Then, in 1990, Elizabeth Dole made a career change that reflected her inner pilgrimage. She became president of the American Red Cross—the first female president since Red Cross founder, Clara Barton. She once said, "I had to realize that Christ could not be compartmentalized. It was time to submit my resignation as master of my own universe, and God accepted my resignation." In response to His guidance, she began a new journey into a new area of service.

POINTS TO PONDER

Political clout can hold great power over an individual—the prestige, the ability to make things happen, and the control over important events can be almost intoxicating. Elizabeth Dole's story demonstrates her personal commitment to God's sovereignty and direction.

POWER BUILDER

**MICHAELA AND
AUGUSTO ODONE**

Persistent Parents

THE MOVIE *LORENZO'S OIL* brought the story of Michaela and Augusto Odone's son Lorenzo to the attention of the world. Lorenzo suffers from a rare genetic disease affecting his nervous system called ALD, which strikes only boys between the ages of five and twelve.

Unwilling to accept a "hopeless" diagnosis of their son, the Odones began to research the disease. Doctors were cynical. However, as Christians, the Odones had a sense of destiny: "We came to believe that God chose us to help find a cure. As painful as it was, we accepted that the hand of God put us on this path. When I asked Lorenzo if he was proud that Jesus chose him, he said 'yes' with his hands."

The Odones discovered information in an obscure Polish medical journal that led to their development of a cooking oil—"Lorenzo's oil"—that prevents the symptoms of the disease. Lorenzo's condition continued to deteriorate during the three years his parents researched the disease, although he has made some improvement. But boys with the disease who have undergone the treatment soon after diagnosis display no symptoms of nerve deterioration.

In the face of disease and discouragement, the Odones combined personal faith with a powerful sense of purpose. Their reward was the discovery of a treatment modern medicine had overlooked.

POWER QUOTE

We can provide faithfulness to a commitment; God alone can bring results.

SCRIPTURE

Proverbs 16:3

Share your plans with the LORD, and you will succeed.

POINTS TO PONDER

Do the commitments we keep always promise us happy endings? For the Odones, the results were mixed. Their son's health improved, but was not restored, and yet they were able to significantly help other youngsters with the same disease. They were committed to a task they believed God had chosen them to do. In that higher calling, they found success.

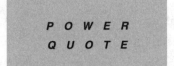

POWER BUILDER

HAROLD MCARTHUR
Farm Implement Dealer

POWER QUOTE

God never breaks His promises to us; He expects us to keep the same faith with one another.

SCRIPTURE

Proverbs 15:33

Showing respect to the LORD will make you wise, and being humble will bring honor to you.

THE CIVIC LEADERS OF Burlington, Colorado, could not find a doctor to settle in their rural area. They didn't want to rely on the federal government for help. Then Harold McArthur, age eighty-two, came up with an idea. "I've been lucky," he told them, talking about his farming equipment dealership. "I've made potfuls of money. . . . I like this idea so much I'll pay for it myself."

McArthur was willing to finance medical school tuition and books for two Burlington High School graduates who would promise to stay in the area after completing their education. McArthur, who came from a low-income family of twelve, was thrilled with the two prospective doctors. Sacramento Pimentel and James Perez were born in Mexico to migrant workers, and both had worked in the fields with their families.

Colorado State University awarded the young men undergraduate scholarships, and once they were ready for their graduate program, McArthur stepped in with his aid. The two young men agreed on a handshake to keep their part of the bargain by staying in the area. And Harold McArthur promised to see that the two young men were prepared to serve their communities as physicians—a commitment acted out in the power of good faith.

Friday
Week

8

POINTS TO PONDER

Is it really possible to do business on a handshake in this litigation-mad world? Sometimes men and women are inclined to promise the moon, their selfish motives masked by flippant vows and quickly forgotten reassurances. God expects better things of His children. As we represent Him in this world, our personal integrity becomes a treasure we offer to others. Our word, like His, becomes trustworthy. Our name comes to represent honesty and truth.

W

RITE A FEW LINES that describe your beliefs and your behavior with regard to commitment.

_____

_____

_____

_____

Weekend
Week

8

Lord,

sometimes my selfishness gets in the way

of my fair treatment of others.

Make me over from the inside out:

faithful, trustworthy, and motivated

by compassion and grace.

Please forgive me, Lord.

Help me to overcome my selfishness

and to submit to Your commandment

to love others the way I love myself.

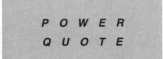

POWER BUILDER

POWER QUOTE

Regret and faith are incompatible. If we really trust God, we trust Him with everything—the good and the bad.

SCRIPTURE

Psalm 139:1

You have looked deep into my heart, LORD, and you know all about me.

A GUN SAVED THE life of Ruben Fuentes, an Austin, Texas, police officer. He shot a man who was pointing a .357 magnum pistol at him, saying, "Your time has come!" Ruben managed to knock the magnum aside, and he fired four rounds into the huge raging suspect. The fourth round killed him. The man's six-year-old daughter, hysterically crying, rushed to her father's side.

Although Ruben's life was spared in the incident, the act of taking another man's life deeply wounded his mind and emotions. Again and again he relived the horror of the shooting. The case was pursued in the courts. Four years later, Ruben's marriage ended, and he left the police department, weary in body and soul.

Ruben began to attend a Bible study, where he learned the meaning of God's grace and mercy. He began to realize that God had allowed the shooting incident for His own reasons, and unresolved endless guilt was futile.

Ruben Fuentes discovered that the power of prayer is greater than the power of a gun, bringing healing and hope. As he prayed for the family of the slain man, his own life was blessed by increasing opportunities for Christian ministry.

POINTS TO PONDER

No amount of sorrow can reverse tragic circumstances. But for believers, a sense of God's providence can help explain the unexplainable: "He allowed it for reasons of His own, and I don't need to understand." Sometimes, over the course of years, the reasons emerge, and we do understand. Otherwise, we are left with the task of trusting His wisdom and accepting His promise to work things out for the best.

POWER BUILDER

RED BARBER

Sportscaster

RED BARBER WAS WELL known for his intelligence and his varied interests. He wrote columns, guested on radio programs, and provided play-by-play commentary on countless Brooklyn Dodgers baseball games.

He recalled the challenges faced by the first African-American to play big-league ball. Jackie Robinson joined the Dodgers in 1947 only to be assaulted with bean balls, obscenities, and death threats. When Dodgers president Branch Rickey told Red he was planning to integrate baseball, Red first thought he should quit. He had grown up with strong prejudices, and was shocked by Rickey's idea. Then a deep sense of justice and truth overwhelmed him. He later explained, "All I had to do was treat Robinson as a fellow man, and broadcast the game."

Red Barber became a supporter of Jackie Robinson. Later in his life, Robinson credited Red with helping him win the heart of the Brooklyn fans. And Red felt Robinson had given him the gift of unprejudiced thinking: "If there were any thanks involved, I thank him. Jackie Robinson did far more for me than I did for him."

After Red's death, his friends remembered one thing he always said: "Our games or athletes have less importance than the wonders of God."

POWER QUOTE

Acceptance of the unfamiliar opens the door to learning and personal growth.

SCRIPTURE

Psalm 147:11

The LORD is pleased only with those who worship him and trust his love.

POINTS TO PONDER

People who overcome a personal prejudice set aside their own interests for a higher cause. Red Barber's prejudices from his upbringing could not steer him away from the greater causes of equality and human respect. And the wonderful, often unanticipated by-product of overcoming prejudice through acceptance is the learning process that follows. Acceptance of things we don't understand draws us into new levels of understanding, new experiences, and new friendships.

POWER BUILDER

FRANK PATTON, JR.

Crime Victim

POWER QUOTE

When we accept the work of God's Spirit in our lives, we willingly reject ungodly, unforgiving emotions.

SCRIPTURE

Mark 11:25

Whenever you stand up to pray, you must forgive what others have done to you. Then your Father in heaven will forgive your sins.

WHEN FRANK PATTON, JR.'S wife was kidnapped and subsequently murdered, his world collapsed.

Frank was, for a time, considered a suspect. No one except him had heard the brief phone conversation with the killers. Nobody had collected the ransom. Perhaps he had been trying to extort money from his own bank account.

But Frank was soon recognized for something else—his faith in God and the power it gave him to make it through the investigation, the apprehension of the real killers, and the trial. When asked if he wanted the death penalty for his wife's murderers, who were eventually convicted, he said, "My hope and prayer would be that these men come to know Jesus Christ and be forgiven and have their lives changed. . . . Who knows? Someday, we may all be in heaven together."

Frank Patton later wrote, "I suffered an awesome sense of emptiness, but also became aware of a spiritual consciousness that was not my own. God filled this emptiness in my heart with His love before it could be filled with hate. That is why I could do nothing but forgive the killers and express no hatred."

POINTS TO PONDER

When we are filled with a human emotion such as hatred, we have a choice. We can feed the hatred, allow it to grow within us, and use it to energize ourselves. Or we can choose to reject the hatred, love as God loves us, and express God's love to those who have wronged us. Frank Patton was robbed of his wife by greedy criminals. There was no reason for him to choose to love her killers—except for the knowledge that God forgives all sin and loves His children, and we are all sinners. That, along with the Spirit's empowerment, made it possible for him to accept love and to turn away from hatred.

POWER BUILDER

SHARON APPIER
Volunteer Counselor

SHARON APPIER LOST HER fifteen-year-old son to suicide. When she heard about her church's Hope Line, she thought the pain she had been through might be of help to others, so she volunteered to be a counselor. Six months later, her other son was accidentally electrocuted.

At first she thought she could never again counsel or encourage another person. After intense soul-searching, Sharon decided to return to the Hope Line. She took her first call, which wasn't anything particularly difficult for her. Then the phone rang again. It was a widow whose only son had just been killed.

Sharon's worst fear materialized. But rather than fall apart, she found within herself unexpected strength and wisdom. She cried with the woman and shared with her the pain she had encountered. Not only did she help the woman make it through the night, Sharon learned that she could handle the very situation that threatened her the most.

About her ministry, she says, "I believe God gives us the calls we need—the one we can help. No two griefs are exactly alike, so I try not to say, 'I know what you're feeling.' But I do tell them, 'I understand your pain.'"

POWER QUOTE

When we comfort others from the depths of our own pain, we sanctify our tragedies.

SCRIPTURE

2 Corinthians 1:3–4

The Father is a merciful God, who always gives us comfort. He comforts us . . . so that we can share that same comfort with others.

POINTS TO PONDER

Accepting our fears and facing them release us from their power. In Sharon Appier's case, the worst seemed to have happened—she had lost two sons tragically. She must have struggled with spiritual doubt. And she must have feared that if she began to talk about her losses, she would start to cry and never stop. But Sharon chose to confront the pain head-on. She put herself in a vulnerable position and used her devastation to comfort others. How could she have more eloquently demonstrated her humble acceptance of God's sovereignty?

POWER BUILDER

ERMA BOMBECK
Writer

POWER QUOTE

Acceptance comes before gratitude, and gratitude comes before joy.

SCRIPTURE

1 Thessalonians 5:18

Whatever happens, keep thanking God because of Jesus Christ. This is what God wants you to do.

WHEN ERMA BOMBECK LEARNED that she had breast cancer and would need a mastectomy, she was able to confront the situation with her usual good humor—until after the surgery. Then the reality of her loss began to trouble her. She cried every time she had to undress to take a shower, grieved that her days on the beach were over. She struggled with her reflection in the mirror. She snapped at her husband, "You just don't get it, do you? This isn't some little scar from a wart removal!"

When Erma visited her doctor for a checkup, he asked her what was bothering her. After hearing her grumble about her disfiguring surgery, he said, "I think it's time for my 'you're alive' speech. You're one of the lucky ones. Your cancer was small, and the lymph nodes are clean. Without regular checkups, you might not have been so lucky."

After that sobering lecture, Erma began to appreciate the power of gratitude. She wrote, "Every time I forget to feel grateful . . . I hear the voice of an eight-year-old named Christina, who had cancer of the nervous system. When asked what she wanted for her birthday, she thought long and hard and finally said, 'I don't know. I have two sticker books and a Cabbage Patch doll. I have everything!' The kid was right."

POINTS TO PONDER

When we are unable to explain the difficulties in our lives, we become frustrated and shake our fists at heaven, demanding *why*. In a sense, this attitude places us in judgment of God, declaring the things He has allowed to be unacceptable to us. Ultimately, if we are wise, we choose to "accept the things we cannot change." At that point, our eyes are opened to the blessings in our lives, and we are able to say, "Thank You," once again.

CAN YOU RECALL THINGS in your life that were difficult to accept? Take a moment to write them down.

_____

What have you learned about those things?

_____

Lord,

I know You are far wiser than I am

and Your ways of working

are often beyond my understanding.

But sometimes I struggle with

hurts You could have prevented,

injuries from which You could have protected me,

losses You could have restored, and

physical problems You could have healed.

Lord, I don't want to rebel against You,

so my prayer is that You will help me

accept those things, believing You know best.

Enable me to seek Your will.

Help me let go of my anger

and see clearly enough to thank You

for the many great things You have given me.

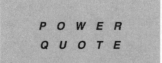

**POWER
BUILDER**

DAVID JACOBSEN

Administrator,
American University Hospital in Beirut

**POWER
QUOTE**

God's timing is perfect. He is in
control. And He never makes
mistakes.

SCRIPTURE

Ecclesiastes 3:1 NKJV

To everything there is a season,

a time for every purpose under

heaven.

ON A MAY MORNING in 1985, as he walked to work, David
Jacobsen was kidnapped. He and several other Americans quickly became
international political pawns.

A Christian at the time of his abduction, David and his fellow
hostages Terry Anderson, Tom Sutherland, Father Martin Jenco, and Rev.
Ben Weir formed their own ecumenical church—the Church of the
Locked Door, complete with hymns, liturgies, and Communion. David
eventually received a Bible for his exclusive use. Among other passages, he
clung to this one: "To everything there is a season." He knew God was
calling him to be patient.

One morning he awoke and vividly remembered a dream in which he
was set free early in November. As his faith increased, he recognized other
signs of God's presence in his daily life.

When David stretched out on his mat the night of November 1, he
firmly believed that his captivity was about to end. And it did. On
November 3, 1986, David Jacobsen was set free from his cell. His patience
had paid off, and he was released into a new life. He was a changed man
who had known the tender care of God through the worst of times.

Monday
Week

10

POINTS TO PONDER

Whatever the worst-case scenario may be, it, too, will pass. But we need
the emotional strength to weather a crisis.

Learning patience is more than developing a personal virtue. It is an
act of faith. Patience demonstrates that we believe in God's sovereignty.

POWER BUILDER

LEE BUCK

Insurance Executive

Tuesday
Week

10

WHEN THE CHAIRMAN OF the board of New York Life Insurance Company summoned him, Lee Buck's heart pounded with excitement—after twenty years of hard work, perhaps the promotion of his dreams was finally his. As he headed upstairs, he remembered that he hadn't prayed, so he stopped abruptly and leaned against the banister. "Okay, Lord Jesus," he whispered, "I've given my life to You and I don't know what's going to happen during this visit, but all I want is peace. I want Your peace in my life and I want to be in the center of Your will."

An unexpected lifting of his anxiety surprised him, and he walked through the chairman's door. "I want to make you senior vice president over group marketing," the executive explained. "Will you do it?"

Lee was stung with disappointment. Although it was the last job he wanted, he was calm. He threw himself into the new position, researching, restructuring, and praying. It wasn't long before he had raised both profits and eyebrows with his performance.

The chairman called again, five years later. By then, Lee had made a name for himself as a man who had turned around the toughest assignment in the company. When he finally got the senior vice presidency he really wanted, he was well prepared, and no one deserved it more than he did.

POWER QUOTE

Delay means that the power of God is still at work in our lives as well as in other lives and circumstances.

SCRIPTURE

Psalm 27:14

Trust the LORD! Be brave and strong and trust the LORD.

POINTS TO PONDER

How difficult it is when the long-awaited answer we receive is "No, not yet." We feel we have done everything possible to prepare ourselves for a particular opportunity. And the truth is, we probably have done everything we can do. But God hasn't finished *His* work yet. As people of faith, we are to submit our personal timetables to His approval and at times accept the "not yet."

THOMAS MURPHY
Chairman of the Board, General Motors

THOMAS MURPHY OFTEN RECALLED three separate detours that had prepared him, through hardship and frustration, for the extraordinary prosperity he ultimately achieved.

At sixteen years of age, Thomas had a backbreaking summer job in a Chicago icehouse. He futilely struggled to find better work. Tom's devout mother encouraged him, "The Lord is making you wait for a reason. One day you'll see." That hard labor convinced the impatient young man that a college education was worth the effort. After graduation, he went to work at GM.

Then came World War II. While separated from his wife and family, Thomas again wrestled with impatience. However, he had ample time to decide what to do with his future.

Ten years later, a lengthy hospitalization found Thomas fighting the old, familiar battle with frustration. Once he was well, he found that he had established a more loving relationship with his family.

Thomas Murphy wrote, "I think that the Lord gives us these waiting periods for a reason—so that we may use them as rest stops to learn more about ourselves. When we accept detours as signals of God's plans for us, He will show us eventually how to use them."

Wednesday
Week

10

POINTS TO PONDER

Seasons of unavoidable waiting are not unusual for people who walk with God. Scripture is replete with references to "waiting on the Lord." Clearly, when we submit to the sovereign will, we also submit to an eternal schedule. Our faith in Him is always strengthened when we wait. Waiting stretches us, refines our motives, and increases our patience. Waiting is part of God's transformative work in our lives.

POWER BUILDER

JACK FRIES

Christian Layman

JACK FRIES, A MAN with a heart for mission work, was about to go into a McDonald's. After reading a brochure about a ministry, he threw it in the trash. Then for some reason he picked it up and reread it and threw it away again. He said, "I had no idea that those few seconds would save my life. As I stepped up on the sidewalk heading toward the door of the restaurant, I was startled by a loud explosion in the restaurant and saw the people inside getting down."

Jack was nearly caught in the shooting that took place on July 18, 1984, in San Ysidro, California, when James Earl Huberty opened fire on McDonald's customers. Jack's life was spared, although several others died.

Later on, Jack learned that on the other side of the country, a Presbyterian pastor had experienced a vision while praying for Jack. He had seen him in an arched building with a heavy dark cloud of danger hanging over his head. The pastor prayed until he felt the danger lifted. This took place several days before the actual incident occurred.

Jack Fries learned a profound lesson about the power of prayer: "No matter where I go, I know that God has a communication system at work through the Holy Spirit that surrounds me at all times with the prayers of God's people. Nothing can happen to me outside of God's will."

POWER QUOTE

At this very moment, God is at work in your life with an eye to the past, the future, and your present protection.

SCRIPTURE

Psalm 139:5

With your powerful arm you protect me from every side.

POINTS TO PONDER

At times, God acts with split-second timing. Can this be the same heavenly Father at work whose delays seem endless, whose waiting periods stretch us to the breaking point? Yes. In His incredible intelligence and wisdom, He is in the midst of it all—aware, alert, and ready to act on our behalf.

POWER BUILDER

Healing is God's gift to us, and passing time is often His best medicine.

Ecclesiastes 3:8

There is also a time for love and hate, for war and peace.

WHEN JIM AMMERMAN REALIZED that the U.S. was moving into the war against Saddam Hussein, he had mixed reactions. He had served in World War II, Korea, and Vietnam. He had experienced first-hand the death and devastation of war. And yet he knew that tyranny is worse than war, and as the U.S. prepared for Desert Storm, Jim saw a powerful movement of God's Spirit in the process.

He wrote, "As August became September, and more Americans were called to serve, I watched and listened. . . . Our military men and women wanted more services than ever before. In-depth Bible studies were available to those who hungered for a greater understanding of God's Word. Tens of thousands were saved, with thousands rededicating their lives to the Lord.

"On the home front, members of . . . churches joined with people of all faiths in praying for our troops overseas. Congregations set aside special services, initiating prayer circles. Evangelism was being reborn in congregations that had not been spiritually active in years. School children were writing and praying for our servicemen and women. . . .

"It had taken a long time, but Vietnam's old wounds were being healed."

Friday
Week
10

POINTS TO PONDER

Healing, whether in the lives of individuals, relationships, or nations, is often a process rather than an event. Frequently, the passage of time brings new understanding along with distance from old injuries. As we seek healing, we are wise to be persistent in our prayers and patient in our efforts. God's balm of passing times and seasons may be the very thing necessary to bring about permanent health.

I S YOUR PATIENCE BEING tested right now? List the things you are most anxious to see happen, and write the reasons you believe God might be causing you to wait.

_____

_____

_____

_____

Weekend
Week

10

Lord,

I am so tired of waiting—

tired of watching the clock,

tired of seeing days turn into weeks,

realizing I'm getting older

and I haven't yet fulfilled my goals.

Please remember me, Lord.

I know Your purpose is, in part,

to increase my patience and faith.

Help me to learn Your lessons, Lord,

and to become the person You want me to be.

POWER
BUILDER

KATHIE LEE GIFFORD
Entertainer

POWER QUOTE

God loves the real you—His unique creation—just the way you are.

SCRIPTURE

Luke 6:45

Good people do good things because of the good in their hearts.

KATHIE LEE GIFFORD IS known and loved by millions of Americans for her happiness and upbeat good humor. She is a Christian, and she has an interesting perspective on happiness.

"Being happy is different than having joy in life," she explains. "One of my favorite verses has always been Nehemiah 8:10 which says, 'The joy of the Lord is your strength.' Even when I'm going through things that are not particularly happy in my life, I always have an underlying joy in knowing who I am in the Lord and knowing that He loves me.

"I feel content knowing my parents loved me and then later discovering how much God loves me. When the world doesn't love you so much, you've got those things that are so innate and so true to your whole being that the world really can't hurt you."

Kathie Lee believes that people can never be contented in life without grasping the reality that God really loves them. She maintains that if every human being truly believed that, war would be eliminated, and violence would be squelched. The free gift of God's love is available to everyone—a power that can change the life of every person on the earth.

POINTS TO PONDER

We hear all sorts of talk about the importance of self-esteem, and some of it is undeniably true. But upon what is our self-esteem based? If we find self in our careers, our looks, our money and possessions, or our relationships, we are vulnerable to deep losses. But if we find our true selves in the love of God, in the new person He is creating through rebirth, self-esteem then becomes a form of gratitude: "He has made us, and not we ourselves."

POWER BUILDER

LES BROWN
Lecturer

Les BROWN SPEAKS TO employees of Fortune 500 companies and conducts personal and professional seminars around the country. Les knows the power of personal confidence. He was born into extreme poverty and was adopted by a single mother, who lovingly raised him. Although he was identified as having a learning disability, his adoptive mother's love changed his life. He developed intellectually and socially, and he eventually served two terms in the Ohio state legislature.

In his book *Live Your Dreams*, Les suggests four questions to ask to boost self-approval:

1. What are your gifts? What do you do well? If you have good health, acknowledge it. Be thankful if your family and your friends love you.
2. What are five things you like about yourself? You could include your appearance and/or qualities such as punctuality, honesty, and a loving spirit.
3. What people make you feel special? These individuals inspire something within you. What is it?
4. What moment of personal triumph do you remember? Take a moment to recall it.

"Find out what it is you want and go after it as if your life depends on it," Les Brown challenges his audiences. "Why? Because it does!"

POINTS TO PONDER

Love has matchless power to encourage us, make us aware of our potential, and help us reach for the stars. God's love, above all others, most effectively increases our self-esteem. He loves us as we are, but He encourages us to become more like Him. Because He believes in us, we begin to believe in ourselves. We find new courage because He walks with us.

POWER QUOTE

God believes in you so much that He already sees you as a glorious new creation, fit for heaven.

SCRIPTURE

Proverbs 19:21

We may make a lot of plans, but the LORD will do what he has decided.

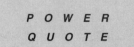

POWER QUOTE

A sincere quest for truth ultimately leads us to God, and God brings us into relationship with our true selves.

SCRIPTURE

Proverbs 4:5–6

Be wise and learn good sense. . . .

If you love Wisdom and don't

reject her, she will watch over

you.

Wᴴᴱɴ THOMAS BANKS WAS young, his father became ill, and the boy had to quit school to support the family. He worked as a sharecropper with two great dreams: he wanted to be independent, and he wanted to be able to read the Bible.

As an adult, still illiterate, Thomas toiled all week as a stone cutter. He cooked barbecue pork, collard greens, and black-eyed peas and sold them on weekends. His diligence gave his seven children a good life. Although he attended church, he felt distant from God because he was unable to read the Bible. One day the preacher read from Proverbs: "Wisdom is the principal thing. . . . Exalt her, and she shall promote thee: she shall bring thee to honour" (4:7–8 KJV).

Thomas realized that he had been working for "things" all his life. It was high time his two dreams came true. He applied for a $75,000 loan to start a restaurant, and he also began to study at the adult learning center.

Today, his restaurant is wonderfully successful. But his greatest satisfaction comes from reading. He especially treasures reading the family Bible.

Wednesday
Week

11

POINTS TO PONDER

Learning is a tremendous source of self-esteem. Not only do students gain understanding, but they experience the satisfaction that comes from accomplishment. They set educational goals, and as they meet them, they feel a new kind of self-respect. Thomas Banks had a particularly good reason to desire learning—he wanted to be able to read God's Word without assistance so he could grow spiritually as well as intellectually. Hardworking as he was, he had enough faith to believe that once he had done all he could do to attain his dreams, God would take care of the rest.

POWER BUILDER

LUCIANO PAVAROTTI

Opera Singer

Luciano Pavarotti's mother imagined that he would be a banker. His father constantly reminded him that he had a wonderful singing voice. And his grandmother frequently said, "You're going to be great—you'll see!"

Falling short of everyone's expectations, Pavarotti taught elementary school. Dissatisfied and frustrated, he rarely sang. His father was unrelenting, reminding him of his unused talent.

Finally, at age twenty-two, Pavarotti had heard enough complaints. He quit his job as a teacher and sold insurance so he would have enough time to pursue vocal training. Today, Pavarotti's name is familiar throughout the world, even among those who are not opera fans. Yet Pavarotti nearly missed the road to his future.

"Studying voice was the turning point of my life," he says. "It's a mistake to take the safe path in life. If I hadn't listened to my father and dropped teaching, I would never be here. And yes, my teacher groomed me. But no teacher ever told me I would become famous. Just my grandmother."

Thursday
Week

11

We'll never know what we might have become unless we take the necessary risks to find out.

SCRIPTURE

Proverbs 4:18

The lifestyle of good people is like sunlight at dawn that keeps getting brighter until broad daylight.

POINTS TO PONDER

Pavarotti's story brings together several elements that contribute to healthy self-esteem: the love and encouragement of others, the development of personal talents, and the Providence that blesses our efforts when we take risks. It seems that we shine brightest when we follow our hearts. Luciano Pavarotti probably would never have gained a sense of personal satisfaction as an elementary teacher. His talents as a singer were too great to be locked into a classroom. And what unlocked that classroom door? His father's nagging, his grandmother's optimism, and his courage to take the more difficult course, to develop his talent, and to risk everything.

POWER BUILDER

BOB McKIGNEY

Self-Esteem Teacher

POWER QUOTE

In the midst of our powerlessness, we find the transforming power of God's love, and through Him, we are restored to our true selves.

SCRIPTURE

Colossians 3:9–10

You have given up your old way of life with its habits. Each of you is now a new person. You are becoming more and more like your Creator.

Friday
Week

11

IN GRADE SCHOOL, BOB McKigney was diagnosed with "defective intelligence . . . infantile speech patterns . . . clumsy coordination." In adulthood, he was addicted to drugs, alcohol, and sex. On a good night, he slept in an abandoned car or a skid row hotel. On a bad night, he was on the streets.

In his despair, Bob determined to try something "absolutely different." He attended church. Four weeks later, Bob committed his life to Jesus Christ. A work of inner spiritual transformation was begun in him.

Along with that inner work, the love of a local church profoundly touched Bob. He learned to read; he learned to speak clearly. He said he felt as if the power of God was "blowing the circuit breakers of [his] mind."

In a step of personal choice, Bob also turned away from a sexually promiscuous lifestyle. For the first time in his life, he gained a measure of self-esteem. As he continued to grow, he gave his testimony on the *700 Club* and was asked to teach a class on self-esteem. "Take it from someone with the most messed-up life you can imagine," Bob McKigney writes, "God's dynamic control can thoroughly change any life."

POINTS TO PONDER

The way people live influences self-esteem. When they are trapped in unhealthy behavior patterns, they continuously pass judgment on themselves, and they feel powerless to overcome shortcomings. They cannot change themselves, and they cannot love themselves. In this state, millions of men and women like Bob McKigney have turned to God in desperation. In Him, they find the supernatural power they desperately need. And in learning to accept His unconditional love, they grow up in Him; they grow out of their unhealthy behavior into a new healthy and fulfilling life.

HOW MUCH TIME DO you spend thinking about self-esteem? Do you struggle to like yourself, or are you content with the person you are? Reflect on some of the questions Les Brown raised, and write your answers on the lines below.

What are your gifts?

_____

What are five things you like about yourself?

_____

What people make you feel special?

_____

What moment of personal triumph do you remember?

_____

Lord,

I know that You have called me to deny myself,

take up my cross, and follow You.

Lord, that's what I want to do.

I pray that as I follow You,

You will help me be

at peace with You,

at peace with myself,

and at peace with others.

Help me find my real self in You.

POWER BUILDER

FRANK PETERS
Chiropractor

POWER QUOTE

God is big enough to rule the universe, yet small enough to live in our hearts.

SCRIPTURE

Deuteronomy 33:27

The eternal God is our hiding place; he carries us in his arms.

FRANK PETERS WAS ON a fishing trip to Costa Rica when a tractor trailer hit his truck. He had five broken ribs, a broken nose, a broken jaw, a punctured lung, and crushed sinuses. He sank into a coma for several weeks and was not expected to live.

Because his wife, Mary Kay, believed in prayer, she faced the tragedy with tremendous faith, although the first sight of her husband nearly devastated her. Faithfully sitting by his side, she repeated the same prayer, "Okay, with faith in You, Jesus, I know You can restore him."

One crisis after another plagued Frank's recovery. His family struggled to get him flown back to the United States. Most of all, his friends and family prayed without ceasing.

Finally, Frank awoke from his coma, and as he regained consciousness, he experienced a startling encounter. He said, "When I returned to consciousness . . . two arms were around me, hugging me. I looked to see if it was Mary Kay, but nobody was in the room. Then I heard a voice: 'Frank, this is Jesus and I love you. . . .'

"At first I thought I was losing my mind, or that I had somehow invented this experience. But when a nurse walked into the room, the voice faded and the hug gently subsided. That's when I realized Jesus had visited me."

POINTS TO PONDER

Now and then God chooses to break through from the supernatural into the natural world; He moves from His transcendent glory across our temporal view. He does not reveal Himself because we beg Him, manipulate Him, or seek to have an experience with Him. He comes to us when we need Him, acting in grace and mercy to comfort, encourage, inspire, or correct us. He proves Himself to be "closer than a brother," and He meets us in the midst of our humanness.

POWER BUILDER

VAN BRUNER

Architect

Tuesday

Week

12

WHEN VAN BRUNER FIRST learned that his only son was dying of sickle-cell anemia, he turned to alcohol. Then the mother of an old friend said, "Call a man of God."

Van stared at her and asked, "Are you some kind of a fanatic? I need a scientific answer. . . . What do you mean 'a man of God'? Come on!"

That night Van's son, Scottie, collapsed in severe pain, and he had to be rushed to the hospital. The disease was attacking his spleen. The doctors shook their heads, saying, "There's nothing we can do."

Van later wrote, "Suddenly, my 'greatness' faded into nothingness. Pride in my accomplishments seemed hollow." In his despair, Van frantically dialed the number of the "man of God" his friend's mother had given him. The man wasn't a minister; he was a janitor with a big smile. And the first thing he did was to lead Van and his wife, Lillian, to Christ. Then he accompanied them to the hospital.

Van reported, "When we arrived, there he was . . . walking around! . . . His doctor stood there, looking dazed. 'I don't know what happened. But his hemoglobin is way up. Above what it should be.'"

"Praise God!" Van Bruner laughed. "God did that!"

Young Scott Bruner's healing was complete and permanent. He recently graduated from Harvard, and he is assistant district attorney for Cook County, Illinois.

POWER QUOTE

When we have an encounter with God, we see ourselves as small as we really are, and we realize how mighty He really is.

SCRIPTURE

Ephesians 3:20

His power at work in us can do far more than we dare ask or imagine.

POINTS TO PONDER

Our encounters with God often reveal the condition of our souls. In His power and holiness, He serves as a mirror, reflecting to us our weakness and pride. In His healing strength, He reveals to us our inability to find physical, emotional, or spiritual health. In His wisdom, He reveals to us the foolishness of our overinflated egos.

POWER BUILDER

DANNY HOLT

Construction Worker

Our encounters with God confirm His sovereignty, remind us of our dependency on Him, and assure us of His love.

SCRIPTURE

Luke 1:50

He always shows mercy to everyone who worships him.

DANNY HOLT FACED HIS intestinal cancer with all the courage he could muster. And because he was a Christian, he knew God could heal him if He chose to do so. Danny struggled with the fact that his cancer remained, despite surgery and chemotherapy; he firmly believed God had promised to heal him. He endured treatments and stubbornly thanked God—publicly—for the miracle that had not yet happened.

One day Danny experienced immense pain in his abdomen. He cried out, "Jesus, thank You for healing me." He was rushed to the hospital for emergency surgery. After several days in intensive care, he awoke and found his wife, Bonnie, standing beside his bed.

She said, "Danny, I've got something incredible to tell you. When the doctor opened you up, he couldn't believe what he saw. The tumor has completely disappeared. . . . The lab test revealed that the cancer has completely disappeared. No residual cells."

Bonnie related the surgeon's words to her: "I've been a surgeon for twenty years. I've studied in England and many other places, and I've never seen anything like this. Your husband has had a touch from a greater Power. He has had a touch from God."

Wednesday
Week

12

POINTS TO PONDER

God's desire to heal us is often revealed to us through a gift of faith. At times He places within us a certainty that seems to go against reality. When God promises healing, we find it irresistible and cannot escape it. The tenacity of our prayers comes from Him, not from us. He encounters us with a gift of faith and follows it—in His time—with His gift of healing. The good work begins and ends with Him, not with us.

POWER BUILDER

DENNIS EISENHART
School Bus Driver

Once DENNIS EISENHART WAS sure all the departing children had crossed the street, he checked the mirrors on the school bus. He saw nothing, so he reached for the lever to turn off the flashing red lights: "As I reached my hand out, something stopped me just inches from the lever . . . a force . . . an inner feeling said 'Wait.'"

Dennis studied the street in front of the bus. He checked the mirrors again, flicked off the overhead alternating light, and reached for the gearshift lever.

The feeling of "Wait!" was stronger than ever. Again he checked his mirrors. Nothing. He says, "I took my foot off the brake. The big bus started to move. Suddenly in the front mirror there was a flash of color . . . something moved.

"My foot went to the brake instantly.

"It was a little girl. She stood up, her arms clutching loose papers and books. My heart stopped. She had been out of my sight down under that big bus on her hands and knees picking up her papers. I knew right then and there that it was the hand of God that kept me from running over that little girl. I had always believed in God. But it wasn't until that day that I knew He was beside me in that bus."

Thursday
Week

12

POWER QUOTE

People who have encountered God recognize that His ways are mighty, marvelous, and profoundly mysterious.

SCRIPTURE

Isaiah 58:11

The LORD will always guide you.

POINTS TO PONDER

What is God's purpose in meeting us in the midst of our earthly lives? Perhaps our cynical natures require an occasional reminder that we are not alone. In a world that honors the scientific method and denies the unseen spiritual world, God is not mocked. He reaches boldly from one dimension into another, stopping the bus, shielding the little child, and letting us know that He is profoundly aware of the smallest details of our lives.

ELDREDE JARMAN

Pilot

POWER BUILDER

POWER QUOTE

When God answers our prayers, He partners with us, making us participants in His limitless power.

SCRIPTURE

Mark 4:41

They were more afraid than ever and said to each other, "Who is this? Even the wind and the waves obey him!"

ELDREDE JARMAN'S ROUTINE FLIGHT home from Washington, D.C., to Florida was interrupted by a powerful storm. His small private plane lurched and plunged, and both engines spluttered dangerously. He would have to ditch his plane in the ocean.

"Lord," he prayed, "save me." He was making a reasonably easy descent, planning how to land on the choppy water, when his right engine suddenly came to life. He strained for control, then dive-bombed into the water, ripping off both wings.

Despite multiple injuries, Eldrede managed to swim toward shore. A yacht rescued him from the stormy waters, and he was rushed to the hospital. "There was no possible way for you to survive that crash," he was told, "but you did."

A day later, the yacht's captain walked into Eldrede's hospital room. He said, "While you were still in the ocean, before the first mate pulled you up, I saw a circle of calm water gather around you. . . . Yet, beyond that area, it was choppy. What was that I saw? How could that be?"

Eldrede Jarman explained, "I knew something was going to happen, and I prayed, 'Lord, save me!' God did what you saw."

POINTS TO PONDER

How often do we wish we had been present when Jesus was walking on earth? What incredible faith we would have if we had actually seen Him heal the sick, raise the dead, or calm the raging sea. Are we able to believe that He is still working miracles? A story like Eldrede Jarman's assures us that God still does the impossible. And at times, He allows us to accomplish impossible things on His behalf.

H

AVE YOU EVER HAD a powerful encounter with God? Try to remember the details, record them, then thank Him for revealing Himself to you in a unique way.

_____

_____

_____

_____

Weekend
Week

12

Lord,

You have called me to walk by faith,

not by sight.

But now and then You have chosen to break through

the barrier between here and eternity,

and You have let me catch a glimpse of You

through an act of healing,

through miraculous intervention, or

through a message of guidance and truth.

Thank You for Your immensity

and for Your amazing ability

to reach into my world

just when I need it most.

AMY CARMICHAEL
Missionary

Truth opens the door to problem solving.

John 8:32

You will know the truth, and the truth will set you free.

Amy Carmichael left her native Northern Ireland to serve God just before the turn of the twentieth century, during a time when Christian work was glorified and the struggles of missionaries were hidden even from friends and families.

Amy was not afraid to speak about the difficulties of life in foreign lands. She wrote in her book *Things as They Are,* "You go to a hut and find nobody in. You go to the next and find nobody wants you, you go to the next and find an old woman who says yes, you may talk if you like, and she listens in an aimless sort of way." She recounted the prostitution that trapped young girls in service to Hindu deities. She was called "the child-stealing woman" because she provided shelter to runaway girls who came to her home.

In the early 1900s, proper Christians didn't speak openly about sexual abuse, and Amy wasn't detailed in her descriptions. But she described the temples as strongholds of principalities and powers, which Christians should battle with the power of God.

Amy Carmichael's life was a fresh breeze of reality that refused to allow pretense, artificiality, or dishonesty to invade the kingdom she so faithfully served.

Monday
Week
13

When we are not truthful with ourselves, before long we are dishonest with others as well. And once we begin the cycle of dishonesty, we have to continually support our lies, inaccuracies, and cover-ups. Truth, as Jesus said, sets us free to deal with the realities of life—pleasant and unpleasant. Living in truth removes the complicated web of intrigue we weave to maintain denial. Best of all, truth makes it possible for us to go to God with open requests that address real situations and seek real answers.

POWER BUILDER

JIM VALVANO
Basketball Coach and Sportscaster

Tuesday
Week

13

JIM VALVANO WAS AN enthusiastic, funny man, admired by friends and foes alike. He moved from a successful career in college basketball into television broadcasting on ESPN and ABC. Then he learned that he had cancer. With his usual good humor, Jim continued to rib his friends and tell his stories.

When he was given the Arthur Ashe Award for Courage, Jim Valvano said, "To me there are three things everyone should do every day. Number one is laugh. . . . Number two is think—spend some time in thought. Number three, you should have your emotions move you to tears. If you laugh, think, and cry, that's a heck of a day. Ralph Waldo Emerson said, 'Nothing great was ever achieved without enthusiasm.' I urge all of you to enjoy your life, to be enthusiastic every day. To keep your dreams alive in spite of your problems.

"I know I gotta go. But I have one last thing to say. Cancer can take away all my physical abilities. It cannot touch my mind. It cannot touch my heart and it cannot touch my soul. And those three things are going to carry on forever."

SCRIPTURE

Proverbs 16:21

Good judgment proves that you are wise, and if you speak kindly, you can teach others.

POINTS TO PONDER

By accepting the reality of his impending death, Jim Valvano was able to reach countless others with words of wisdom and encouragement. Ever the optimist, he turned his misfortune into an opportunity. He used his life-and-death situation to remind his listeners about priorities and values he held dear. And he allowed himself to express real emotions so that those who heard him would grow through his experience and not be diminished by it. What are the issues we're hiding from? As we accept them and live with them, we are able to strengthen others as well as ourselves.

BRUCE COLLIE

Professional Football Player

God's truth provides a firm foundation in a world of shifting values and unclear boundaries.

SCRIPTURE

James 4:8, 10 NIV

Purify your hearts, you double-minded. . . . Humble yourselves before the Lord, and he will lift you up.

BRUCE COLLIE HAD A successful NFL career. Five seasons with the San Francisco Forty-Niners. Two Super Bowl rings. Yet as he started training for his sixth football season, Bruce was unmotivated. An empty ache intensified. Bruce called his mother, a Christian, who advised him to read the small book of Psalms she had given him.

He describes the unexpected power in the words he read: "I started at chapter one, verse one, 'How blessed is the man who does not walk in the counsel of the wicked.' I read on and it made sense to me. . . . It was describing my life . . . what I had been doing wrong. I had been 'walking in the counsel of the wicked.'. . .

"It was at that moment that I saw myself as God saw me—a pretender and a sinner. Pretending to live the life of a Christian, but in reality, living the life of a willing sinner. I was doing those things described in Psalm 1, and more!"

Bruce fell on his face and repented his double-mindedness. He was soon traded to the Philadelphia Eagles, where he found several strong Christian teammates. Thanks to the truth he found in God's Word, he says, "Jesus Christ was finally real to me. . . . I accepted Jesus' sacrifice for my sins and became a new creature in Christ."

Wednesday

Week

13

POINTS TO PONDER

What is truth? Truth is revealed in the pages of the Bible. The truth in Scripture is constant and unchanging. It doesn't ebb and flow with emotions. It doesn't adapt itself to changing cultures and styles. When Scripture says that ungodly people do not receive God's blessing, we learn a life-changing truth for all generations. And when we receive the truth—along with the One who spoke it—we become willing and able to live in truth, and we welcome the Spirit of truth to live in us.

POWER BUILDER

BRIAN MOLITOR

President, Molitor, Inc.

BRIAN MOLITOR PROVIDES LEADERSHIP training principles to companies throughout America. He believes that as people unify, organizations turn around.

After managers of a Fortune 400 company asked him to visit corporate sites around the country, Brian assessed three areas that needed work: leadership, teamwork, and problem solving. He developed business principles that he believes God helped him discover: assess a situation; develop leadership to address it; and foster teamwork to solve it.

Brian observes, "As I grew up as a Christian and understood more of the character of God, He taught me more about the principles of unity, leadership, communication, listening, and the power of words. He also showed me their scriptural foundations.

"Take the image of Jesus as a humble servant, washing feet and helping multitudes, though He was the greatest man to ever walk the face of the earth. That's the kind of leader that workers will respond to. I once thought ministry meant preaching from a pulpit. But today I know that God wants His people everywhere, so the gospel of Christ will be carried to all corners of the earth. Given that calling, I pose this question: how well are you managing His business?"

Thursday

Week

13

POWER QUOTE

God's truth is not a religious system. It is a way of life.

SCRIPTURE

Ephesians 6:7

Gladly serve your masters, as though they were the Lord himself, and not simply people.

POINTS TO PONDER

How vital it is for us to take God's truth into the marketplace! In what has been described as a post-Christian world, we cannot afford to selfishly keep spiritual truth to ourselves. It is not enough for us to share God's love with those who do not know Him. We must integrate that truth, and the values that represent it, into our businesses, our professional relationships, and our daily habits.

HERMAN CAIN

Businessman

POWER BUILDER

POWER QUOTE

The truth about success is that every good thing comes from God.

SCRIPTURE

Philippians 1:6

God is the one who began this good work in you, and I am certain that he won't stop before it is complete.

WHEN HERMAN CAIN TOOK over as president and CEO of Godfather's Pizza, the company was financially troubled, and he turned it around to profitability within twelve months. At age thirty-four, he was vice president at Pillsbury. Then he resigned his position and entered the restaurant business. He began by broiling hamburgers at Burger King.

He believes in living in God's truth, and he attributes his success to three factors: (1) focus, (2) follow-through, and (3) faith.

Of focus, he says, "First you must define your goal. Just saying, 'I want to be successful' is not a goal, but 'I want to earn a master's degree' is. To be focused, define your goal."

Of follow-through, Herman explains, "Take life one day at a time, and take your career one step at a time. As long as you're making progress toward your goals, that's fine. It's better to make steady solid progress than to suddenly catapult to the top."

And of his faith? "My secret is my belief in Christ and almighty God—and They are no secret! I have to give God the glory in everything I do and in every success I've achieved. It's not that I am so great, but that God has blessed me so much."

POINTS TO PONDER

When we approach our business decisions with a commitment to truth, as Herman Cain demonstrates, we add a significant element to the professional success equation: God's power. By including God in our work as well as in our worship, we infuse our daily schedules with His presence and present our agendas for His guidance. Furthermore, we can eliminate stress by shifting the final outcome of our efforts to Him. After all, God is the source of success, prosperity, and personal fulfillment.

Is IT EVER DIFFICULT for you to tell yourself the truth? Remember and record an occasion when you refused to admit something to yourself and therefore could not deal honestly with the circumstances.

_____

_____

What are the truths that mean the most to you in your spiritual life? Why?

_____

_____

Weekend
Week

13

Lord,

sometimes I fear the truth,

and by avoiding it, I cheat myself out of its benefits.

Lord, stay close to me

while I learn to confront reality head-on.

Teach me the value of personal truth.

Teach me the power of spiritual truth.

And teach me to commit myself to

the ironclad truth of Your Word,

building my life on its firm foundation.

DOUG MARLETTE

Pulitzer Prize–Winning Cartoonist

Our power to succeed increases as we overcome emotional weaknesses.

SCRIPTURE

Ecclesiastes 10:10 NKJV

Wisdom brings success.

Pressure is valuable to people who work with constant deadlines and have to achieve creative output in little time. Doug Marlette has learned to greatly appreciate that challenge. He says, "Some people cannot imagine drawing a cartoon every day. 'I'd be a nervous wreck,' they say. But with practice, I adjusted to being on the high wire."

Then Doug gives an example. He talks about the Boston Celtics' Larry Bird and why he was so dependable when a big game was at stake: "Lots of players want to be the hero and take the last shot when the score is tied, but only a handful want the ball when their team is down a point. That's the mark of a champion.

"It is the same with cartooning. I have learned to love a blank sheet of paper on deadline. It braces me with its endless potential. When the game is on the line, put me in, coach!"

Monday
Week

14

POINTS TO PONDER

The ability to create quality work is indispensable for anyone who wishes to succeed. But the ability to create quality work under pressure is more challenging. Emotions play a large role in our ability to accomplish great things in the world. Feelings can make or break us despite our talent, intelligence, and education: fear keeps us from risking; anxiety causes us to choke when the pressure is on; anger distracts us from our focus. Practice, self-talk, and determination enable us to keep hitting the emotional wall until we break through it. As people of faith, we include prayer in this process of overcoming emotional barriers, asking God to partner with us as we seek to make the most of our talent, unhindered by our feelings.

POWER BUILDER

SIGERU MIYAMOTO

Computer Game Designer

SIGERU MIYAMOTO'S IMAGINATION HAS affected the minds of millions of children as well as transformed Nintendo Entertainment Systems into one of the most successful corporations in the world. Sigeru attributes his achievements in designing computer games to his understanding of children's sense of wonder.

As a boy growing up outside Kyoto, Japan, Sigeru discovered a cave. He longed to explore it, but he was afraid. He returned to the site several times before he gathered up enough courage to go inside. He carried a small lantern with him as he delved deeper and deeper into the cavern, where he encountered another cave. Shaking with excitement and fear, he climbed through.

"That state of mind, when a child enters a cave alone, must be realized in my games," Sigeru explains. "Going in, he must discover a branch off to one side and decide whether to explore it or not. Sometimes he loses his way. But through perseverance, wit, luck, and practice, he will improve."

Tuesday

Week

14

POWER QUOTE

Childlike faith is the primary source of spiritual maturity.

SCRIPTURE

1 Corinthians 13:11

When we were children, we thought and reasoned as children do.

POINTS TO PONDER

The ideas we developed as children can become the source of adult success. A child's pure imagination, unlimited by the grown-up limitations of "it won't work," or "be careful," or "that's a silly idea," can create marvelous new and innovative concepts. The same is true in matters of faith. When Jesus remarked that men and women should become as little children to enter His kingdom, He was making a similar observation. A child's mind is not cluttered with doubts, fears, and cynicism. When a responsible parent says, "I'll take care of you," a child believes that promise. When God says, "I will care for you and meet your needs," we need to take Him at His word with childlike enthusiasm, choosing to follow Him into the unknown with full confidence that He knows the way.

ORVILLE REDENBACHER
Gourmet Popcorn Developer

Great ideas require many good minds to move them from vision into reality.

SCRIPTURE

Proverbs 24:6

Battles are won by listening to advice and making a lot of plans.

Hᴇ RESEARCHED POPCORN, PLANTED it, harvested it, and tested it. And it was the best because he scientifically determined just how much moisture each kernel needed to contain for maximum popping.

Orville Redenbacher could do just about everything well when it came to popcorn—except sell it. His product "Red Bow" popcorn was going nowhere fast, and he was incredibly discouraged. Suddenly, he remembered a fragment of a biblical verse, looked it up, and located the whole proverb: "For by wise counsel you will wage your own war, and in a multitude of counselors there is safety" (Prov. 24:6 NKJV).

Seeking wise counselors, Orville hired an advertising and marketing firm, which promptly renamed his product "Orville Redenbacher's Gourmet Popping Corn." Once he sent some of the newly labeled popcorn to Marshall Field's in Chicago, the store couldn't keep it in stock. It soon became the best-selling popcorn in the world.

Wednesday
Week

14

POINTS TO PONDER

Creative, imaginative people often come up with astonishing and exciting ideas. But they are sometimes limited by their own rugged individuality— they want to find success all by themselves. The unique giftings of God have filled the world with every imaginable sort of human talent. On the other hand, individuals who are gifted in one sphere of influence are sometimes all but useless in another. Orville Redenbacher was a gifted farmer. But it took others with talent in advertising and promotion to make a powerful impact in the food industry. He was wise enough to reach beyond his area of specialization and to retain the talents and ideas of others with unique abilities. The result was success for all involved.

POWER BUILDER

PHIL JACKSON

Coach, Chicago Bulls

Onl y A PREACHER'S KID could take his church background and apply it to professional basketball. One of Phil Jackson's most challenging jobs is working with superstar Michael Jordan. Michael's achievements on the court are legendary, and he enjoys incredible support from his fans. But early on Jackson had to convince Michael that to build a better team, Michael would have to sacrifice personal statistics from time to time. Then his teammates could excel, and the team's opportunity to reach the NBA Finals would improve. Michael Jordan was responsive to his coach's request. And for the first time in fifty years, Chicago won back-to-back championships.

Thursday
Week

14

Jackson credits his Bible-believing parents for his persuasive manner, which he describes as "friendly": "Perhaps it's learned behavior from my father, a pastor. . . . You don't talk down to people, and you don't have to talk up to them. We're working together. It's not me telling them what to do."

POWER QUOTE

Love and respect are the most powerful motivators on earth.

SCRIPTURE

Proverbs 24:3

Use wisdom and understanding to establish your home.

POINTS TO PONDER

The ideas that motivate people are the same, no matter whether they are applied to sports, corporate endeavors, creativity, or physical labor. When human beings are respected, treated with dignity, and spoken to with compassion and understanding, they are more easily motivated. Perhaps that is why God chose to take human form and live within the confines of humanity. In humility, He walked among His creatures, identified Himself with us, and experienced the ups and downs of daily life. Ultimately, He chose to die a human death, an act that He overcame with His divine power. What enormous love and respect He has demonstrated to us. Can we show each other anything less?

POWER BUILDER

JOHN HETRICK
Industrial Engineering Technician

Success is measured not in dollars and cents but in good character, love, and kept commitments.

SCRIPTURE

Proverbs 13:12

Not getting what you want can make you feel sick, but a wish that comes true is a life-giving tree.

THE POWER OF A good idea can generate more than money. John Hetrick was driving over a rough road in 1952 when he hit a rock. He slammed on the brakes and instinctively flung out his right arm to protect his child from smashing into the dashboard or windshield.

"Why," John asked himself, "couldn't some object come out to stop you from hitting the inside of the car?" He turned his question into a series of possible solutions. A year later, John patented a Safety Cushion Assembly for Automotive Vehicles. John Hetrick had designed and patented the first air bag.

He was ahead of his time. His patent ran out shortly before General Motors released the first air bag on a passenger car in 1974. Consequently, John never made a cent on his invention. Forty years later, 90 percent of all cars come with at least a driver-side air bag.

Since air bags became widely available in the mid-1980s, more than four thousand people have been saved from death or major injury. "That," John Hetrick says, "makes it worth it."

POINTS TO PONDER

Our competitive world often judges the value of ideas by their financial success. But a man like John Hetrick reminds us that money isn't everything, and financial success doesn't necessarily equate peace of mind. Seeing lives transformed should be the rightful focus of our lives. If the car isn't new, the house needs repair, or clothes aren't designer originals, we may still think of ourselves as successful if we are living to a higher calling, which lifts us out of the material and into the spiritual realm.

MAKE A LIST OF some ideas you have had. What have you done about them? What could you do if you started tomorrow?

_____

_____

_____

_____

Weekend
Week

14

Lord,

thank You for Your immense creativity,

and thank You for sharing it with me

by giving me creative ideas,

possibilities, and solutions.

Your Word says that all good things come from You,

and so I ask You to help me implement

the good ideas that You have given me.

Help me bless people's lives with them.

And once I have done my best,

enable me to let go.

The rest is up to You.

MAC GOBER

Founder, Canaan Land

POWER BUILDER

POWER QUOTE

God is doing the work of our transformation—minute by minute, year by year.

SCRIPTURE

1 Peter 1:3

By raising Jesus from death, he has given us new life and a hope that lives on.

MAC GOBER WAS ONE of the toughest bikers in California. He rarely bathed and was often stoned and angry.

One day someone gave him a leaflet informing him that God loved him. Two weeks later, he found another pamphlet about God. "What if God's real?" he asked himself. That night he returned to his apartment, still thinking about God.

He says, "Entering an upstairs room at 2 A.M., something startled me worse than any Vietnam firefight. I looked up and saw Jesus hanging on a cross. . . . I realized that Christ had died for me. Not just for the world. For ME. A smelly, dirty, rotten hood who terrorized society. I burst into tears.

"'I love you, Mac,' the Lord said. . . .

"Shaking my head I said, 'But You couldn't love somebody like me.'"

Three times, Jesus told Mac that He loved him. Mac finally cried out, "Please let there be room at the cross for one more."

Mac made two requests that night. He asked Jesus to allow him to find his mother and apologize for all he had put her through. And he prayed that he would be allowed to help young people find the truth. Both prayers were answered. Today, Mac serves as founder and president of Canaan Land in Autaugaville, Alabama. He ministers to bikers and student groups.

POINTS TO PONDER

God is more interested in the needs of our hearts than in the attractiveness of our bodies. He reaches past all the externals and reminds us that He loves us and that He sent His Son to die on our behalf. Once we have received that amazing offer—His life for ours—He begins the work of transformation. He works from the inside out and changes the way we think and behave as well as the way we look.

POWER BUILDER

BARRY TAYLOR

Former Rock Band Crew Member

H E WAS A MEMBER of the rock band AC-DC's road crew, so Barry Taylor had access to all the drugs and good times he could hope for. He had always yearned to explore life's ultimate meaning, but his lifestyle kept getting in the way. He had never seen insanity quite like that of AC-DC and the fans who thronged to hear the group.

Then something even more "insane" happened. One of Barry's closest friends wrote to him from Los Angeles and told him about his newfound relationship with Jesus Christ. Barry made up his mind to set his friend straight. He bought a Bible, determined to arm himself for the coming confrontation with his friend. Instead, he started reading it for himself.

One night, after a particularly uproarious AC-DC concert, Barry returned to the bus. He didn't do drugs with the others. He didn't watch the porn video or have a drink. He picked up his Bible and said a prayer aloud: "God I want the life You have for me. . . . I want to live for You on the earth." Since then, Barry has gone from powerful rock music to an even more powerful ministry, both in America and in Russia, where he has led thousands of men and women to Christ.

Tuesday

W e e k

15

POWER QUOTE

People who wholeheartedly seek God inevitably find Him.

SCRIPTURE

2 Corinthians 5:17

Anyone who belongs to Christ is a new person. The past is forgotten, and everything is new.

POINTS TO PONDER

A search for ultimate meaning can be a philosophical ego trip, or it can be a sincere yearning for something greater than ourselves. If we genuinely seek truth, God will respond to our quest. He will meet us unexpectedly, and He will lead us into a totally new life—the one He had planned for us all along. God's purpose for everyone on earth is a close personal relationship with Him. That is the new life He makes available. The only thing that keeps us from having it is our refusal to submit to Him as Lord and King.

DENNIS TINERINO

Bodybuilder

POWER BUILDER

DENNIS TINERINO HELD THE titles of Mr. America, Mr. Universe (three times), and Mr. Natural America. He mastered the world of physical power, but his personal life was out of control. Drugs. Gambling. His own prostitution ring. Before long, Dennis was behind bars, where life was even sicker than life outside.

During the times of his arrests, probations, and sentences, Dennis encountered many who tried to tell him how to be saved from his self-destruction. He avoided them all. Finally a former bodybuilder named Ray McCauley called long distance every week to talk about the Bible, and he did it for months. One day he said, "If you'll pray now, God will change your life."

Dennis later wrote, "I couldn't fight anymore . . . I said, 'Lord, forgive me for everything I've done.'"

A new power entered Dennis's life—the power of God's life-changing Spirit. He wrote, "A black cloud lifted from my presence. . . . God said, 'Dennis, don't look back. You're a new creation today.'. . . The world deceives you into thinking you have to achieve something to be somebody. I realized my value because Somebody died for me."

Wednesday
Week
15

POINTS TO PONDER

Physical power is virtually useless in matters of faith. It can become a hindrance when we allow ourselves to depend on our own strength instead of relying on the omnipotent God of the universe. Dennis Tinerino needed a new point of view after seeing his personal power vanish into powerlessness. He had gratified his desires in every imaginable way, and he had come up empty. After years of struggle, he was ready to reach out to God. When he did, he was transformed on the inside from weak to strong, from self-absorbed to God-centered. He was a new man living a new life.

POWER BUILDER

CHARLES DUKE

Apollo 16 Astronaut

CHARLES DUKE ENJOYED AN unforgettable experience when he "walked in wonder on the moon." Then came the aftermath: "After coming back to earth—the dramatic splashdown, debriefing, hero's welcome and ego-inflation—came the inevitable letdown. . . . I wondered, 'What am I going to do now? I'm on a downhill slope at thirty-six.'"

As he struggled with his identity, his marriage and family were under incredible pressure. Charles's wife, Dottie, was despondent, and she became nearly suicidal. Charles quit NASA and became a highly successful beer distributor, a business that he eventually sold.

During those stressful years, Dottie came to know Jesus Christ, and she asked Charles if he would accompany her to a Bible study. He did, and he later wrote, "The scales suddenly fell from my eyes. I saw that God had loved Charlie Duke from the time He created Adam—now and forever—and had created him as an individual."

After he affirmed that Jesus was indeed the Son of God, Charles's life was radically changed. He was given a purpose, a sense of dedication, and more love than he had ever known before. He said, "Walking on the moon cannot begin to compare with walking on earth with Jesus."

Thursday

Week

15

POINTS TO PONDER

Human accomplishments deserve congratulations and affirmation. But they have a transitory nature. Athletes who win "the big one" have to wake up the next morning and start training all over again. Scholars who receive a graduate degree have to seek other goals. A new life in Christ brings us into an eternal realm where we are investing in a permanently satisfying future. This world's greatest glory will pale when we see His unimaginable kingdom with our own eyes.

POWER QUOTE

People who believe in eternal life know that the best is yet to come.

SCRIPTURE

John 8:12

I am the light for the world! Follow me, and you won't be walking in the dark. You will have the light that gives life.

POWER BUILDER

PHIL AGUILAR

Pastor

POWER QUOTE

New life in Christ is the beginning of a growth process that takes a lifetime to complete.

SCRIPTURE

Micah 6:8

The LORD God has told us what is right and what he demands: "See that justice is done, let mercy be your first concern, and humbly obey your God."

Friday
Week
15

PHIL AGUILAR WAS AN angry man when he first got involved with the Hell's Angels. He was enraged at God for allowing his family to disintegrate, and he wanted nothing more than to pay God back for all his pain. Several suicide attempts failed. He acted out this rage by physically abusing anyone who crossed him. He became brutal and uncontrolled.

Phil was imprisoned at Chino Institution for Men in southern California. There a chaplain told him that Jesus Christ would forgive him for everything he had ever done wrong. Once he received that forgiveness and was released from prison, Phil went to church. But he didn't look much like the other Christians. And when he brought bikers, punkers, surfers, or homeless people to church with him, frightened believers shunned them.

Guided by his experience and by God's direction, Phil started a new ministry called Set Free. Dressed in black, mounted on a Harley-Davidson, he rode for Jesus. He reached out to the people nobody else wanted to touch. Not fitting into the mainstream sometimes creates challenges, but Phil Aguilar has learned that the power of love and acceptance can transform the most unlikely individuals into the image of God.

POINTS TO PONDER

Phil Aguilar was part of a rough-and-tumble world that seemed ill-suited for worship at the church on the corner. In his desire to bring others into a new life in Christ, he created a come-as-you-are environment in which they could worship Him in spirit and in truth.

D O YOU REMEMBER THE beginning of your new life in Christ? Recall and record the changes that happened in your life.

_____

_____

_____

If you aren't sure you have begun a new life in Him, take a moment to ask Jesus Christ to forgive your sins, and start your new life today.

Lord,

thank You for new beginnings.

Thank You for giving me a new life,

for forgiving the past

and promising me an exciting future.

I need to share the opportunity

of new life with others, Lord.

Give me courage and ability to do so,

and make me available to help them

while they are being transformed into Your image.

POWER BUILDER

POWER QUOTE

Answered prayer confirms
God's personal involvement
in our daily lives.

SCRIPTURE

2 Chronicles 30:27 NKJV

Their prayer came up to His

holy dwelling place, to heaven.

Monday
Week

16

AS POWERFUL AS HOLLYWOOD moguls are, a group of them sensed a need to rely on a greater Power than their own, and they started gathering for prayer. They keep their identities anonymous and set aside their high-level connections. Humbling themselves before the Lord, they call themselves Key Men.

One Key Man had constant back pain. Seven doctors had prescribed dangerous surgery as his only hope. But as the Key Men prayed, two new physicians recommended a radical noninvasive approach to healing, which relieved the pain.

A meeting in a network boardroom was interrupted by the news that the car belonging to a Key Man's daughter had been found, abandoned in a remote area. The men gathered and prayed for the young woman. They specifically asked that she be kept safe, and that she reestablish contact in twenty-four hours. By noon the next day, the daughter had called home.

A film company vice president asked the group to pray that he could locate other believers in his studio. Within hours, he had found two influential Christians, and he learned that the secretary he had hired days before was a follower of Christ.

These Key Men in Hollywood have learned the difference between media power and God's very real power, appropriated through humble, sincere prayer.

POINTS TO PONDER

God left instructions for us to join together in agreement, praying over even the smallest concerns. God wants us to talk to Him, even though He already knows our thoughts, our needs, our desires, and our plans.

POWER BUILDER

JIMMY ROGERS
President, Rogers-Wood and Associates

Jimmy Rogers heads a company that sells around $10 million worth of insurance every year. But all the insurance in the world was unable to protect him from the tragedy of a son who lost his way in the world of drugs.

Jimmy, a committed Christian, was brokenhearted by the young man's behavior. He felt responsible, and he did what he could to help. Jimmy turned to the Bible, where he read voraciously from the Gospels. There he learned that Jesus had often used the Word of God to accomplish His greatest miracles.

Jimmy stated, "Suddenly I realized that coupled with the power He demonstrated while on earth, He gave us authority to use His name to accomplish the same tasks, to heal the sick, empower the lame, and open blind eyes. Armed with that scriptural awareness, I saw that we needed to do what we could do best. Pray, speak the Word, and trust in God to deliver the results."

Jimmy began to pray authoritatively for his son. About a year later, a long-haired, bearded stranger showed up at his office. He stood to meet the individual and looked into the eyes of his son. The young man quietly explained that he had made a decision to straighten out his life, and that he had decided to follow Christ.

The power of God had done what earthly success could not do for Jimmy Rogers—it had brought a prodigal back to his father's arms.

Tuesday
Week

16

POWER QUOTE

God has already responded to a prayer, even before we ask. He is preparing us for His answer.

SCRIPTURE

Psalm 4:1

Please answer my prayer. I was in terrible distress, but you set me free. Now have pity and listen as I pray.

POINTS TO PONDER

When we pray, we are essentially telling God that we are powerless to contend with some circumstances. Or we are choosing to set aside whatever power we may seem to have, relinquishing our ability to His sovereign might. Sometimes years pass, and our prayers seem to be unanswered. But after He has completed His process, He acts and brings forth an answer—better than we could have hoped or imagined.

POWER BUILDER

SAM HUDDLESTON
Prison Minister

POWER QUOTE

We may be good at hiding the truth from ourselves, but God will not allow us to lie persistently to Him.

SCRIPTURE

2 Chronicles 7:14

If my own people will humbly pray and turn back to me and stop sinning, then I will answer them from heaven. I will forgive them.

Sam HUDDLESTON STARTED HIS teenage years using drugs, stealing, smoking, and having sex with every girl who was willing. His godly father tried to tell him about Jesus. But Sam was angry—his mother had left him, his friends had betrayed him, and things hadn't gone his way. For nineteen years, he absolutely would not pray.

But years and prison sentences added up, and Sam began to wonder about the child he had fathered out of wedlock. Would that boy ever respect him the way he respected his godly father? He remembered that his own father had said, "God will always be there, waiting."

Sam said, "I flopped down on the grass and looked up at the stars. Where was God? All I heard was my own voice: 'It's their fault. . . . It's God's fault.'"

That night Sam wrote to his father and acknowledged that he had prayed. He began to read the Bible and to walk with the Lord.

Sam commented, "True freedom began the moment I quit blaming others and accepted responsibility for my life. But I knew my journey would never have taken this path if my family hadn't kept praying, talking to me about the Lord, and loving me."

Wednesday
Week

16

POINTS TO PONDER

If we are wise, we begin to face ourselves and our weaknesses, and we accept accountability for our failures. When we speak that truth to God, He immediately forgives us. Then the process of change can really begin.

POWER BUILDER

KWABENA DARKO

Owner, Darko Farms

Thursday
Week

16

TORMENTED BY SPIRITS THAT tried to strangle him in his bed, Kwabena Darko turned to God when he was sixteen years old, seeking deliverance from the terrors that haunted him. The spirits vanished, and he received a new vision. Kwabena clearly heard the voice of God speaking in his heart: "I want you to be a businessman to support My work."

Kwabena and his bride combined their resources, leased five acres of land, and started an egg farm. They made a commitment to tithe their income. Before long their investment grew. Kwabena prayed, borrowed money, and repaid it. He continued to pray and borrow and repay. In less than twenty years, the original nest egg of 2,000 cedis was literally multiplied into the billions.

Kwabena Darko says, "Today, almost 27 years since our Farms started, Darko Farms is ranked as one of the most efficient farms in Africa. It is a highly integrated operation . . . with a highly motivated work force of 300 . . . and computerized facilities in some of our key areas of operations. God's blessing has been quite tremendous. . . .

"From the utmost dark tunnel that I found myself in 40 years ago, today I can join the chorus of other believers in saying that 'His love has lifted me' out of the miry clay and state of hopelessness. To God be the Glory!"

POWER QUOTE

Prayer is a personal interaction with God that enables us to agree with His perfect plan for our lives.

SCRIPTURE

Matthew 21:22

If you have faith when you pray, you will be given whatever you ask for.

POINTS TO PONDER

Which comes first: the desire or God's intention to meet it? Many times, it seems that He stirs us up to pray, and when He does, His answer is immediate. Our greatest danger in prayer is determining what we want and then convincing ourselves that it is His will. When we impose our will on Him, we unfailingly encounter disappointments. But when the desire springs forth from some source beyond ourselves, it is probably His Spirit at work. In this way, He gives us the desires of our hearts by placing them there in the first place.

POWER BUILDER

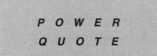

POWER QUOTE

Prayer puts the power of God to work against life's seemingly impossible odds.

SCRIPTURE

Proverbs 15:29

The LORD never even hears the prayers of the wicked, but he answers the prayers of all who obey him.

RICH SPRENKEL WAS AMAZED to be running again when he entered the world-famous Boston Marathon in 1989. Five years earlier, he had been in a serious automobile accident. Rich suffered a skull fracture, a pelvis broken in four places, and multiple lacerations. He was in a coma, and the attending physicians tried to prepare his parents for the brain impairment they foresaw.

Although Rich was not a believer at the time, his Christian family prayed in earnest about his life-and-death predicament. Twenty-eight days after the accident, Rich regained consciousness. And he could spell words when asked to do so.

Rich says, "The night before the surgery, I attended a prayer meeting and was anointed with oil and baptized in the Holy Spirit. I actually felt a surge of power through my neck during prayer. I knew God touched me. The next morning when the doctors X-rayed, they discovered the vertebrae were in position. I was elated to have that surgery canceled and breathed a prayer of gratitude . . . God was real!"

One year after the accident, Rich was running again. He has since competed in triathlons, marathons, and 10Ks. He finished in the top 20 percent of the Boston Marathon. Tears streaming down his face at the finish line, he prayed, "Is there anything You can't do, my Father in heaven?"

Friday
Week
16

POINTS TO PONDER

There is much talk of alternative medicine in our society. Some people turn to Eastern herbalists for help. Others seek shamans and psychics for mysterious cures. But Jesus Christ is the Great Physician. And He is still in the business of answering prayers for physical healing. He uses healing to remind us of His power, His wisdom, and His love.

THE PLAQUE ON THE Sunday school wall reads PRAYER CHANGES THINGS. Take a moment to remember some answers to prayer that have changed your life. Write them down, with thanks.

_____

_____

_____

_____

_____

Weekend
Week

16

Lord,

thank You for hearing my prayers—

the loud, angry outbursts,

the quietly whispered requests,

even the silent thoughts that I don't

stop to verbalize.

You hear them all

and supply my needs.

Thank You for being so deeply involved

in my life

and for inviting me to communicate with You.

ROBERT SNYDER

Major, U.S. Marine Corps

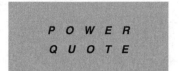

We may lose our way from time to time, but we cannot lose the battle if God is on our side.

SCRIPTURE

2 Corinthians 10:4

[We don't] fight our battles with the weapons of this world. Instead, we use God's power.

R OBERT SNYDER WAS FLYING in a Harrier formation across the Pacific Ocean when an unexpected and violent storm interrupted their refueling efforts. As Robert pulled away from his refueling aircraft, he lost his airspeed slightly and began to fall behind the other three aircraft.

He fixed his eyes on the three rapidly disappearing dots on the horizon. He spent all his energy trying to accelerate and catch up with the others. Suddenly, Robert sensed a presence to his left, where he saw another Harrier flying next to him. It appeared to be upside down, but it was in perfect wing position. Where had it come from?

Checking his instruments, Robert realized that he had lost more than a mile of altitude and was flying nearly upside down. He was diving full speed toward the ocean.

After righting himself, he looked around for the other Harrier. It was gone. When he radioed for position, the only planes visible to the navigation aircraft were the other three. Once he landed in San Francisco, Robert realized that he had enough fuel left to fly only four more minutes. If the fifth Harrier hadn't appeared precisely when it did, he would never have made it back.

Monday
Week

17

POINTS TO PONDER

In the Bible, our walk of faith is often compared to military service. God's army has a unique advantage, however. Although we will certainly be involved in ongoing struggles, the battle has already been won. And in the moments when we are overwhelmed by impossible odds, we find, like Major Snyder, that our God is on our side, guiding us, protecting us, and doing the impossible on our behalf.

POWER BUILDER

GRADY JACKSON
Rear Admiral, U.S. Navy

GRADY JACKSON, WHO TAKES his Christianity into the military service with him, had a third class petty officer in his squadron named Scotty. The tough young sailor had fallen ill with a rare blood disease while in the Philippines. His family was flown to Clark Air Force Base Hospital because he wasn't expected to live.

When he heard that the doctors had given up hope, Rear Admiral Jackson called a prayer meeting in the chapel of the USS *Enterprise*. Scotty was a popular crew member, and the chapel was more packed than Jackson imagined possible. Jackson read Matthew 18:20: "Whenever two or three of you come together in my name, I am there with you." The group prayed together for half an hour. Jackson then explained that the situation was in God's hands, and the meeting ended.

The first day, Scotty's condition was no different. The next day, he seemed slightly better. Then there was a dramatic change—Scotty was completely healed. Believers or not, nearly everyone aboard agreed—there was no explanation for the young man's turnaround except a miracle from God, accomplished through the power of prayer.

SCRIPTURE

James 5:16 NKJV

The effective, fervent prayer of a righteous man avails much.

POINTS TO PONDER

The saying goes that there are no atheists in the trenches—that is, when a matter of life and death arises, human beings instinctively turn to God for help. In navy life, spiritual concerns are not the most common topic of discussion. In fact, those who consider the things of God to be of central concern may find themselves on the outside of many conversations. But when a shipmate's life is threatened, God is quickly recalled. His power is quietly acknowledged. And when He accomplishes His wonders, He is worshiped, however briefly, as "eternal Father, strong to save."

CINDY DILLON

Lieutenant Commander, U.S. Navy

God goes into battle before us, follows behind us, and surrounds us with His powerful protection.

James 5:15

If you have faith when you pray for sick people, they will get well. The Lord will heal them.

CINDY DILLON WAS A weather officer in a remote U.S. Navy support facility on the Indian Ocean island of Diego Garcia when a strange, frightening condition overcame her. A medevac C-5 aircraft flew her to the Philippines, the nearest U.S. armed forces major medical facility, which was eleven hours away. Two CAT scans and two spinal taps revealed hemorrhaging, probably in the brain.

Cindy's commanding officer was a believer, as was Cindy. He initiated prayer for healing for her. Along with other concerned personnel, he was saddened to hear that her husband was being flown in for her surgery—that could only mean that the doctors expected her to die. The officer and a few fellow believers got together to pray, and they pleaded for Cindy's life.

In advance of the operation, the medical team did a routine angiogram. To their amazement, it appeared to be perfectly normal. They ran exhaustive tests. Every test came back normal. The doctors canceled the surgery. From the farthest reaches of the earth, the prayer of faithful friends had been heard and answered on her behalf. Her illness never recurred.

Wednesday

Week

17

The concern of a commanding officer for the troops is an earthly metaphor for God's love for us. As our commander in the spiritual battle, He is responsible for our well-being, for our placement in the conflict, and for our care when we are injured or ill. He knows about our special abilities, and He places us in positions that best suit our talents. And when we fall into difficulties or dangers, He stirs up our fellow soldiers to pray for us and to come to our aid. Most important of all, God goes ahead of us into the most dangerous warfare, fighting for us, clearing a safe pathway for us through the deadly assault of the enemy.

NED COLBURN
Fighter Pilot

As A FIGHTER PILOT during the Vietnam War, Ned Colburn had a dream: "I saw a MIG coming in for the kill, and I attempted to call a warning to the other EB-66's in the flight—but no one heard me. The MIG fired its missiles, but missed us. Relieved, I looked down at my radio-interphone connections and saw that they had come apart, which was the reason my warning calls were not heard."

Twelve hours later, Ned's dream became reality. A MIG appeared on his radar screen and fired its heat-seeking missiles. His first warning call was not heard. The second warning was heard, and the aircraft broke left just as the missiles passed harmlessly over the right side.

After the war, Ned returned home. He says, "My mother asked if I had been in some sort of danger on the previous January 17 at 1 A.M. Kansas time. I thought for a moment, adjusted the time difference to what it would have been in Vietnam. Incredibly, it was exactly the same time we were under attack by the MIG."

At that moment, Ned Colburn's mother was praying for him. Once she fell asleep, a dream assured her that her son was safe.

He will not abandon us in our weakness, and He will not leave us in doubt about His strength.

SCRIPTURE

2 Corinthians 10:3

We live in this world, but we don't act like its people.

POINTS TO PONDER

In His deep concern for His army, God continuously involves Himself in our protection. When necessary, He uses any means possible to communicate to us that He is caring for us, even in the midst of the battle. He speaks through His Word. He communicates through His still, small voice. He reveals His purposes through dreams. He discloses Himself through the words of other men and women. Once He has assured us that He is prepared to defend us, He allows us to enter the battle. And then He acts. The enemy is defeated, and the victory is God's, not ours.

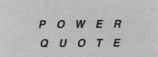

WWI SOLDIERS

German and British Forces

POWER QUOTE

The peace of God is available to His people, even in the heat of the battle.

SCRIPTURE

Luke 2:14

Praise God in heaven! Peace on earth to everyone who pleases God.

Nearly an entire generation of young Britons was lost in World War I, and the casualties were no less dramatic on the opposing side of the conflict. But on Christmas Day, 1914, the Prince of Peace seized control for a few hours, and bitter opponents momentarily became friends.

It began when German troops lit candles on Christmas trees so the British sentries could see them. In other places, the British lit bonfires, announcing a truce. In some places, they sang carols together, traded names and addresses, and even played soccer.

One soldier wrote to his parents, "Just you think that while you were eating your turkey, etc., I was out talking and shaking hands with the very men I had been trying to kill a few hours before! It was astounding!"

As the soldiers exchanged portions of their food gifts from home, their generals were horrified. In later years, their diaries revealed deep concern that their soldiers' will to fight would be gravely weakened by fraternizing. On December 19, Germany declared fraternization to be high treason. But for less than twenty-four hours—the guns of World War I fell silent, and the front lines resounded with laughter, conversation, and Christmas music.

Friday

Week

17

POINTS TO PONDER

Although the people of God are enlisted in an ongoing spiritual conflict, God's ultimate goal for us is peace. "Peace on earth" was His promise on the night of His Son's birth, and His Son bears the title of Prince of Peace. God wants us to have peace in our hearts and serenity in our surroundings. He has not called us to compromise truth, but He has instructed us to seek peace and to pursue it. Ultimately, the battle will be over, and only peace will remain for His victorious army.

I S YOUR LIFE AS peaceful as you would like it to be? Reflect on some steps you could take that would bring greater serenity to your inner world and your outward circumstances. List them.

_____

_____

_____

Weekend
Week

17

Lord,

I'm a nervous soldier in Your army.

I often find myself becoming edgy,

irritated, and grouchy.

I get caught up in my day-to-day battles,

I react to other people's trouble making,

and I worry needlessly.

Even though the Christian life is filled with warfare

I know that peace is a choice I can make.

Lord, I choose peace right now.

Please teach me how to let go

without giving up.

Show me how to relax within my responsibilities.

And as I commit my future to You,

grant me the special peace

that goes beyond my understanding.

POWER BUILDER

GENE ELLERBEE
Executive, Procter and Gamble

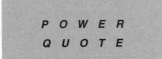

POWER QUOTE

Bowing the knee to God is a humbling act, but it introduces great power and potential into our lives.

SCRIPTURE

Proverbs 16:7

When we please the LORD, even our enemies make friends with us.

GENE ELLERBEE HAD NEVER met a Christian businessman. His wife believed in Jesus and prayed for him regularly, but he viewed her faith as a "woman's" issue. He didn't know that she was praying for godly Christian businessmen to cross her husband's path.

On a trip to Breckenridge, Colorado, Gene was reunited with a friend who was a former football player and fighter pilot. He and Gene were out splitting logs when the man said, "Something has happened to me since I saw you last." He went on to explain that he had become a born-again Christian. Gene was uncomfortable, so he was glad when his friend left for home.

Another newly converted friend arrived from Denver in his four-wheel-drive truck, proclaiming that Gene needed Jesus Christ in his life. More uncomfortable than ever, Gene got on a plane for home, relieved to be away from his suddenly "fanatical" friends.

A stranger sat down next to him on the plane. The man said, "I just got back from the Vatican." But he didn't want to talk about the pope. "Either you accept Jesus Christ as your personal Savior," he told Gene, "and have everlasting life with Him, or you reject Him."

By that time, Gene had seen more than enough real men who believed in Christ. When he got home, he humbled himself, prayed with his wife, and invited Jesus into his heart.

POINTS TO PONDER

Success in the marketplace is a powerful motivator for competitive men and women. And accomplishment can create a sense of personal power that causes people to feel no need for God. But God wants to come into our lives to change us from within into a new kind of people living a new kind of life. His eternal agenda for us certainly takes our business concerns into consideration, but His big picture involves every aspect of our lives here and now as well as the life to come.

POWER BUILDER

BILL MCCARTNEY
Former Coach, University of Colorado Buffaloes

THE POWER OF GOD'S love can overcome seemingly insurmountable threats to personal relationships. Bill McCartney learned in August 1988 that his 19-year-old daughter was pregnant, and the father of the baby was his star quarterback—Sal Aunese. Sal was not in love with Kristyn, and he suggested that she abort the baby, which she refused to do.

Coach McCartney assured Sal that his position on the team would not be affected by the pregnancy, but as a father, he struggled desperately with his daughter's pain. He needed to forgive the young man for hurting Kristyn so deeply. Could he? A few months later, even more shocking news emerged: Sal was dying of cancer.

Meanwhile the press publicized the pregnancy story. The family members clung to their Christian faith and to each other.

Sal's condition worsened, and his sister asked Coach McCartney to lead Sal to Christ. As the two men wept, Bill McCartney prayed the sinner's prayer with Sal, and the dying young man received eternal salvation. The baby, Timothy Chase, was born before Sal's death in 1989, and Sal described him as "the gift of life God has given me." Bill McCartney had given him an even greater gift—God's powerful and unconditional love.

Tuesday
Week

18

POWER QUOTE

When we refuse to be vindictive, we make it possible for the True Judge to mandate both justice and mercy.

SCRIPTURE

Psalm 112:5–6 NKJV

A good man deals graciously. . . . He will guide his affairs with discretion. . . . The righteous will be in everlasting remembrance.

POINTS TO PONDER

Films and television shows often depict revenge as a glorious act, and vindictiveness seems to indicate a heroic character. But how much more difficult it is to let go of our rage and retaliation and to seek God's better way—forgiveness and love. The strength of character necessary to love someone who has wounded us or someone we love requires far more courage than any act of vengeance. This response to injury is evidence of God's power at work in us—and oftentimes in spite of us.

POWER BUILDER

DON ARMSTRONG

High School Hockey Coach

POWER QUOTE

Personal heroism often requires overcoming our fears and confronting a potential disaster head-on.

SCRIPTURE

1 Corinthians 13:7–8

Love is always supportive, loyal, hopeful, and trusting.

DRIVING HOME FROM PRACTICE, Don Armstrong noticed that a car was stopped at the crest of a bridge with its blinker on. Its driver was slouched, smoking a cigarette. When Don tried to get his attention, he waved him on.

Don parked and headed back to the car on foot. "Hey, buddy—you ain't thinking of going over, are you?"

"Yeah. Now go away and leave me alone."

Don kept talking about the thing he knew best—hockey. He explained that he was a coach, and that he had been a little down—his team had lost a few games in a row.

The man glanced up. "My son played hockey."

Having won his confidence, Don asked the man what was wrong. He explained that his wife was ill, and that he had been laid off from his job. He was fifty-three years old, and as far as he was concerned, life was over.

"Don't do this. Come to my office and we'll talk."

Don drove the man to a local college, where a counselor talked to him. Later on, local police took him to a hospital for treatment. Once the man was released, Don picked him up and drove him home. In the midst of a losing hockey season, Don Armstrong won the big one.

POINTS TO PONDER

Our world urges us to follow a better-safe-than-sorry credo: don't get involved. When Don Armstrong reached out to a suicidal stranger, he set aside his own comfort zone, he risked exposing himself to someone's potentially troublesome personal life, and he gave of his time and emotion without seeking compensation. Isn't that precisely what Jesus has done for us? How can we do less for others?

POWER BUILDER

NOLAN RYAN

Former Professional Baseball Player

NOLAN RYAN HAD MORE than five thousand strikeouts, more than three hundred wins, and more no-hitters than any other player in baseball. When he retired from baseball, he was the oldest player in the game, approaching fifty years of age.

He attributes his success to the power of dedication and determination, and to his love of hard work: "I've accumulated a lot of money, and I suppose I could coast for a good while if I chose to. But I'd go crazy not working. I enjoy manual labor; I enjoy working cattle. I get a lot of satisfaction out of doing a good job, whether it's mowing a yard, raking leaves, doing a flower bed, or building a fence.

"I don't like doing shoddy work or spending my time on something that isn't what it should have been or isn't going to last. I don't want to have to go back and redo.

"I'll always be able to look in the mirror and know that the guy looking back gave the game and the fans and his ball club everything he had to give for as long as he could."

Thursday

Week

18

Hard work reflects good character, and good character is powerful.

SCRIPTURE

Hebrews 6:10 NKJV

God is not unjust to forget your work and labor of love which you have shown toward His name.

POINTS TO PONDER

A strong work ethic is a major component of good character. In a leisure-oriented culture, many individuals have learned to take the easy course and to cut corners. They get by, but they do not excel. On the other end of the continuum are the workaholics who use work as a distraction from painful relationships and personal problems. Keeping work in its proper perspective means giving our best to every task, but knowing when to stop. It means, in the case of Christians, doing all things for the pleasure and approval of God, without placing undue priority on professional concerns.

POWER BUILDER

ALFRED E. FERGUSON

Chief Judge, Cabell (West Virginia) County Circuit

POWER QUOTE

If you were accused of being a Christian, would there be enough evidence to convict you?

SCRIPTURE

1 Corinthians 15:58

Stand firm and don't be shaken. Always keep busy working for the Lord. You know that everything you do for him is worthwhile.

ALFRED E. FERGUSON BECAME a powerful public witness for his Christian faith. A state prison inmate filed a lawsuit against a local citizen, involving allegations of homosexuality, blackmail, and corruption. Judge Ferguson noted that the plaintiff was a worshiper of Satan, and he wrote a letter to the West Virginia Supreme Court, asking to be removed from the case because he felt his personal Christian faith should disqualify him. Six weeks later, he returned from out of town to a flurry of news stories. His correspondence had been made public.

Judge Ferguson received letters from all over the country. One read, "In this day and age it takes more courage to speak out for Christianity. Good for you . . . the final victory will be Christ's."

And it was. Courthouse employees and lawyers quietly sought out Judge Ferguson to share their faith and to express appreciation for his stand. Scores of believers whose faith had been strengthened by his stand contacted him.

Judge Ferguson says, "Though I never expected to become a public witness when I wrote that letter to the Supreme Court, the Lord showed me how He uses seemingly ordinary incidents to make a dramatic impact on people. He also let me know what He wants me to do in my position—at the right time, in the right place, to the right people—share my faith."

Friday
Week

18

POINTS TO PONDER

When we stand by our convictions, we rarely do so in hope that we will set a public example with our actions. But God is aware of our efforts to do right, and sometimes He chooses to make our choices known to others. Our Christian witness is made up of small decisions and large commitments. Ultimately, when it comes to our faith, we are known by what we do.

Wᴴᴬᵀ DO YOU CONSIDER the qualities that contribute to powerful Christian living? List some of the attributes that reflect a strong Christian commitment.

_____

_____

_____

_____

_____

Weekend
Week

18

Lord,

I know Your desire for me is that my character

reflect the character of Your Son.

I want to do right and to behave appropriately.

But I have learned that I'm not able,

by using my own power,

to be the person You want me to be.

I am not always courageous,

I don't always do my best,

and at times I insist on

taking things into my own hands

instead of trusting You.

Please work on my heart and mind

so that I am continuously being transformed

into a new creation by Your power.

POWER BUILDER

JOHNNY LANHAM
University Professor

JOHNNY AND MEGAN LANHAM went to the People's Republic of China where Johnny was invited to be a guest university professor. The Lanhams were well aware of the tightly controlled environment, but they felt no particular sense of alarm. Then whooping cough struck the playmate of Rebekah, the Lanhams' two-year-old daughter.

A few days later, Rebekah awoke, coughing in spasms that left her desperate for breath. After a long, terrifying night, Johnny and Megan took their exhausted child to a local hospital. The results wouldn't be available until the next day.

That night, the coughing struck again with a vengeance. The parents tried to ease it with various remedies. Nothing helped. Never had they felt so alone, so helpless.

Johnny was not a believer in miracle cures, but in his desperation, he placed his hand on Rebekah's chest and began to pray. He prayed so long that the child fell asleep. Still he prayed. Hours passed. Rebekah slept quietly.

The following day, although hospital tests verified whooping cough, Rebekah's cough never returned. The power of the miracle touched Johnny's and Megan's lives as well as some of their new Chinese friends. The Lanhams say, "At home . . . we would have relied on the best doctors, medicines, paramedics . . . having never been driven to prayer, we might never have witnessed a miracle . . . born of desperation."

POINTS TO PONDER

When we turn to God for healing, we set aside our scientific understanding of medicine. That doesn't mean we fail to go to the doctor. But it does mean we have chosen to rely on God's power and not solely on human solutions. God works in many ways, and He often uses physicians as healers. When we pray, we turn over the controls to Him, knowing that He is able to work in a multitude of ways to restore physical, mental, and spiritual health.

POWER BUILDER

LARNELLE HARRIS
Gospel Singer

Tuesday
Week
19

THE POWERFUL VOICE OF Larnelle Harris has touched the hearts of millions of listeners since his first album was released in 1975. He has won Grammys and Dove Awards.

But before his first album was ever released, Larnelle lost his voice, and his musical career very nearly ended. While touring with the Spurrlows, a Christian group that performed in high schools and churches, Larnelle had sung in two or three performances a day. The schedule was so exhausting that it had injured his vocal cords.

"Why?" Larnelle asked himself again and again. He sank into tremendous self-pity, wondering how a God of love could allow him to be robbed of his best gift—his ability to sing. Finally, Larnelle came to terms with God's power over everything: "God loves me and cares for me."

After consulting with countless physicians, he learned that rest for his voice was the best treatment. He also discovered that he had to rest in the Lord and allow Him to deal with his life and future. Eventually, Larnelle's voice returned, strong as ever. But more important, his immature Christianity developed into a faith that respected God's infinite wisdom and power.

POWER QUOTE

The Good Shepherd makes me to lie down in green pastures—whether I want to or not.

SCRIPTURE

Luke 9:11

Jesus welcomed them. He spoke to them about God's kingdom and healed everyone who was sick.

POINTS TO PONDER

Relaxation may seem self-indulgent, even irresponsible, to us. But this belief is not appropriate for Christians who understand that the human body, because of Christ's indwelling presence, is an actual temple of God. Scripture reminds us not to harm that temple. It is not unusual, when we need a break, for God to allow some unforeseen ailment to come along, forcing us to rest and restore ourselves. It is His gracious way of caring for us.

DAVID YANIV
Israeli Farmer

**POWER
BUILDER**

God sometimes creates a need
in our lives so He will be able
to meet us in the midst of
that need.

SCRIPTURE

Matthew 4:24

People with every kind of sick-

ness or disease were brought to

him. . . . Others could not

walk. But Jesus healed them all.

DAVID YANIV WAS THE son of German Jews who had immi-
grated to Israel after World War II. David's father was an avowed atheist.

After he served in the Israeli army, David and his wife joined an agri-
cultural commune along with 165 other families. There David slipped
while milking cows and injured his back. The injury caused intolerable
pain. Finally, he consented to minor surgery, which was to completely correct his painful condition.

David awoke from the surgery paralyzed from the waist down. His
emotional world collapsed. He struggled with depression for seven and a
half years.

David's only diversion was television. After watching Christian pro-
gramming, he accepted Jesus Christ as his Savior. Then one day a guest on
the *700 Club* said, "There is someone who has been paralyzed for many
years . . . this person will feel a certain sensation and will be healed."
David said to himself, "I receive that healing in the name of Jesus."

That night, David felt a sensation move from his spine into his legs,
which began to tremble uncontrollably. The next day, feeling returned to
his legs. Days later, twenty-five neurosurgeons examined him in amazement. David Yaniv told those physicians, and continues to affirm today,
that the power of Jesus the Messiah is still performing miracles in Israel.

Wednesday
Week

19

POINTS TO PONDER

God is not willing for anyone to be without Him, and He uses every
resource at His disposal to gain our attention. Frequently, in the midst of
adversity we become aware of our need for Him. And when, as in the case
of David Yaniv, the body is so assaulted that it cannot function normally,
God finds opportunity to step in and make His power known, not only
for the sake of healing, but for the purpose of providing eternal life.

POWER BUILDER

LELA GILBERT
Writer

LELA GILBERT SUFFERED THROUGHOUT her childhood from a serious skin disease that refused to respond to medical treatment. Her skin became red and peeled. The constant itching was agonizing and humiliating.

Depressed and bitter, Lela attended a 1963 Billy Graham crusade in Los Angeles. She surprised herself by giving her future to Jesus Christ.

Four years later, Lela was walking down a southern California street when an uninvited thought came to her with overpowering conviction. It was as if a voice said, "I want to heal your skin." She told her mother, who shook her head skeptically. "Well, just don't get your hopes up," she warned her daughter.

Thursday
Week

19

But Lela did get her hopes up. Within weeks, she was healed so totally that she went on to become a fashion model. She learned three things from the experience: "To get up and get going, no matter how painful the circumstances. To show compassion to the diseased and despairing." Most important, she says, "It's all right to get my hopes up, when God is in the world." Although skin disease controlled her life for more than two decades, the power of God intervened and dramatically changed her, both inside and outside.

POWER QUOTE

Physical illness is sometimes a tool in the hand of God, carving beauty into our souls through patience and suffering.

SCRIPTURE

Psalm 119:71 NKJV

It is good for me that I have been afflicted, that I may learn Your statutes.

POINTS TO PONDER

Some people focus on physical healing. They hold seminars and quote Scriptures that verify God's healing power. Although Jesus performed many healings during His ministry, He did not come into the world only to heal. He came for a greater purpose—to redeem our souls. There are times when God allows disease and physical discomfort to deepen us, to prepare us for a greater work in our lives. Once He has accomplished His purpose through our illness, He may well remove it so that we can move on to other areas of growth and maturity.

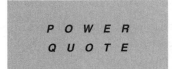

**POWER
BUILDER**

SHAWN WHALEN

Baseball Player

POWER QUOTE

God is listening to everything you say. Are you listening to Him?

SCRIPTURE

Psalm 107:19–20

You were in serious trouble, but you prayed to the LORD, and he rescued you. By the power of his own word, he healed you.

WHILE PLAYING BASEBALL WITH the San Diego Padres class A team, Shawn Whalen began to have trouble coordinating his eyes and muscles. Doctors discovered that his thyroid gland wasn't functioning. That was corrected. But then Shawn became excessively fatigued. His elbows and knees swelled, and the surrounding skin felt red hot.

"You've got an incurable muscle disease," the doctor reported, "and I don't feel capable of treating it." A second opinion was even more grim: "Forget baseball. Let's see how long we can keep you out of a wheelchair."

Shawn and his wife, Lisa, had been attending Bible studies, and they quickly turned to prayer. They reassured themselves after reading Proverbs 4:20–23 that God's Word would be medicine and health to Shawn's flesh.

Shawn began to feel better, and by the time he reported for further tests, he felt great. The doctor shook his head. "It's not there anymore," he said as Shawn and Lisa smiled at each other. "You're normal. What did you do?"

Shawn explained that he and his wife had prayed to God for healing.

"Right. Okay. But what did you do?"

Shawn says, "He never listened. Some can't accept the truth that God is alive and well and heals His people."

Friday
Week

19

There seem to be two kinds of people—those who have spiritual hearing and those who don't. The Bible talks about this phenomenon, suggesting that certain individuals should unstop their ears. Jesus frequently said, "He who has ears to hear, let him hear!" Perhaps we should pray that our spiritual hearing is healed before we seek God's help with our other infirmities.

THERE ARE MANY FORMS of healing—physical, emotional, mental, and spiritual. Can you remember an occasion when God healed you or used your prayers to heal someone else? Take a moment to record that story and to thank Him.

_____

_____

_____

_____

Weekend
Week

19

Lord,

I come to You today

seeking the touch of Your hand.

My body is hurting,

my mind is weary,

and my emotions are troubled.

Touch me, Lord, with the same hands

that gave health to the diseased and

hope to the desolate.

In the process, Lord,

show me the purpose of Your work in my life.

What would You have me see and hear?

What would You have me do?

SHELLEY SMITH GULMON
Hospice Volunteer

POWER BUILDER

POWER QUOTE

Compassion is the gift we bring forth from the depths of our suffering.

SCRIPTURE

Proverbs 14:21

God blesses everyone who is kind.

SHELLEY SMITH GULMON HAD problems throughout her pregnancy. She deeply desired to bring her baby into the world. But Andrew John Gulmon arrived three months early—stillborn.

Shelley and her parents were shopping for a burial outfit for the tiny infant when they met Lanette Davis, a salesclerk who was touched by their tragedy and their evident heartache. They couldn't find anything small enough to fit the little boy. Lanette contacted her mother, who was an excellent seamstress, and asked if she could tailor an outfit to fit the Gulmon baby. The woman agreed to do so for no charge.

When the Gulmon's arrived at the chapel before the funeral, they noticed an inscription in the guest book: Ronald, Sharon, Laura, and Lanette Davis. The Davises had also left a plant and a card reading, "To Andrew John's daddy and mommy—our prayers are with you."

After her grief had passed, Shelley Gulmon reflected on the kindness of the Davis family. She chose to follow their example. She volunteered at a local hospice where she continues to serve as a group leader in the infant-loss program.

POINTS TO PONDER

Our suffering often brings forth our greatest gifts, and frequently, these gifts include being compassionate and giving comfort. Having been through personal pain, we are quick to recognize similar pain in the lives of others, and empathy with them is as natural as breathing. We feel their heartache as if it is our own. When we offer comfort from the depths of our woundedness, we make our suffering meaningful and allow God to use it for His good purposes.

POWER BUILDER

JONNIVAR D'ANGELO

Representative, Southwest Airlines

FRANCES LUSK RECEIVED THE troubling news that she might have a malignant brain tumor, and she was referred to the Barrow Neurological Institute in Phoenix, Arizona, for further testing. If necessary, brain surgery was to be performed there.

A friend who might have accompanied her was also scheduled for surgery. And so, terrified and feeling utterly alone, Frances called Southwest Airlines to make a reservation. As she spoke to Southwest representative Jonnivar D'Angelo, she broke down. "She wanted to call me back later, but I said, 'No, Stay on. We'll talk. Take your time,'" Jonnivar remembers.

Jonnivar made the flight arrangements and a hotel reservation, and she also informed Frances that she was going to pick her up at the airport and take her to the doctor.

Tuesday
Week
20

Flowers in hand, Jonnivar met Frances's plane. "Now you have a friend in Phoenix," she explained.

The surgery was performed, and the brain tumor was not malignant. Every day Jonnivar called or visited Frances at the hospital, and she took her out to dinner several times. In gratitude, Frances bought Jonnivar a gold pin and presented it to her. "You just don't find people who welcome strangers like that," she says, amazed at her good fortune.

POWER QUOTE

Showing compassion means getting involved with troubled people and making their problems ours.

SCRIPTURE

Proverbs 15:30

A friendly smile makes you happy, and good news makes you feel strong.

POINTS TO PONDER

We have to remind ourselves that we have a responsibility to those who are in need because Jesus set an example for us. He set aside His glorious life in heaven and came to walk the dusty roads of the Middle East because He wanted to share our lives with us. Ultimately, He came to give His life in exchange for ours. Are we willing to do the same for others?

POWER BUILDER

HARRIET BEECHER STOWE
Writer

POWER QUOTE

When we act in compassion, God gives greater purpose to our pain and greater power to our prayers.

SCRIPTURE

2 Corinthians 1:5

We share in the terrible sufferings of Christ, but also in the wonderful comfort he gives.

"SO YOU ARE THE little woman who wrote the book that made this big war!" Those were the words of President Abraham Lincoln when he was introduced to Harriet Beecher Stowe in 1862. He knew how profoundly the book *Uncle Tom's Cabin* had shaken the foundations of American life.

Mrs. Stowe was not particularly well prepared for her fame. Although her father was a well-known evangelist and temperance advocate, and one of her brothers was a great preacher, all was not well in Harriet's family. Two of her brothers committed suicide. Her sister rejected Christianity. Another brother was brought to trial for his belief in evolution. Harriet's children did not fare much better. Of the six she bore, three died tragically.

Out of this agonizing reality flowed the fiction of *Uncle Tom's Cabin*. The book galvanized readers at a time when many had grown apathetic about slavery and refused to see its horrors.

Where did Harriet Beecher Stowe derive the power to write her novel? When asked the question, she was quick to respond, "God did it!" God had used the heartbreak and devastation of her own life to enable her to empathize with African-Americans whose families were also torn apart by tragedy and loss.

Wednesday
Week

20

POINTS TO PONDER

The New Testament tells us that Jesus Christ endured the same kinds of pain we experience, and that He shares in our suffering. Although He did not have to cope with the troubles we bring on ourselves by doing wrong, He still understands the emotions that those troubles arouse. In His compassion, He hears the prayers we offer up in tears, and He identifies with us. There is great power in His compassion because He puts it to work for us, bringing good out of evil, overcoming evil with good.

LARRY WAGNER

Business Administrator

Thursday

Week

20

THE BOY LEARNED THAT by stealing tires from a local junkyard, he could earn a few dollars. He was pleased with his new vocation, that is, until someone at the junkyard started shooting at him and his friends.

Late that night, after Larry Wagner sneaked into the house, his mother entered his bedroom and quietly reminded her son that he should say his prayers before he went to sleep. Her tear-stained face indicated that she had been praying for Larry. "Lord," he prayed as he drifted off, "don't let me take the wrong road in life."

Both Larry's brothers had worked hard in school, graduating with top honors, only to find themselves in menial jobs. *Why try?* Larry thought angrily. *Only white people get good jobs.*

Stephen Rose came to Larry's school. He was a white businessman who had founded the Vocational Information Program. He took his young charges to visit dozens of career sites, and he saw that they were tutored by executives every Saturday morning.

With Stephen Rose's no-nonsense guidance, Larry was able to enroll in a local college. He graduated and began a white-collar career in business administration in one of Mr. Rose's affiliated corporations. Larry recognizes that hard work and diligence opened the door to his future success. But the compassion of a white businessman toward a discouraged African-American boy turned the key.

POWER QUOTE

Our compassion for others is God's gift to them, given with our hands.

SCRIPTURE

Isaiah 49:8

I will answer your prayers because I have set a time when I will help by coming to save you.

POINTS TO PONDER

What causes us to care about less-fortunate people? Sometimes we have been through similar difficulties. But now and then, God places a special concern in our hearts. It seems to have no particular reason for being there, except for His providence. It is, in essence, God's way of granting us the privilege of doing His work through us.

ROY MCKEOWN

Founder and President, World Opportunities

SCRIPTURE

2 Corinthians 9:7, 11 NKJV

God loves a cheerful giver. . . .
You are enriched in everything
for all liberality, which causes
thanksgiving through us to
God.

ROY MCKEOWN IS OFTEN at the scene of disasters. But he was never closer to personal tragedy than on the day of the Northridge earthquake. At 4:31 A.M., January 17, 1994, Roy and his wife, Marianne, were awakened by a terrifying jolt. Marianne was thrown violently from the bed just as a jagged piece of the window hurtled across the room and stabbed the mattress—in the same spot where she had been lying.

Dazed and shaken, the couple fell to their knees and prayed. They didn't know it at the time, but their Granada Hills home was very close to the earthquake's epicenter. Outside, gas mains exploded; water geysered from broken water pipes. Neighboring houses were ripped apart with a deafening sound.

The McKeowns' home was found to be unlivable. And the World Opportunities Headquarters, in nearby Hollywood, was also damaged. Only the warehouse, filled with food and supplies, survived intact.

Grateful to be alive, Roy McKeown found strength beyond himself. By the end of the day, he was passing out food, clothing, and medical supplies to victims of the earthquake. He was back on the job, doing what he does best—caring for those who need a helping hand.

Friday
Week

20

POINTS TO PONDER

Bearing one another's burdens is a demonstration of a strong faith. Although much has been written about the dangers of focusing on the needs of others and avoiding the issues in our own lives that need attention, we can find great pleasure and reward in setting aside our needs for a few hours and helping those who can't make it on their own. And in God's economy, we invariably find that as we meet the needs of others, God meets our needs in unexpected and exciting ways.

COMPASSION CAN BE A powerful force in the life of a hurting person. When have you been touched by someone's compassion? How did it affect you?

_____

_____

Reflect on your sense of compassion and on any changes you would like to see in yourself.

_____

_____

Weekend
Week

20

Lord,

You have always treated me with great compassion.

You have forgiven my sins,

and You are helping me change my behavior.

You have provided for my needs

and given me good things beyond my basic needs.

You have heard my prayers

and sometimes answered me before I asked.

You have met me in my darkest hour

and lifted my spirits.

Many times, You have used others

to love me with Your love.

Help me do the same, Lord,

for others, demonstrating Your compassion.

It's the least I can do for You.

DAVID RING

Motivational Speaker

POWER BUILDER

True empowerment is God's strength working through our weaknesses.

2 Corinthians 12:9

My kindness is all you need. My power is strongest when you are weak.

A POWERFUL MOTIVATOR WHO speaks more than 250 times a year, David Ring has a loving wife, four healthy children, and a talented management staff. Week after week huge crowds welcome him. David is, in every visible way, a success. But it wasn't always so.

David was "born dead"—without oxygen—and this deficiency resulted in cerebral palsy. His brothers died of hemophilia. His parents were divorced. When David was eleven, his father died of cancer. His beloved mother died of the same disease when he was fourteen, leaving him orphaned. David's family wanted to institutionalize him; he was so angry and self-pitying. He hated God. Most of all, he hated himself.

David was confronted with a choice. Either he could receive a new beginning through Jesus Christ, or he could go on wallowing in his acute misery. David chose to accept God's purposes for his life—cerebral palsy and all. He received Christ, and in doing so, he was immediately embraced by other Christians. Best of all, he learned to accept himself and to thank God that he has been "fearfully and wonderfully made."

Today, David still walks with a limp and speaks with an impediment. But in his unique way he tells people, "Don't ask WHY, ask WHAT— What do You want me to do with my problems, God? How can I glorify You with them?"

Monday
Week

21

POINTS TO PONDER

Empowerment isn't a gift. Empowerment is a choice. We have to make a choice. If we choose to be victims rather than to make the most of our difficulties, we miss out on the very things that can make us powerful. Instead, we need to identify our limitations and then ask, "What can God make out of this?"

POWER BUILDER

DENNIS BYRD

Former Professional Football Player

Dennis Byrd was drafted by the New York Jets. A Christian man of faith, he had learned to rely on God when he was a small child. And as the summer of 1991 came and went, Dennis had a strange and definite sense that his faith was about to be tested.

In 1992, the Jets were playing the Kansas City Chiefs. Dennis collided violently with another player. He struggled to get up off the ground, but his body wouldn't move. He knew instantly that he had broken his neck. *My football career is over*, Dennis thought.

The prognosis was not good. Although no one directly told him he would never walk again, the signs were there. Fear and depression haunted Dennis during long months of surgery and rehabilitation. Yet a single thought drove him: *Take back your body*. Rehab was a battle to reclaim turf.

Dennis and his wife prayed together, along with a vast network of concerned friends and fans. Every time he felt the slightest response from a nerve or muscle, he worked on it night and day. As God renewed his strength, Dennis Byrd put that strength to work.

Today, Dennis Byrd is walking. He says, "If I've learned anything from my experience, it's that the Lord is with us if we falter, He is with us if we fail, He is with us when we break, and He can help make us whole."

Tuesday

Week

21

POINTS TO PONDER

"Dear God, I need a miracle!" is a familiar prayer. We've brainstormed our best ideas. We've experienced our resources. We've faced a thousand frustrations. In times like these, faith can provide peace of mind. And when a crisis occurs, a powerful miracle may very well follow.

But sometimes prayer isn't enough. Some miracles require both belief and a hefty application of elbow grease.

POWER QUOTE

Faith plus fortitude is an indomitable equation.

SCRIPTURE

Psalm 42:5

Why am I discouraged? Why am I restless? I trust you! And I will praise you again because you help me.

T O M   L A N D R Y
Former NFL Football Coach

POWER QUOTE

Nothing can destroy a man or woman whose plan, purpose, and posterity are founded on the Rock of Ages.

SCRIPTURE

Luke 6:48

[He] is like someone who dug down deep and built a house on solid rock.

T OM LANDRY WAS ONE of the most successful coaches ever to work in the National Football League, and his name is still synonymous with that of the Dallas Cowboys. Their coach for twenty-nine seasons, Landry led five Cowboys teams to the Super Bowl during the 1970s.

Years ago, Landry found good reason to commit his life to Christ: "I had always figured I was a pretty good person. Now here was the Bible saying I was as much a sinner as anyone else in the world." Landry's calm approach to wins and losses, his coaching style, and his off-the-field morality made him a paragon of Christian living.

For a number of reasons, the Cowboys in the 1980s didn't have the winning records of the earlier teams. Fingers of blame pointed Landry's way. Finally, in 1989, without a word of warning or consultation, Landry was out of work. Before he was so much as informed, a new Cowboys owner and head coach were toasting each other in a Dallas restaurant—in front of press cameras.

How could Tom Landry, who had experienced ultimate power and success in his field, cope with such a humiliating end to his brilliant career? He wrote, "My relationship with Christ gives me a source of power I would not have otherwise. . . . The knowledge that my life is in God's hands helps me to keep my composure or regain it in tough situations."

Wednesday
Week

21

POINTS TO PONDER

When things are going well, we're on top of the world, proudly wearing the label: SUCCESSFUL. But sometimes unwelcome changes come. Are we able to survive a major crisis? Or are we left empty-handed, asking, Who am I? Is my life over? If we've built our lives on earthly success, we may be swept away. But if we've built on the reality of God and His love, we have a solid foundation when life's storms howl around us.

POWER BUILDER

GRACIE OLIVER

Actress

Gracie Oliver's power-packed little body lays to rest any idea that size equals strength. She is thirty-four inches tall. Gracie is one of six children born to an alcoholic father prone to violence. Her physical condition made her early years challenging. But family troubles made life nearly impossible.

Yet Gracie learned that even though her body was small, it worked quite well. And she could sing beautifully.

Recent years, however, have taken their toll. A car accident in 1992 led to spinal surgery that left her unconscious and on life support for thirty-five days. She struggles through ongoing physical therapy in an attempt to regain use of her legs.

Thursday
Week
21

But Gracie is an overcomer, and she can still sing. She can still work as an actress. And she donates her time to raise funds for men, women, and children with disabilities.

Despite many trials and ongoing physical pain, Gracie Oliver believes in positivism, humor, and endless effort. Her friend and pastor Rev. Gus Krumm says of her, "She has every reason to be down in the dumps and be angry with life but she never is. She shames me sometimes because she's so up and so independent."

POWER QUOTE

A positive attitude is one of the most powerful weapons we can bring into the battle for success.

SCRIPTURE

1 Chronicles 28:20 NKJV

Be strong and of good courage, and do [the work]; do not fear nor be dismayed, for the LORD God . . . will be with you.

POINTS TO PONDER

What makes some people without challenges complainers and whiners, while others with major challenges somehow seem to look on the bright side? The answer is attitude. And those who have overcome adversity, survived tragedies, and beat the odds are invariably individuals who focus on the good things in life. They accomplish amazing things because they want to try, and in trying they want to succeed. People such as Gracie Oliver are winners—no matter what happens to them.

POWER BUILDER

HEATHER WHITESTONE
Former Miss America

HEATHER WHITESTONE WAS CROWNED Miss America because of her beauty, poise, and talent. But she brought far more than a pleasing persona to her audiences. Heather, who lost her hearing at eighteen months, is a powerful spokesperson for people with hearing impairments. A highly skilled lip-reader, she is able to speak eloquently wherever she goes.

Heather frequently addresses schoolchildren. She communicates to them a powerful message about beauty: "I've seen a lot of young ladies who are beautiful but have a hard heart. Nobody wants to be around them. When your heart is beautiful, you become more beautiful; your smile becomes more beautiful." This is something her mother taught her. And she wants boys and girls to know that "anything is possible if you believe in yourself and are willing to work hard."

As she visited schools around the country, she noticed that small children sometimes forgot what she was trying to tell them. In response, she developed her "Stars" platform. "A Star," Heather Whitestone explains, "has five points: have positive attitude; believe in your dreams, especially education; face your obstacles no matter how great; work hard; and build a support team."

POINTS TO PONDER

Overcoming disabilities makes strong people stronger. The compensatory skills we develop in the process of working around our limitations often become our greatest strengths. And when we combine our positive attitudes with faith in God, we become irresistibly powerful. Those who know God and have won the battle against tragedy, disability, and loss emphatically thank Him for the hard times. They know that without their struggles, they wouldn't be the overcomers they are. And they know that without His sovereign permission, the struggles would have never blessed their lives.

W HAT WAS THE SINGLE most difficult challenge you've ever faced in your life?

_____

_____

_____

How have you allowed that challenge to make you stronger?

_____

Weekend
Week

21

_____

Lord,

there have been many times in prayer

when I have choked out the words Thank You,

knowing I should be grateful for the bad things

as well as the good.

But I was emotionally unable to agree with my words.

Yet now, as I look back,

I can see the good You have accomplished

in those very disappointments and disasters.

I can see the changes You have made in my life,

and the way You have protected me.

Continue to strengthen me, Lord.

Take my self-pity and turn it into praise.

Take my scars and turn them into stars.

POWER
BUILDER

JOHN GRISHAM
Author

POWER
QUOTE

When God is at home in our lives, He understands our dreams, and He hears them as if they were prayers.

SCRIPTURE

Psalm 138:8

Your love never fails. You have made us what we are. Don't give up on us now!

THE LITTLE ARKANSAS BOY was in the third grade when he began to listen carefully to his Sunday school teacher's words about Jesus. That afternoon, he asked his mother what it meant to "ask Jesus into your heart." After she led her young son to Christ, he made a public confession of faith at church the following Sunday.

The boy especially enjoyed the wonderful stories told by missionaries who brought their slide projectors and showed pictures of far-off lands. The boy dreamed that someday he would be a missionary, too. But life took a different course for him. He began to practice law, and his desire to do missionary work was put on hold.

Ten years passed while he worked as an attorney. Then he decided to write a novel about lawyers and courtrooms—the subject he knew best. His novel was published, along with four others. *A Time to Kill, The Firm, The Pelican Brief, The Client,* and *The Chamber* have sold more than 40 million copies. John Grisham, the author, is no longer practicing law. He is one of America's best-selling authors. And he is able, at last, to be deeply involved in missions work.

He and his wife went to Brazil with forty other Americans, building a church and providing medical assistance. Grisham is also able to help financially support many other mission projects. Of his success, Grisham says, "I don't know why it happened to me. God has a purpose for it."

POINTS TO PONDER

The dreams we dream and the prayers we pray are often identical. Dreams may be unspoken prayers that God hears and answers. Of course, we sometimes entertain self-serving dreams, and we hardly dare bring them to God. But even then, He sees the genuine needs behind our dreams, and when things happen just the way we'd imagined, we feel as if a dream has come true.

POWER BUILDER

RICHARD KUGHN
Founder, Kughn Enterprises

TRUDGING HOME, RICHARD KUGHN was discouraged about his schoolwork. As he walked past a trash can, he found a discarded Lionel train. He rushed eagerly home with the battered engine, cars, and tracks.

Dick and his dad were both spiritually and emotionally close. So Dick's father was as excited as his son about the treasured discovery. What a gift God had given the struggling youngster!

Two years later, on Christmas morning, Dick woke up to find a sleek new Lionel train under the tree. He continued to collect trains. Even after managing to overcome his visual difficulties, graduate from a university, and establish his own corporation—Kughn Enterprises, handling real estate, commercial, and industrial enterprises—he never lost his love for trains. He became one of the world's outstanding collectors.

Forty years after Dick found his first Lionel in the trash, another gift came his way. The Lionel Train Company was for sale. He prayed and asked God for direction. Although warned that the Lionel Company was in financial trouble, Dick felt God was guiding him to buy it. He did. Before many years had passed, the fortunes of Lionel trains were, as Dick Kughn put it, "back on track." God's love had been demonstrated to him in the most personal, powerful way imaginable—He had given Dick the desire of his heart and more.

Tuesday
Week

22

POINTS TO PONDER

Sometimes our fondest longings are based on gifts that God has invested in us. Then when we are ready, He gives us the things we have always dreamed about. This is His way of rewarding us for our faithfulness in using our gifts wisely: He gives us more.

POWER QUOTE

When we take responsibility for His small gifts to us, God is able to entrust us with greater gifts.

SCRIPTURE

Psalm 139:16

Even before I was born, you had written in your book everything I would do.

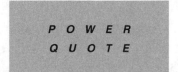

CARL LEWIS

U.S. Olympic Gold Medal Winner

POWER BUILDER

POWER QUOTE

God works within our dreams to accomplish His will for our lives.

SCRIPTURE

Isaiah 40:31

Those who trust in the LORD will find new strength. . . . They will walk and run without getting tired.

A T FIFTEEN YEARS OF age, the scrawny African-American boy looked into the eyes of the soccer coach he admired. The season was over, and the coach's words nearly broke the boy's heart: "You'll never amount to anything. You're a disgrace, a nobody."

Carl Lewis fought off that discouragement to face another one—a continuous struggle with injuries in junior high school. With the encouragement of his close family, however, Carl persisted and found his way into national competition in track and field. In 1981, another dimension was added to his life.

At an NCAA Track and Field Championship in Baton Rouge, Carl was invited to a chapel service. There he came to see that although he knew all about Jesus Christ, he had never invited Him into his life. After accepting Christ, Carl shared his new decision with his family. His brothers went with him to the next chapel, followed by his sister and his parents.

Three years later, in the Los Angeles Olympics, came the realization of Carl's dream—he won four gold medals and equaled Jesse Owens's record. He says, "When I'm competing I have peace of mind. I feel like there is nothing else in the world at that time. I seek the Lord's help in even the simplest things."

POINTS TO PONDER

Many times dreams come true because of the courage, discipline, and determination to fulfill them. Whether dreamers know God or not, they often remain committed to their goals and accomplish what they want. How much more rewarding it is, however, to partner with God in dreams. With His supernatural power at work on our behalf, we know He has a higher purpose for our accomplishments than self-satisfaction once those dreams come true.

POWER BUILDER

BOTTIA SEGAL
Computer Typesetter

BOTTIA SEGAL GREW UP in an Orthodox Jewish family in Jerusalem. As a very young girl, she often prayed that she could know God in a personal way. And in her early twenties, she persistently asked that He would show her the truth about eternal life.

Bottia took a job at a printing company as a computer typesetter. Her very first assignment was to typeset the New Testament in Hebrew. She was fascinated with the text but unclear about its message. Never before had she read the words of Jesus Christ. Other Christian books also came her way, adding to her confusion.

One night Bottia cried out, "God, I am in a place where I really want to know the truth. If Yeshua is the true Messiah of God, I would like to follow Him. And if He's not, please, I would like to forget about it." The words had hardly left her mouth when she had a vision of an angel of the Lord.

The next day, while waiting for a bus, she saw the same angel, moving closer and closer to her. Bottia glanced around, wondering if anyone else could see the angel. When she looked back, the vision was gone.

Thrilled by this revelation, Bottia Segal asked Jesus to come and live in her heart. Her desire had been met by the One who had first placed it in her heart—the Messiah.

Thursday
Week

22

POWER QUOTE

A longing for a relationship with God is one dream that will most certainly come true.

SCRIPTURE

Psalm 27:4

I ask only one thing, LORD: Let me live in your house every day of my life.

POINTS TO PONDER

How can we know whether our dreams have been placed within our hearts by God? We can examine our motives and reflect upon how self-serving our desires may be. But the true test probably lies in the outcome. If God has placed a desire in our hearts, He will bring it to pass, and it will reflect His values and principles. A desire to know Him better surely tops the list of personal longings that He will most willingly fulfill.

POWER BUILDER

POWER QUOTE

By seeking God first, we ready ourselves for all the other things He wants to give us.

SCRIPTURE

Psalm 37:4

Do what the LORD wants, and he will give you your heart's desire.

W HEN TIM BURKE, RELIEF pitcher for the Montreal Expos, first began to play class A ball, drinking filled his off-hours and eased his anxiety about becoming a big-league player. He was determined to find his way to the top.

Tim's closest friend stopped drinking after becoming a Christian. Then Tim was moved to Buffalo to play with a class AA team where a new teammate invited him to a Bible study. The invitation couldn't have come at a better time—Tim and his wife were having monumental marital problems, and his drinking problem was worse.

Tim and Christine received Christ as their Savior. The desire for alcohol was removed from Tim's life, and the Burke marriage was miraculously healed. Meanwhile, Tim learned to play ball a revolutionary new way: "Whatever you do, do it with all your heart as if working for the Lord and not for man." No longer did he strive to please managers. Or to improve statistics. Or to ensure a promotion to the major leagues. He played his best. God would have to take care of the rest.

And He did. Tim became a major league relief pitcher, and he got on the National League All-Star team. He says the Lord spoke to his heart, "See, this is from Me, and I will give you the desires of your heart, if you just live for Me and seek after Me and let Me call the shots."

Friday
Week

22

POINTS TO PONDER

Although God's love is unconditional, at times His answers to our prayers have certain conditions. When we long for success in some field of endeavor, He knows the toll that success may take upon the spiritual life. He may require us to commit ourselves wholeheartedly to Him before He begins to give us the things we want. He is bringing us into a deep and lasting relationship with Him before we have the other things we want.

WHAT ARE THE DREAMS that never quite leave your heart? Have you doubted God's love for you because He hasn't made them come true? Take a moment and write down the desires of your heart that are unfulfilled.

_____

Can you think of any reasons He might be waiting to give you the things you want the most?

_____

Weekend
Week

22

> *Lord,*
>
> *sometimes my dreams haunt me,*
>
> *they are so ever-present in my thinking,*
>
> *and I plead with You to make them come true.*
>
> *Other times I think they have become too important,*
>
> *and I try to set them aside,*
>
> *choosing to seek You first.*
>
> *Now and then I try to manipulate You by being good,*
>
> *so You'll do what I want.*
>
> *Or I try to get Your attention by being depressed,*
>
> *and I become angry because I'm having to wait.*
>
> *Lord, please remember me and my dreams.*
>
> *Do whatever work You must in my heart*
>
> *to prepare me,*
>
> *and if they fit into Your will,*
>
> *please make them come true*
>
> *in Your time, in Your perfect way.*

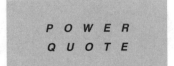

BERT HAMILTON
Businessman

POWER QUOTE

We are wise to reevaluate our priorities before a crisis forces us to do so.

SCRIPTURE

Psalm 18:4

Death had wrapped its ropes around me, and I was almost swallowed by its flooding waters.

Monday
Week

23

BERT HAMILTON WAITED IMPATIENTLY for his flight to take off for Tampa. A cold January storm was bearing down on the Washington, D.C., area.

Bert knew something was not right the minute the Boeing 737 took off. The jet lifted only slightly and then began to shudder. Bert saw the 14th Street bridge as the plane dropped past it.

They crashed across the bridge after being airborne only thirty-two seconds. Icy water flooded in, and Bert automatically unbuckled his seat belt. He floated out of his seat toward some light in front of him. Once he was out of the plane, he didn't know what to do. He yelled for help, but no help came. "Lord!" he prayed, "I know You didn't get me out of that plane so I could freeze to death in the Potomac."

Finally a helicopter arrived. Bert was pulled from the river. He had a shattered right wrist, a broken forearm, other broken bones, and cuts and bruises. But he was one of five survivors; seventy-eight people died.

Bert says, "My brush with death opened my eyes and broadened my focus. My concerns had been limited to my own ambitions and family. Now I see how different the world would be if we reached out in love to others, like some of the many heroes at the crash scene."

POINTS TO PONDER

Death remains a stranger to many of us. We tend to feel immortal until the aging process makes us aware of our mortality. In the meantime, however, we are occasionally confronted with circumstances that remind us of the fragility of life. How quickly our priorities change when the question "What if this is the last day of my life?" arises. Bert Hamilton's experience dramatically changed his perspective.

POWER BUILDER

DANA CRANEY

Geologist

DANA CRANEY WAS FLYING out of Denver, Colorado, when the call suddenly came across the plane's loudspeaker: "Prepare for an emergency landing!"

Dana was a pilot, and he knew enough about aircraft to see that the plane was in serious trouble. Both engines had died at twenty thousand feet while the plane sailed above the fourteen-thousand-foot Rocky Mountains. He pondered the reality of sudden death, focusing his mind on prayer.

Buena Vista Airport was a possible landing site, but there was no way the pilot could make it onto the runway. To make matters worse, mountains loomed ahead.

Dana glanced around the cabin. Hopeless men and women sat slumped in silence, their coats on, awaiting their doom. Dana realized, to his amazement, that he wasn't afraid. He recognized that God's promise of eternal life had overpowered his fear of death.

At two hundred feet, the orders were shouted: "Everybody get down, stay down!" A huge shock followed. The nose pitched down; the plane shook violently. Finally, it came to a halt, its nose in the ground. Everyone headed for the doors—no one was seriously injured. Dana Craney spent the time on the ground sharing his faith with those who could not face death without fear.

Tuesday
Week

23

POINTS TO PONDER

The process of dying is not a pleasant thought, and the idea of leaving our loved ones makes us hurt for them and for ourselves. But the fear of what is beyond death really grips those who are not assured of their destiny. As Christians, we have a wonderful gift from God who has done all the work to guarantee our eternal life. We know we aren't good enough, can't try hard enough, and haven't given enough to pay our own way into heaven. But through our faith in Christ, our journey there is guaranteed.

POWER QUOTE

The greater power of eternal life has removed the power of death.

SCRIPTURE

Psalm 23:4

I may walk through valleys as dark as death, but I won't be afraid. You are with me.

ALLAN MAYER
Businessman

Do we remember God in the celebrations of life, or do we wait to plead with Him during our darkest hours?

SCRIPTURE

Matthew 16:25

If you want to save your life, you will destroy it. But if you give up your life for me, you will find it.

FOR TWENTY-FOUR YEARS, Allan Mayer worked in the family business, Oscar Mayer and Co. Then Allan and his wife left Oscar Mayer to start a new life managing business interests. The transition went well for nine months. Then they learned that their five-year-old daughter Kathy had a malignant brain tumor.

Allan knew how to run a business, how to make a profit, how to wield power. But Kathy's illness showed him that he was powerless. The little girl wasn't expected to live more than a few months.

Although he had always maintained a humanistic philosophy, in his desperation Allan began to seek God. At first he went into a church and read the prayer book. Then he began to read Christian books on healing and to pray more frequently. Finally, he fell on his knees and asked Christ to come into his life.

Meanwhile, to the amazement of everyone, his daughter's tumor was reduced. Allan writes, "I had concentrated on pursuit of things of this world—making money, gaining social prestige, power, and recognition. After becoming a Christian, I recognized that these are very temporary. Now it frightens me that I spent so much time planning and pursuing worldly things and gave hardly a thought to my eternal destiny."

Wednesday
Week

23

POINTS TO PONDER

The threat of losing a beloved child or spouse is more frightening to us than our own death. Most loving family members would rather endure suffering than see a dear one in pain. When the threat is real, we begin to seek help, and we may learn that there is little we can do but pray. God meets us in those prayers. He reminds us that He is always with us, in life and in death. Although we may have ignored Him, He has never been more than a prayer away.

DAVID LEESTMA
NASA Mission Specialist and Astronaut

Thursday
Week
23

MATTERS OF LIFE AND death were familiar to David Leestma. He found the courage to deal with the challenges of his career through his faith in God. Then a month before *Columbia* blasted off in 1989, David learned that his wife had breast cancer. She would require an immediate mastectomy and chemotherapy. The doctor also reported that Patti was pregnant. He recommended abortion.

David and Patti were stunned by the news, but abortion was not an option for them. After seeking a second opinion, they found an alternative. Another doctor suggested that with careful monitoring, Patti could have chemotherapy and not endanger the baby's life. The surgery was scheduled, and when David was launched into space aboard *Columbia*, Patti was in Florida to watch the liftoff.

Patti had her last chemotherapy treatment in mid-December, and Caleb was born on December 28, full term and perfectly healthy.

The power of the family's faith saved young Caleb's life. And the power of God brought Patti and David through the greatest challenge of their lives.

POWER QUOTE

God is the source of all life, and when we honor life, we honor God.

SCRIPTURE

Matthew 17:20

If you had faith no larger than a mustard seed, you could tell this mountain to move from here to there. And it would. Everything would be possible for you.

POINTS TO PONDER

A respect for life is a natural by-product of our faith in God. As we see His fingerprints on all creation and recognize that all things are held together by His power, we honor Him in the living things He has made. And His crowning accomplishment, human life, becomes even more sacred when the lives we treasure are those we love best. Choosing to preserve life, to fight for it, to treasure it, is a form of worshiping the Creator of life. He, in turn, demonstrates His ability to accomplish the impossible in our lives as we reverence the works of His hands.

ROBERT P. CASEY

Governor of Pennsylvania

Human existence belongs to God, and He alone has the power to grant us life or to authorize death.

SCRIPTURE

Ezekiel 18:31 NKJV

Get . . . a new heart and a new spirit.

ROBERT P. CASEY WAS beginning his second term of office when he was diagnosed with a rare hereditary liver disease that would eventually cost him his life. Determined to accomplish his political goals, he continued to work twelve-hour days. One of his causes was the trouble that simmered in the inner cities of the state. He worked particularly to help communities like Monessen, where drug abuse and unemployment were destroying the quality of life.

Finally, the disease wore Casey down until he was admitted to the hospital. A heart and liver transplant could save his life, but a donor would have to be found—soon. The family prayed and waited.

During that difficult week for the Caseys, another family was struggling. In Monessen, an African-American man named Mike Lucas was brutally beaten. The beating left his brain so damaged that he hung between life and death. His despondent mother, who had already lost one son to violence, quietly agreed to donate his organs. Soon thereafter, Mike died.

And so it was that Robert Casey received a new heart and liver. The transplanted organs came to him from the mean streets of a struggling community he tried to rehabilitate. He recuperated from the surgery with astonishing speed, and he served out his four-year term.

Friday
Week

23

POINTS TO PONDER

What can we learn from Governor Casey's story but that life and death are in the hands of God? There is great mystery in the ways He works, but certain issues are clear: God gives us our breath, and He takes our breath from us at the end of our lives. He knows the length of our days, He has a purpose for every one of us, and He will complete the good work He has begun in our lives, according to His sovereign plans.

D O THE ISSUES OF life and death make you uncomfortable? Record your thoughts about life's end and the beginning of a new life in the world to come.

_____

_____

_____

_____

_____

Weekend
Week

23

Lord,

I get so caught up in life

that I rarely give a thought to death

unless it confronts me in some unavoidable way.

I have many fears about death and dying,

and talking about it makes me feel vulnerable.

Please teach me to dwell safely in the present

and to trust You with the future.

Help me to understand the wonders of heaven

as well as I appreciate the pleasures of earth.

Thank You for Your gift of eternal life, Lord,

and for what You did to make it possible for me.

GINNY THORNBURGH

Advocate for Persons with Disabilities

POWER QUOTE

The very circumstances that might well destroy us can become enormously beneficial to others when handled God's way.

SCRIPTURE

Genesis 50:20

You tried to harm me, but God made it turn out for the best.

DICK THORNBURGH WEATHERED COUNTLESS conflicts in his many years of public service. But one long, quiet battle was going on in his home, carried on by his wife, Ginny.

When Peter, Dick's son, was four months old, he was in a car accident that killed his mother, Dick's first wife. Peter sustained extensive brain damage.

Peter was four years old when Ginny married Dick in 1963. Ginny became the boy's champion, his guardian, and his best friend. As she researched the problems Peter encountered, she realized that she was discovering the tip of an ugly iceberg. Ginny set out to improve conditions for persons with disabilities.

She was rewarded in 1990, standing beside her husband at a White House ceremony, when George Bush signed into law the Americans with Disabilities Act. It provides legal protection and consideration for America's people with disabilities.

Meanwhile, Peter blossomed. Today, he lives in an apartment with a roommate, and he attends church regularly. His faith in Jesus is an encouragement to all who know him. Ginny Thornburgh describes her efforts, which began as a heartfelt response to Peter's needs, as "a drop in the bucket." However, the ripple effect from her concern continues to be felt across the United States.

Monday
Week

24

POINTS TO PONDER

When we are hurt or see loved ones suffer, we can resign ourselves to the plight, or we can pray for help and get busy.

By our choice to act, changes begin—first inside us, then around us. When we take positive action, our sphere of power extends far beyond ourselves.

POWER BUILDER

DAVE CORNELSON
Hand-Cycling Competitor

Tuesday
Week
24

DAVE CORNELSON WAS A thirty-five-year-old athlete, professor, and doctoral student when he headed for Mexico for a sports-filled Fourth of July weekend. The trip included four friends.

A car accident changed all that for Dave. Ironically, his seat belt caused his back to be broken, and his legs were paralyzed.

Dave had always believed in God, but his faith had been more intellectual than personal. The accident drove him and his family to prayer. He began to ask some strategic questions: Can I still have a high-quality life? Can I still experience joy in the same way?

At first the struggle was with the process of regaining physical strength and learning to use a wheelchair. But avid sportsman that he is, Dave found a new reason for living and a sport that answered his questions with a positive yes—he could enjoy life again.

Hand-cycling uses a three-wheeled bike with the pedals at chest level instead of at the feet. Because of Dave's passion for competition, he tried to beat a transcontinental record, which he did. By speaking and competing, Dave Cornelson encourages all athletes, disabled or not, to make the most of their talents. He hopes to build up their spirits as successfully as God has helped him to build up his own.

POINTS TO PONDER

Our bodies are reasonably healthy. Only when we lose something important do we begin to appreciate the blessing that it was. We can learn from Dave Cornelson to make the most of the things that remain—the talents we still have, the skills we can still put to work. By focusing on the remaining qualities and abilities, we can overcome our adversities and restore our zest for life.

POWER QUOTE

We often fail to appreciate blessings until they are lost.

SCRIPTURE

Romans 8:28

We know that God is always at work for the good of everyone who loves him. They are the ones God has chosen for his purpose.

DAVE DRAVECKY
Former Professional Baseball Player

SCRIPTURE

Isaiah 55:8

The LORD says: "My thoughts and my ways are not like yours."

DAVE DRAVECKY'S LEFT ARM was his fortune. As a pitcher, he had been the pride of the San Francisco Giants. But powerful as it was, his arm was not immune to malignancy. After every other kind of cancer treatment failed, on June 18, 1991, Dave's left arm was amputated.

The morning after surgery Dave was horrified by his reflection. His arm and shoulder were gone, along with the left side of his collarbone. What would his family think of him? What would other people say about him? It didn't take long for him to learn. He says, "As important as my left arm had been [to me], it meant nothing to them. It was enough that I was alive."

His major career as a league pitcher was clearly over. Yet Dave gratefully understood that he was about to experience a deeper level of existence than he had ever known before.

On October 5, 1991, for a special event at Candlestick Park, Dave wore his Giants uniform one last time. It was officially Dave Dravecky Day, and he received a standing ovation as he was driven around the park with his family, lifting his hat happily to the crowd. He could see the pain on many faces as people wept in response to what they perceived as a tragedy.

Dave views his brush with death far differently. He writes, "When I look back over all I've learned from other people who have suffered, all I've experienced of their love and all God has shown me of His mercy, I think: if I'd have continued as a ballplayer and missed that, now *that* would have been a tragedy."

Wednesday
Week

24

POINTS TO PONDER

The disappointment we tried to avoid. The calamity we never expected. The unhappy ending no one predicted. Our casualties may be financial, relational or physical. What we do with them is the key to our future success. We can give up. Or with faith that God's ways are above our ways, we can start again.

POWER BUILDER

FRED AND ALANNA NILES

Firestorm Survivors

ALONG WITH HUNDREDS OF other southern Californians, Fred and Alanna Niles lost their home during the firestorms of 1993. They had lived in the same Malibu cottage for thirty-two years of marriage.

Fred was a former geologist, employed as a real estate broker. During the week of fires, every house he had listed for sale was burned. Alanna, a literary critic whose work was nationally acclaimed, lost all her manuscripts along with seven thousand books.

All the Nileses' photographs, recipes, paintings, and keepsakes from around the world were burned to ashes except for one. As Fred raked through the debris, he reflected on how archaeologists often find objects that speak of the lifestyles and beliefs of ancient peoples. He found the one remaining artifact of his and Alanna's life—a plate that was inscribed "Rise Above the Storm and You Will Find the Sunshine."

Fred and Alanna wept in the ruins of their life, inspired by the word of encouragement they felt sure God had given them. As they walked away, plate in hand, they noticed that narcissus buds were already making their way through the blackened soil and charred plants. "We're beginning new life again, too," they told each other. "We're going to rebuild."

Thursday

Week

24

POWER QUOTE

Nothing returns us to proper priorities more quickly than the thought of losing everything but our souls.

SCRIPTURE

Isaiah 61:1, 3 NKJV

The LORD has anointed Me . . .

to give them beauty for ashes.

POINTS TO PONDER

If you had ten minutes to take your most valuable treasures out of your house, what would you reach for? Why? We ask these questions when we hear of evacuations and natural disasters, and we wonder how to identify our most precious possessions. When all is said and done, our lives, the people we love, and our faith in God make us who we are. Everything else can be taken from us, but nothing can rob us of the priceless inner life.

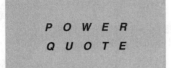

POWER BUILDER

SHANNON SCHATT

Adult Child of an Alcoholic

POWER QUOTE

When our lives are ripped apart, we have the opportunity to rebuild them on a firmer foundation.

SCRIPTURE

Jeremiah 31:16

Dry your tears. . . . All you have done . . . will be greatly rewarded.

TERRIFIED, SHANNON SCHATT WEPT and pleaded with God. In a drunken rage, her mother had chased her with a knife and tried to kill her. Shannon had barely escaped when her mother wildly plunged the knife into a bedroom door, missing her by inches.

In desperation, the teenager located a phone and dialed a counseling number. The man on the other end of the line patiently listened to her hysterical words. He calmed her, then he provided her with some practical suggestions. At that point Shannon had two important things in her favor: courage and prayer.

When her church provided Alcoholics Anonymous literature, she left it lying around the house, hoping her mother would see it. She did, and it infuriated her because she denied that she was an alcoholic. One thing she could not deny, however, was the knife incident. Although she could not remember what happened, the knife was still lodged in the door.

After a year of persistent prayer and prodding, Shannon's mother finally went for help with her drinking problem. "My mom resented the light in me because her world was so dark," Shannon now understands, "but now we're both walking with the Lord—we've both got beautiful lights glowing."

POINTS TO PONDER

Tragedies confront us with reality. There is no room for pretending or posturing when life-and-death circumstances come our way. We can become victims, resigning ourselves to ongoing misery. Or we can rise to the occasion by overcoming evil with good. Things can never be the same because we cannot turn back the clock and erase the events. Instead, with new awareness and determination, we have the opportunity to respond to the tragedy, learn from it, and make the changes it requires in our lives and in our circumstances.

Reflect on the tragedies that have touched your life, involving either you personally or people you know. What has been the result of those events? What lessons were learned in the process?

_____

_____

_____

_____

_____

Weekend

Week

24

Lord,

I am horrified by the tragedies I read about

in the newspaper

and see on the television.

Floods, fires, accidents, wars, and diseases

are tearing people's lives apart.

They make me fearful, Lord.

They make me run to You for protection

for myself and my loved ones.

I ache for those who have

lost so much.

Teach me through them,

and when it's possible,

use me to reach out to them with love and caring.

**POWER
BUILDER**

CLEVELAND WALKER
Custodian

A POWERFUL COMMITMENT TO young people was forged in the heart of Cleveland Walker when his son Victor was shot to death outside a Washington, D.C., nightclub after getting into an argument. Grieving his loss, Cleveland, a high-school custodian, turned his attention to other students—especially those in trouble for skipping class, being tardy, or getting bad grades.

"I tell them life is not a game. You need to learn. Get your education. Stay away from drugs and alcohol because these things will kill you. I used to tell another young man the same thing," Cleveland quietly states, "but he didn't listen and he got killed."

Students who cannot be reached by anyone else will listen to Cleveland and his ceaseless demands for greater discipline and harder work. Students explain their acceptance of the tall, thin man and his message by saying, "I trust him."

When he was offered a promotion as an area supervisor, Cleveland would have no longer been required to work so hard at his custodial duties. But he would have had to leave Edison High School. After very little consideration, he said no. The students at Edison need him, he concluded.

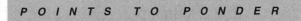

POINTS TO PONDER

How will we be remembered? Will we be praised for our world-class accomplishments? A man like Cleveland Walker will leave behind a priceless legacy—he has given hundreds of young people a clear awareness of right and wrong. From his humble responsibilities at his work and out of his heartache over his lost son, he has brought forth pure gold: a trustworthy, caring heart.

POWER BUILDER

JOHN GRINALDS
Major General, U.S. Marine Corps

JOHN GRINALDS WAS A high achiever from boyhood until his education at West Point provided him a Rhodes scholarship and a direct commission into the Marine Corps—one of the first such commissions awarded since 1814.

In Vietnam, John had to consider his mortality and his powerlessness in the face of overwhelming danger. Of the eight hundred young men in his battalion, half were dead within six months. At home, John's inability to control life-and-death circumstances was reconfirmed when he saw his five-year-old son fall from a diving board and crack his skull from one ear to the other. Only prayer saved the boy's life and restored him to perfect health.

Back in Vietnam, after experiencing a flashback of his son's injury, he thanked God for saving the boy's life. He heard a clear word in his mind: "John, I have given you your son's life. Now you must give Me yours."

After the war, John began to recall his accomplishments and to see them in a new light—there was something unworthy in every one of them. He eventually concluded, "After reviewing all the opportunities for achievement this world holds out to us, I am certain that they all miss the mark; nothing compares to the decision to accept Jesus as Lord and Savior and to share the Good News of what Jesus offers with others."

Tuesday
Week

25

POWER QUOTE

An awareness of our powerlessness is our first step toward true greatness—God's greatness at work in us.

SCRIPTURE

Matthew 16:26

What would you give to get back your soul?

POINTS TO PONDER

Competitive people struggle with being humble. It seems self-defeating for them to give up the battle to be number one. The fact is, before our lives are over, we will always reach a point at which we realize that we can't win. We can't control everything and everybody. And when death approaches, we realize most clearly our powerlessness and our desperate need for God.

POWER BUILDER

PHILIP SMITH
Trumpet Player, New York Philharmonic Orchestra

POWER QUOTE

Our humility demonstrates to God that we honor Him and rely on Him for everything.

SCRIPTURE

Philippians 2:5–7

Think the same way that Christ Jesus thought. . . . He did not try to remain equal with God. He gave up everything and became a slave, when he became like one of us.

PHILIP SMITH IS CONSIDERED one of the finest classical trumpet players in the world, and tickets to his performances sell for extravagant prices.

When asked about his success, Philip Smith attributes it to two things. First, he mentions his love for music and his commitment to his art. But his second reason for success is more unusual.

Philip is a lifelong member of the Salvation Army. His first public performances occurred when he was a small child, playing along with the Army band while his father was bandmaster. Even after achieving world-class recognition as a musician, every Christmas Philip stands outside a department store or a supermarket, playing carols. His purpose is to "work for the betterment of humanity," a cause the Salvation Army has worked for since its inception.

And so it is that the incredibly beautiful tone of Philip's trumpet carries familiar carols across the city. And those who toss their money into the charity pot have no idea how much it would cost to purchase a ticket to hear the same man play his golden trumpet down the street at Carnegie Hall.

POINTS TO PONDER

Why is humility important to God? Scripture is full of statements expressing His favor to those who are humble and His aversion to those who are proud. Perhaps the reason lies in the truth that God wants to be God. Since the Garden of Eden, humankind has exhibited an unhealthy desire to be as God. And when we choose to behave with humility, we acknowledge that God is great, and we are beneath Him in power and authority. In doing so, we invite Him to bring His strength into our weakness. He does so gladly.

POWER BUILDER

TIM BENNETT
Freelance Writer

WHEN TIM BENNETT GRADUATED from college with a B.A. in English literature, he was filled with dreams of glory. He would be a journalist, get his master's degree, and leave his mark on the world as a writer. Instead, Tim served food at a large nursing home.

Tim was ashamed to be doing such menial work. He scanned the want ads for potential career opportunities, but nothing materialized. *Nobody cares about me—not even God!* Tim never verbalized the thought, but it was there.

Meanwhile, Tim was getting acquainted with the staff and the patients. God was giving him specific help in dealing with some of the more difficult characters. Most notable was James, who was violent and verbally abusive.

One day Tim felt that he should take a guitar into James's room and play Christian songs for him. Feeling foolish, he nevertheless obeyed the inner voice. To his amazement, James sat silently, smiling a little and listening serenely to the music. After several visits, James unexpectedly said to Tim, "But who pays you to do this? You need money to live."

Tears burned in Tim's eyes. Through the words of his most difficult patient, he heard the loving voice of God. "You need money to live." Of course, God knew about his difficult circumstances.

POWER QUOTE

Not only does He know about our difficult circumstances; He designs them especially for us.

SCRIPTURE

Genesis 16:13

She called him, "The God Who Sees Me."

POINTS TO PONDER

Humility before honor. The idea repeats itself again and again in the pages of the Bible and in the lives of God's people. It seems that God wants us to learn certain life lessons before He places us in positions of leadership and provides us with recognition. How well He knows our tendency to forget Him when things are going well. So, during the seasons of humility, He teaches us to rely on Him, to listen to Him, to give Him thanks for every good thing.

POWER BUILDER

ROBERT SCHULLER

Pastor

POWER QUOTE

When we fully humble our-selves before God, we also find ourselves serving one another in love and humility.

SCRIPTURE

1 Peter 5:5

God opposes proud people, but he helps everyone who is hum-ble.

WHEN THE SECOND AFRICAN/AFRICAN-AMERICAN Summit was held in Libreville, Gabon, Dr. Robert Schuller was the only white minister invited to attend. Schuller was not prepared for the emo-tional encounter. First of all, the plight and the poverty of the Gabonese people stunned him. Their average annual income is $275 a year, and the average life span is forty-five years. What a contrast to the comfortable world of Western Christians!

Schuller was even more moved by the sight of the Atlantic coastline and the thought of slave ships coming and going, carrying helpless Africans to their fate in Europe and America during the sixteenth, seven-teenth, and eighteenth centuries.

As he walked to the podium, Dr. Schuller looked out over a sea of faces. But he simply couldn't speak. He began to weep, stricken with the horrors of slavery and the pain of the poverty.

All at once a man wearing Muslim attire stood up next to Schuller. Schuller, who then regained his composure, later explained, "He smiled as if to say, 'We won't let you stand up here and cry alone.'"

The unknown man's powerful statement of support and solidarity was deeply humbling to the American pastor. "It was genuine grace—I was supposed to be there to encourage them. Instead, they ministered to me," said Schuller.

Friday
Week

25

POINTS TO PONDER

Humility, according to God's order of business, is supposed to extend beyond our relationship with God into our community with one another. Of course, we are to bow before Him as Lord and King of the universe. But we are also intended to humble ourselves before one another. In doing so, we create a unique equality in God's kingdom, based on our mutual submission to one another and our unified submission to Him.

CAN YOU RECALL SOME circumstances in which humility was difficult for you? Perhaps you are in that situation now, having to submit to someone you do not particularly respect. Write your thoughts about that situation, trying to understand what God is attempting to do in your life.

_____

_____

_____

Weekend
Week

25

Lord,

I understand Your desire for me to humble myself,

and I want You to take charge of my life.

Even though I enjoy feelings

of success and fulfillment,

I know that every good thing in my life

comes from You.

I don't enjoy humbling myself

before people who don't respect me in return.

I feel humiliated, not humbled, when that happens—

ashamed and angry and rebellious.

Help me honor the people

You have placed in my life.

Teach me to love them, pray for them,

and give them the respect You want them to have.

DAVID AIKMAN

Journalist

POWER QUOTE

When we are in agreement with God's calling, everything we do becomes a form of worship.

SCRIPTURE

Romans 12:12

Let your hope make you glad.
Be patient in time of trouble
and never stop praying.

WHEN DAVID AIKMAN WAS contracted to write a book about hope, he was a successful foreign correspondent for *Time* living in Washington, D.C., after spending two action-filled decades overseas. The subject of hope had always intrigued him, but in a detached way. He had little sense of hope as one of the most powerfully life-enhancing elements.

Within months of beginning the book, David and his wife separated. The parental breakup traumatically affected both Aikman daughters. Financial difficulties followed. Then David's mother was suddenly diagnosed with cancer, and within a few months, she died.

David asked himself, "Could the hope that had intrigued me as a book subject also be a quality that could bring light into the darkness of my own griefs?" The answer was yes. As David made his way along the pathways of hope within the Jewish and Christian traditions and the landscapes of other faiths, God's grace reached down and reassembled hope in his life. His marriage was put back together. His daughters were healed. His health improved. He wrote, "Man's reasonableness is always less powerful than God's mercy and forgiveness. . . . He calls us towards Him, of course, but also out of ourselves, into the world—and into hope."

Monday
Week

26

POINTS TO PONDER

What is the calling of God? In every life, calling may manifest itself in a different way, but the result will be the same. God's calling does not allow us to separate the sacred from the secular. We have one life to live for Him in every aspect of existence. The calling of God challenges us to bring Him into our most mundane activities, breathing life into our smallest tasks, and giving power to our greatest challenges.

POWER BUILDER

JORGE SERRANO
Former President, Guatemala

W HEN HE WAS PRESIDENT of Guatemala, Dr. Jorge Serrano led a country torn apart by political turmoil. His personal faith and deep prayer life empowered him to meet his daily responsibilities. And he believed that God called him into the presidential position so he could bring greater justice and prosperity into his homeland. He often spoke of that calling: "If politics is dirty . . . then we must change it. God has a program for us. God made us in His own image—His likeness. . . . Laws should reflect what has been put into the heart of man by God.

"There is no possibility of taking away from man his liberty and dignity. Because man's nature comes directly from God, not from the state or society. If we want to see this—our nature reflected in society—then we have to work in order to obtain that.

"And that is the great responsibility that we have. We have come to power and we have a standard for action. We are not going to act just on expediency or for convenience. We are going to act on conviction."

POWER QUOTE

No matter what our responsibilities entail, communicating God's love is always our first priority.

SCRIPTURE

Romans 13:1, 4

Obey the rulers who have authority over you. Only God can give authority to anyone. . . . They are God's servants, and it is their duty to help you.

POINTS TO PONDER

God's calling may require one person to a quiet role of service in a hometown where few people know what he does. It may send another person abroad to be involved in international negotiations. For a select few, God's calling may elevate them to positions of supreme national power in which He expects them to represent His heavenly principles on an earthly level. Whatever we do, our hearts need to be focused on eternal values—the unchanging truths that God's Word reveals about relationships, morality, and responsibility. When these principles are in place, our tasks will always reflect God's love, and our success will communicate His love to people everywhere.

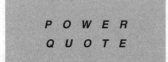

POWER
BUILDER

FILM STUDENTS
Concerned Christians

When we have done our part in the battle, we are called to stand and to witness His victory.

Matthew 18:19

I promise that when any two of you on earth agree about something you are praying for, my Father in heaven will do it for you.

*L*OS ANGELES TIMES ARTS editor Charles Champlin wrote, "I'd never heard 'raunch' used as a verb until the other night when, after the screening of a film at the University of Southern California Film School, a student asked the producer if he had been asked by the distributor to 'raunch up' the film."

"Yes," the producer replied, clearly regretful. He had not wanted to show bare breasts in one scene or to feature a clip from a porn film in another. He had also been instructed to include language that would require an R rating—a PG film wasn't what the distributor had in mind.

To the surprise of Charles and other participants in the program, more than three hundred students burst into spontaneous applause in support of a producer's moral outrage at "raunching up" a film that had every reason to remain clean.

Charles felt the applause was the students' way of saying, "Enough already!" to a film business community that insists on accommodating a sex-and-violence-hungry public. What Charles didn't know was that many young Christian filmmakers were part of the USC Film School audience. Those believers have committed themselves to prayer and to moral integrity, believing that God's power and their eventual influence in the industry will change the future of American motion pictures.

Wednesday
Week

26

POINTS TO PONDER

When our calling leads us into areas where disagreements exist, we may get into conflicts we didn't really want. A personal commitment to God's values sometimes means taking an unpopular position and standing firm, no matter what the cost. We are reminded once again that our calling is sometimes called a spiritual battle. Fortunately for us, Scripture assures us, "You will not need to fight in this battle. . . . Stand still and see the salvation of the LORD, who is with you" (2 Chron. 20:17 NKJV).

POWER BUILDER

NAOMI JUDD

Singer

NAOMI JUDD HAS HAD a true rags-to-riches story. Pregnant and unmarried at seventeen, she struggled with the realities of rural life. Her brother, who had Hodgkin's disease, inspired her to become a nurse. As a single parent, she reared her daughters, Wynonna and Ashley.

After she and Wynonna began to sing together, an explosive eight-year music career brought every imaginable recording award and millions of dollars. Then Naomi was diagnosed with chronic hepatitis, a disease that would continue to weaken her and eventually, apart from divine intervention, would take her life.

Naomi and Wynonna began their farewell tour in 1991. Wherever they went, they spoke of the power of God at work in their lives and how He had always guided and protected them. Following the tour, the disease went into a prolonged remission.

Naomi says, "If I can come from a dysfunctional family in small town America; if I can survive as a single working parent against all odds; if I can come out with the relationship that Wynonna, Ashley, and I enjoy; if I can achieve the success that we've achieved when we had nothing but raw talent and a belief in God's promises . . . then you can too."

Thursday
Week

26

POWER QUOTE

We are called to live out our lives to please God and God alone.

SCRIPTURE

Psalm 144:9

In praise of you, our God, I will sing a new song.

POINTS TO PONDER

God's calling places His people in every conceivable role and responsibility. He has literally shaken us out over the world like salt, evenly distributed across every field of endeavor. Those who, like the Judds, are highly visible are sometimes forced to see their most difficult personal circumstances broadcast around the world. Although they are vulnerable to the scrutiny of millions of people, their only concern has to remain that He is pleased with them. As for the rest of us, He wants us to speak for Him, praise Him, and represent Him, whether our lives are visible or invisible, known or unknown.

POWER BUILDER

POWER QUOTE

When we obey God's calling, we will be remembered for our love, not for our earthly success.

SCRIPTURE

2 Timothy 4:7–8

I have fought well. I have finished the race, and I have been faithful. So a crown will be given to me for pleasing the Lord.

Friday
Week

26

CHARLOTTE DIGGS MOON WAS born into a well-to-do family. She and her siblings received the best possible education from tutors.

Charlotte, who was known as Lottie by her friends and family, initially rejected the Baptist faith of her parents. But at eighteen years of age, she heard a message about Christianity that would not leave her. She chose to follow Christ. Lottie earned her master's degree as a linguist, speaking seven languages. She was soon to add an eighth to her astonishing vocabulary.

Lottie was a teacher at the Cartersville Female High School in Georgia when she heard "a call as clear as a bell." She went to China, where she worked among China's suffering women and children from 1873 until 1912. She began by opening a school. She worked diligently to thwart such inhumane practices as the binding of infant girls' feet. She fought starvation, feeding the hungry at her doorstep. More than a dozen destitute Chinese women lived under her roof at a time.

By the end of her life, she was exhausted financially and physically. She had given up her family's power and privilege to serve. She died on Christmas Eve on her way back to America. She was remembered in the simple words written by those she left behind in the church at P'ingtu: "How she loved us."

POINTS TO PONDER

Some people would have us believe that if we obey God's call on our lives, we will be blessed with prosperity, health, and honor. This is an appealing teaching, and many Christians enjoy the benefits of our affluent Western culture. But God's calling makes no such promises. The Son of God had no home of His own, He allowed His physical body to be broken, and He was mocked and jeered by raging crowds. Are we to expect any greater blessing than He did?

Do YOU SEPARATE YOUR secular life from your sacred life—going to church, praying, or talking about God? Why or why not?

_____

_____

Reflect a moment about the calling of God on your life. What is He calling you to do or to be?

_____

_____

Lord,

You created me for a purpose,

and You drew me to Yourself so I could

live with You forever.

But I don't always know what You want from me today.

What is Your purpose for my life?

What is my spiritual calling?

Please help me understand how I can best please You.

Show me how to use my gifts,

teach me how to use my time, and

reveal to me the direction You want me to take.

I belong to You, Lord.

Help me to serve You well and love You more.

POWER BUILDER

POWER QUOTE

Bitterness is a poison we swallow in hopes that it will harm someone else.

SCRIPTURE

Matthew 6:14

If you forgive others for the wrongs they do to you, your Father in heaven will forgive you.

Monday
Week

27

FATHER LAWRENCE "MARTY" JENCO was serving God in Lebanon when Islamic extremists kidnapped him. He was tied to the underbody of a car where he could hardly breathe because of a bloody nose. His mouth was taped shut. For hours he repeated the prayer, "Lord Jesus, Son of David, have mercy on me." Somehow, he continued to live.

As months of captivity turned to years, Father Jenco was given a Bible, which he read voraciously. Sometimes he blessed his stale bread for Communion. Eventually, he was brought into the company of other hostages. He wrote, "Now, in addition to God's Word and the Eucharist, I discovered a third great nourishment—the nourishment of each other. These three nourishments were how I survived."

When the time of his release arrived, one of the most violent guards asked him if he remembered the rough treatment he had received in the first six months of his captivity. He then said, "Do you forgive me?"

Father Jenco responded, "I need to ask God's forgiveness for every time I hated you, and I need to ask for your forgiveness, too."

"Hate," he later wrote, "is corrosive, and the one that hates does terrible damage to his own character and personality."

POINTS TO PONDER

The act of forgiveness seems, to some, like an unreasonable commandment that lets wrongdoers off the hook too easily. But forgiveness lets us off the poisonous hook of bitterness and hatred. To forgive is to release ourselves of all vindictive emotions and to hand the desire for vindication over to God. We are set free from passing judgment, and we allow Him to do what will best correct the problem—from His perspective.

POWER BUILDER

ADOLPH COORS IV

Former Brewer

ADOLPH COORS IV SEEMED to have everything. He grew up in a famous wealthy family. He married his childhood sweetheart. But inside were a deep emptiness and a malignant hatred for the man who had kidnapped and then murdered his father.

Adolph determined that he would be like his father and make his first million dollars in investments by his thirtieth birthday. He failed. He went to work at the brewery, scrubbing the insides of fermenting tanks. Then a head-on automobile collision nearly cost him his life.

With his marriage on the rocks and his life in shambles, Adolph and his wife came to Christ. The emptiness inside was gone. The marriage was mended. But he knew he had to resolve his rage. He tried three times to visit his father's murderer in prison, but the man refused to see him. Finally, Adolph wrote a note, "I ask for your forgiveness for the hatred I've had for you for seventeen years, and I forgive you for what you did to me and my family."

The note was widely circulated around the prison. Its generosity amazed many inmates. But Adolph Coors was more profoundly affected than anyone: "For me, applying the principles of forgiveness didn't stop at the Colorado State Penitentiary. Forgiveness is to be practiced daily and has extended to many areas of my life, particularly to family and business relationships."

POWER QUOTE

Jesus forgives us for sins that cost Him His life; He expects us to forgive others with similar generosity.

SCRIPTURE

2 Corinthians 2:7

Forgive and comfort them, so they won't give up in despair.

POINTS TO PONDER

To come into relationship with Jesus Christ, we have to receive His forgiveness for our sins. It doesn't take any logical person long to realize that forgiveness is an essential part of salvation. And Jesus made the point abundantly clear when He offered salvation conditionally—if we forgive others, He will forgive us. We dare not ignore His words.

PAUL SCHWARZ
Writer

POWER BUILDER

POWER QUOTE

Whether our unforgiving anger is fiery or icy, it will injure others who get too close to us.

SCRIPTURE

Isaiah 42:16

I will guide them on paths they have never traveled. Their road is dark and rough, but I will give light to keep them from stumbling.

SIXTEEN-YEAR-OLD PAUL Schwarz learned that his parents had been killed in an accident. The other driver, moving at more than 110 miles per hour, had been drunk.

Rage wasn't something Paul exhibited outwardly. But he rejected the companionship of friends and family. He raged silently.

Then a letter arrived from the driver of the car. From New York Penitentiary, the sorrowful man wrote, "I have been unable to live with myself because of what I did to your parents. . . . I want to know if you can forgive me."

When Paul's brothers and sisters responded in Christian love, the driver accepted Jesus Christ into his life as his Savior. Finally, Paul understood. Just as Christ's death had made eternal life possible for Paul, his parents' deaths had made eternal life possible to the drunk driver who had killed them.

Paul wrote, "I then realized that God is too great and His ways are too authoritative to waste my life on a cause as puny as myself. . . . God proved to be sovereign after all; He turned a tragedy into a triumph. . . . He uprooted a recluse from his hiding place."

POINTS TO PONDER

Sometimes our rage and bitterness are hidden, like Paul Schwarz's, behind a silent mask. We don't spew out hot words of anger, but we freeze out everyone who comes near us with a cold, hard exterior. When we are hurt, we experience both rage and fear, and to protect ourselves from more injury, we shut ourselves away in an antisocial shell. In forgiveness, we find freedom from anger, and we release our fears to God, trusting in His protection.

POWER BUILDER

FRANK SHERRY

Minister

Thursday
Week

27

THE SPRINGFIELD, ILLINOIS, PAPER reported, "A drug-crazed man armed with a hammer terrorized a neighborhood on Springfield's southside thirteen years ago, brutally attacking eight men. Two died. The drug-crazed man, now 'born again,' spoke at a local church recently."

In 1975, after a wild weekend of partying and taking drugs, including PCP, Frank Sherry was overwhelmed with something that took over his mind, urging him, "Kill!" He grabbed a hammer and started his murderous rampage.

While Frank was in jail, awaiting his trial, a tiny woman visited him. She had a Bible with her, and she quietly said, "I must forgive you, for the Lord has forgiven me for all of my sins." Her husband was one of the men Frank had bludgeoned to death.

Supported by the prayers of other Christians, the woman's word deeply moved Frank. He accepted Christ as his Savior. Although he was sentenced to thirty years in a maximum security prison, after thirteen years in prison, Frank was released. The murdered man's widow said, "I don't know how anything good can come from this unless you become a minister and turn others to Jesus Christ."

Since regaining his freedom, Frank reports, "My wife and I have traveled extensively, proclaiming the power of God to save, heal, and deliver."

POWER QUOTE

To care about heaven's values, we have to set aside earth's violations.

SCRIPTURE

Psalm 126:6

We cried on the way to plant our seeds, but we will celebrate and shout as we bring in the crops.

POINTS TO PONDER

It takes immense courage to look beyond the faults of a wrongdoer and see the person's needs. How can we get past our hurts and begin to care about eternal concerns? We have to walk very close to Christ Jesus. We must have His mind—His forgiving spirit—to leave behind our brokenness and lovingly restore a person who has severely wronged us. That was the very essence of Jesus' ministry, the ministry He has called us to continue in His behalf.

RONALD "RUSTY" WOOMER

Inmate on Death Row

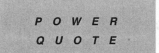

POWER BUILDER

How can we give up on each other when God never gives up on us?

SCRIPTURE

Luke 23:42–43

He said to Jesus, "Remember me when you come into power!" Jesus replied, "I promise that today you will be with me in paradise."

Bob McALISTER VOLUNTEERS WITH Prison Fellowship. He is a regular visitor to death row in Columbia, South Carolina. In that capacity he met Ronald "Rusty" Woomer, a murderer who was about to die in the state's electric chair.

Rusty was sitting on the floor, covered in roaches, his face white as chalk. Unable to communicate with the wretched man, Bob appealed to him, "Rusty, just say the word Jesus."

After a moment, Rusty quietly whispered, "Jesus."

To his amazement, in the moments that followed, Bob was able to lead the notorious killer in a sinner's prayer. Rusty prayed, "Jesus, I've hurt a lot of people. Ain't no way that I deserve You to hear me. But I'm tired and I'm sick and I'm lonely. My mama's died and she's in heaven with You, and I never got to tell her bye. Please forgive me, Jesus, for everything I've done."

Just before Rusty died in the electric chair, he met with some family members of his murder victims, who told him they had forgiven him through Christ. Minutes before his execution, he prayed, "I'm sorry. I claim Jesus Christ as my Savior. My only wish is that everyone in the world could feel the love I have felt from Him."

Friday

Week

27

POINTS TO PONDER

When Jesus forgave the thief who hung on the cross next to Him, He set an example for us: we are never to give up on anyone. Some men and women have carried a burden of wrongdoing and guilt around for decades, and they have never confronted their need for forgiveness. They may be ill. They may be imprisoned, like Rusty. Or they may be church-goers, who hide their guilt and fear behind a cheerful smile. Jesus wants every person alive to experience forgiveness—His forgiveness and ours. It may take place on a deathbed or in a child's nursery. But the results are the same—eternal life to everyone who receives it.

I S FORGIVENESS—OR UNFORGIVENESS—an issue in your life? Who do you need to forgive? Who needs to forgive you?

_____

_____

_____

_____

_____

Weekend
Week

27

Lord,

I thank You for Your incredible grace,

for the countless times You have accepted my apologies

and allowed me to start over with a clean slate.

Teach me to forgive those

who have wounded me.

Help me to seek their forgiveness, too,

for I have not been loving,

and You have called upon us to love.

POWER BUILDER

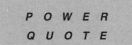

POWER QUOTE

The courage God gives us is a form of trust in Him, knowing that He will be strong, even if we are not.

SCRIPTURE

Joshua 23:10

Any one of you can defeat a thousand enemy soldiers, because the LORD God fights for you just as he promised.

HEATHER STEWART AND ANEETA Campbell were zookeepers in Alberta, Canada. They had fed all the animals but one, a 150-pound jaguar.

As the women stepped into the jaguar's cage with some ground meat, they assumed that he was safely locked away from them. But just as they were leaving, the animal lunged at Aneeta, knocked her down, and tore at her arm.

Heather immediately pulled the big cat's tail, hit him with a bucket, and jumped on top of him. "He held on to Aneeta as if I weren't there," she reported later. Her mind raced, trying to imagine what it would take to get her screaming friend released from the animal's crushing jaws. She remembered a sledgehammer in the pickup.

Heather sprinted for the sledgehammer. By then her friend had stopped screaming, and Heather was afraid Aneeta's heart had stopped. As she lifted the twelve-pound hammer high into the air, she aimed it for the animal's body, knowing that if she missed or failed to hit the big cat hard enough, he would go after her.

She struck him again and again until his body was limp. Then she got Aneeta to a hospital. She said, "I wouldn't be able to live with myself if I'd just run away. What I did wasn't heroic. It was simply an act of humanity."

Monday
Week

28

POINTS TO PONDER

Courage lifts us beyond our fears and causes us to act assertively in the face of threat or danger. Some people are more courageous than others by virtue of their personalities. But real courage comes from a Power beyond ourselves. When circumstances seem to overwhelm us, we are told to call out to God. He will give us the courage that comes from trusting Him, and He will give us the strength we need.

POWER BUILDER

TERRY ANDERSON

Former Hostage

Wh
HILE TERRY ANDERSON WAS held captive by the radical
Shiite Muslims who kidnapped him, he was physically abused, deprived of
all contact with family and friends, and given meager portions of nearly
inedible food. He and his fellow hostages were chained up for years on
end, locked in dark Beirut basements, not knowing whether they would
live or die.

After six years of captivity, Terry was finally released among the last
American hostages. To the amazement of many observers he said, "I have
no room for hatred, no time for it. My hating them is not going to hurt
them an ounce. It's only going to hurt me, and I'm not going to do that."

As he sat in solitude, Terry read the Bible again and again—he figures
he may have read it fifty times. He and the other hostages sometimes
shared Eucharist. He does not see himself as having been courageous: "We
all find it in ourselves to do what we have to do. People are capable of an
awful lot when they have no choice, and I had no choice. Courage is
when you have choices."

Tuesday

Week

28

POWER QUOTE

Sometimes we demonstrate the
greatest courage when we refuse
to give up.

SCRIPTURE

Psalm 68:28

Our God, show your strength!

Show us once again.

POINTS TO PONDER

Although Terry Anderson may not have had choices with regard to his surroundings, he did have choices about his emotions and behavior. His
choice to focus his attention on God's Word, to exercise his mind through
conversation and debate with other hostages, and to worship God reflected
faith in a Power beyond himself. Despair would have been an understand-
able choice of emotion. But Terry Anderson had the courage to choose to
keep faith, to prepare for future freedom, and to believe that God had not
abandoned him.

POWER BUILDER

POWER QUOTE

Sitting still in the midst of trouble requires great courage and self-discipline.

SCRIPTURE

2 Chronicles 20:15

You don't need to be afraid or let this powerful army discourage you. God will fight on your side!

SENIOR CHRIS ERICKS WAS attending the last class of the day when a student marched into the room and ordered the teacher to get out. When the teacher refused to leave, the student pulled out a sawed-off shotgun and pointed it at the teacher.

As the teacher left the room, the student blasted a hole in the wall above his desk. The room fell silent, and Chris watched nervously as the gunman gestured with the gun. He focused on the situation, and he realized that if the police rushed into the room, somebody would probably get shot. Chris determined the gunman would have to be taken out by surprise, and he began to look for an opportunity.

Three and a half hours later, the students were still held in the classroom by the armed student. Chris was still watching and waiting for his chance. He stared as the gunman offered a cigarette to one of the students, then bent over and lit it. In a lightning-quick move, Chris grabbed the shotgun, pointed it at the gunman, and shouted, "Get out, everybody!" Then the police apprehended the gunman.

Chris Ericks was the recipient of a number of honors and awards. He responded by saying, "God was the one who saved us. He gave me the level head and the opportunity to do what I did."

Wednesday
Week

28

POINTS TO PONDER

Each of us is equipped with a unique set of strengths and weaknesses. Those who have walked a spiritual path often credit God with their accomplishments, just as Chris Ericks did. People who have seen God's power at work in their lives know themselves, know God, and know how to give credit where credit is due.

POWER BUILDER

SCOTT CARTER

OSU Cowboys Fan

Oklahoma State University's 1991 basketball team was playing a home game against Cal Berkeley when twelve-year-old Scott Carter was first introduced to the players. Because of surgery to combat his cancer, Scott lost part of one leg. As the players got to know him, Scott's courage impressed them profoundly. He sat beside the team, made irreverent remarks, and high-fived them as they returned to the bench.

One day Byron Houston severely sprained his ankle. When Scott heard Byron wasn't going to play in a key game, he said, "I guess I've got to suit up if you don't play." Byron looked at Scott, sitting in his wheelchair, then at his sprained ankle. He played, although in pain, and scored seventeen points.

Scott's health deteriorated. Tests confirmed more tumors. But the boy showed up at every game, weak as he was. One night he arrived at a game so weak he had to lie down in his wheelchair, and the Cowboys knew it would be his last game. It was.

Scott Carter was buried in his own OSU Cowboys uniform. At his side was a plaque on which was written 2 Timothy 4:7–8: "I have fought well. I have finished the race, and I have been faithful. So a crown will be given to me for pleasing the Lord." Scott Carter remains OSU basketball's model for "player of the game."

Thursday

Week

28

POWER QUOTE

God's gifts are free,
but He doesn't give them to us
until we need them.

SCRIPTURE

Hebrews 10:35–36

Keep on being brave! It will bring you great rewards. Learn to be patient.

POINTS TO PONDER

What was Scott Carter's secret? Was it his outgoing, optimistic personality? The excitement of the games and the friendship of the players? All probably played a part, but a more likely explanation can be found on the plaque displayed at his funeral: "I have been faithful." Scott was a Christian, and he had received a special gift of courage from God to help him deal with his disease and death. That's what kept him going.

THREE CARING MEN

Powerful Mediators

POWER QUOTE

We may have the courage to be heroes, but do we have the courage to be listeners, encouragers, and love givers?

SCRIPTURE

Hosea 11:3–4

They would not admit that I was the one who had healed them. I led them with kindness and with love.

RAJON BEGIN WAS THE first to see Charles Crawford's desperate, suicidal movement along the overpass ledge, his fingers tangled through chain-link fence. Rajon climbed out on the ledge, threw his leg across the larger, muscular Charles's body, and clung to the fence behind him. It was a position that would shield Charles from killing himself or would send Rajon to his death.

"Let me go," Charles pleaded. "I want to die."

Next, a devout Christian arrived. Obeying a sudden urge, he had followed a route home that took him directly past the two men hanging from the fence. "Can we talk?" he asked Charles. Charles began to push away from the fence, crying, "I want to jump!"

Later, Chris Eyre arrived. Chris had experience counseling distraught people. He called the police from his cellular phone, then rushed to the scene. Rajon had been clinging to the fence, his arms around Charles, for more than thirty minutes. As the four men talked, Charles's story of loss and loneliness poured out. Each man shared something of himself with Charles, and his repeated statement of "nobody cares" was quickly denied.

Eventually, Charles consented to be rescued. He later said, "I have gained strength from what these men taught me, that people do care about each other. One of them risked his life to save mine. I can never forget that."

Friday
Week
28

POINTS TO PONDER

Each of the three men who saved Charles Crawford's life brought a different kind of courage to the scene. It took all three of them to get the job done. Perhaps we sometimes fail to allow the gifts of others to have a place in our own heroic scenarios. In Charles's case, it wasn't the heroics that saved him as much as the fact that others cared about his life. Sometimes genuinely caring requires more courage than anything else.

TRY TO RECALL A time when you were aware of courage that came from God, not from your own resources. What happened?

_____

_____

How did God use your courage for His own purposes?

_____

_____

Lord,

I dream of being a hero,

but I'm not really a courageous person.

I might have the strength to rescue

a loved one from danger,

but I'm weak when it comes to taking personal risks,

and I don't always act the way I believe.

Please give me courage, Lord,

to be more like You—fearless, strong,

and willing to die for those You love.

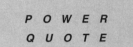
POWER
BUILDER

MIKE PREMO
Evangelist

We become godly when God's strength overpowers our weaknesses.

Hosea 11:8

I can't let you go. I can't give you up. . . . I just can't do it. My feelings for you are much too strong.

Monday
Week
29

*B*ACKSLIDING IS AN OLD-FASHIONED word. But for Mike Premo, it was a way of life. Mike began his adult life as a petty criminal, and when he became a Christian in his early twenties, he thought he was changed forever. He even chose to serve God as an evangelist. But the temptations of sex outside marriage, alcohol, and drugs dogged his steps.

Mike had a familiar pattern—good behavior for a few years, followed by a binge, then a disappearance. Mike's first wife finally gave up on him; his second prayed until at last Mike got involved in a Christ-centered program specifically geared toward backsliders.

Over the course of his rocky spiritual journey, Mike Premo has learned two things that are a matter of life and death to him. He has learned that he is powerless against temptations, and that he must rely on God's power when he feels drawn into trouble. He has also discovered firsthand that God's love is relentless, and that He will never leave or forsake those who have put their trust in Him.

"I know the chastening of God," Mike says, "and I know the love of God. I praise Him for both. I pray that in my weakness the strength of God will prevail and my testimony will relate to others that have failed and are looking for hope."

Oswald Chambers wrote that the church is supposed to be a hospital for sinners, not a museum for saints. Nonetheless, we often expect ourselves to be perfect, and we are surprised at the twists and turns in our Christian walk. God has no illusions about our capacity for wrongdoing. He doesn't give us tests to check up on our growth. Instead, He allows us to walk through our areas of weakness until we acknowledge our helplessness and commit ourselves to His transforming power. Only then do we experience genuine change.

POWER BUILDER

ROBERT SCHULLER

Pastor

ROBERT SCHULLER IS AN avid believer in what he calls Power Thoughts. He says, "God is constantly sending Power Thoughts to communicate with all His human creations who chose by faith (Power Thinking) to connect with Him. . . . On the screen of your imagination the instructions appear, outlining this process called success. Watch the messages come across the screen!"

Schuller describes seven Power Thoughts that the Holy Spirit uses to motivate, monitor, and manage human beings:

1. Potentialize. Ask what you could do and what you could be.
2. Prioritize. Arrange your priorities.
3. Possibilitize. Reject the word *impossible*!
4. Internalize. Enthusiasm means, "God is working in you" (Phil. 2:13).
5. Organize. Get strong help from good people.
6. Revitalize. Take time to worship, rest, and meditate.
7. Patronize. Once you're on top, give to others.

Contemplating humankind's remarkable ability to achieve, Schuller reminds us that God is essential to our success: "The more honestly I study the human being at his or her best, the more convinced I am of the reality of God."

Tuesday

Week

29

POINTS TO PONDER

A unique partnership between us and God enables us to gradually change our way of living. This partnership begins when we come to see that we cannot live the way we should without God's help. Once we have admitted that to Him, and we have asked for His intervention, we add our efforts to the equation: we begin to develop patterns of self-discipline that include God-centered Power Thoughts. As His supernatural inner strength combines with our self-discipline, the process of real change begins.

POWER QUOTE

God is able to transform our lives to the degree that we are willing to cooperate with Him.

SCRIPTURE

Proverbs 24:5

Wisdom brings strength, and knowledge gives power.

POWER BUILDER

WILLIAM B. WALTON

Cofounder, Holiday Inns

POWER QUOTE

Wherever one person is strong, another is weak; this is God's way of making sure we need each other—and Him.

SCRIPTURE

Joshua 24:15

Choose right now! . . . My family and I are going to worship and obey the LORD!

POWERFUL MEN OFTEN HOLD influence over the lives of the people who surround them. William B. Walton was a man with tremendous power. And being in charge was important to him. Unfortunately, his drive had damaged his relationship with his children.

When Walton began to seek change, he wasn't sure who he could trust with his personal concerns. He had few true friendships. Then he met Billy Graham, who graciously invited Walton and his wife to sit on the platform with him at a crusade.

As Graham's sermon ended, Walton watched the faces of the people who were coming forward to receive Christ. Each person came with a need, and tears spoke of the hope for God's intervention. Walton had hidden from the world his guilt about his family—he felt he had victimized them in his incessant drive to succeed and control.

Along with the others at the crusade, Walton confessed his sins, and he asked Jesus Christ to be his Savior. He set aside his immense professional power and received eternal life.

Walton later wrote, "In the Christian family there is only one Lord who is to be loved, worshiped, and served with equal faithfulness by father, mother, and children. That simple truth, put into action, will spare parents a lot of grief and set their children on the only lifetime climb that counts."

POINTS TO PONDER

As well as having special, God-given gifts and strengths, every person has an area of weakness. We confess to God again and again, knowing we still haven't got it right. When we come to Christ, we must come honestly, letting Him know that we need His help and are willing to submit to His correction. Then weakness can be transformed by His strength.

POWER BUILDER

KRISS AKABUSI

British Olympic Medalist

Worldsclass runner Kriss Akabusi was born to Nigerian parents in England. When he was a toddler, his parents returned to their homeland, and they left Kriss behind to live in a series of foster homes. He continuously searched for the love he had never known as a child.

Years later, he experienced a vision of Jesus Christ: "It was as if I were swimming toward a voice which was saying, 'Come to Me all who are weary and I will give you rest.' I pictured Jesus and cried to Him aloud, . . . inviting Him into my life. As I did, an amazing feeling came over me. I felt so happy and tranquil; I felt like I was born again, everything seemed new. . . .

"One of the many changes that followed in my life was an increased inner peace. However, an even more significant change has been in my ability to express and receive love. . . .

"I'm not about to say, 'Now I have no more problems.' I know there are more changes to be made, but I also know that God loves me and that He will help me through the challenges to come. My whole life was really just a search for love. The world says, 'Whatever you want take it!' Many people believe it but deep down inside they know it's a lie. Jesus is the only answer."

POWER QUOTE

God loved you before you were born, when you were only a thought in His mind.

SCRIPTURE

Romans 5:8

God showed how much he loved us by having Christ die for us, even though we were sinful.

POINTS TO PONDER

Why does a perfect, holy God love us? Considering our endless shortcomings, failures, and weaknesses, that is an impossible question to answer. The only thing that matters is, He does. And His Word makes a point of saying that He died for us, "even though we were sinful." God's love is His choice, a reflection of His character, and His gift to us. We don't have to understand His reason for loving us; we need only respond in humility and gratitude.

POWER BUILDER

BEBE AND CECE WINANS
Gospel Singers

Anything we do for others sincerely, and in honor of God, is a powerful performance.

SCRIPTURE

Romans 15:21

All who haven't been told about him will see him, and those who haven't heard about him will understand.

BEBE AND CECE WINANS have been singing together almost as long as they can remember. Their Christian faith is a focal point of their lives, and they often talk about the meaning behind their music. CeCe says, "We get to see first-hand how our music affects people, how our music means something positive. We just give the audiences what God gave us, and that's sharing whatever talent we have. I love to see the change that comes over people during a concert, to see that something we've done makes them feel good."

BeBe adds, "We get to tell them the whole story. Concerts let them know a little bit more about who we are and what we believe in. Sometimes that shatters people's conceptions. They look at us and say, 'Well, maybe they do love Jesus.'"

CeCe concludes, "We never imagined things would go as well as they did, as fast as they did. We just felt called to sing, so I guess our first goal was to do the best we could for the Lord. We'll just keep going until God says to do something else."

Friday
Week

29

POINTS TO PONDER

After all God has done for us, we want to give something back to Him. We offer our time, our talent, and our treasure, hoping to demonstrate our gratitude. But He wants something more, something deeper. God wants us to offer our lives as something His Word describes as "a living sacrifice." That means we present the whole being to Him, available for Him in any way He chooses—serving, praying, listening, loving, or using our creativity in a public way.

HOW IS GOD HELPING you understand His lordship over your life? Record some of your thoughts about His sovereignty and how it affects you.

_____

_____

_____

_____

_____

Weekend
Week

29

Lord,

when You died for me,

You paid an incredible price for my life.

And now I don't really belong to myself anymore.

You have bought me; I belong to You.

I want to live my life according to Your will,

and I offer You my strengths and talents

as well as my failures and weaknesses.

Take it all, Lord.

Most of all, take my will and make it Yours.

Put Your desires in my heart,

and change my mind when it needs changing.

ROBERTA GUASPARI-
TZAVARAS

Classical Violinist

True love means giving without counting the cost.

Galatians 5:6

All that matters is your faith that makes you love others.

Roberta Guaspari-Tzavaras was the daughter of a factory worker. She would have never picked up a violin had it not been for a public school program that offered musical education. Aware that her life had been transformed by music, Roberta took her gifts and talents to Harlem, and she offered them to the children there.

Although some of the students' parents doubted that their sons and daughters had enough discipline to learn such a demanding instrument, Roberta was undaunted. She began teaching in the public schools, demanding that her students practice every day. Budget cuts eliminated her job; she found private funds to keep the program alive. The children's musical performance improved dramatically under their teacher's firm, dedicated instruction.

One night in Harlem, 130 youngsters walked on stage with their violins. They silently studied their teacher's face, bows in hand, awaiting her cue. Then came the music—in tune, in time, and with natural talent and grace that everyone in the room could instantly feel. Tears filled the parents' eyes. It seemed like a miracle.

Virtuoso Isaac Stern was in the audience for the event, which would have never taken place without Roberta Guaspari-Tzavaras's persistence and commitment. "This is not a concert," Stern stated. "This is a way to make these kids proud of themselves. It is an act of living."

Monday
Week

30

When we genuinely care for others, we share with them the gifts we have been freely given. But time is limited. Demands are endless. How can we afford to get involved? When we see the heartwarming results of a caregiver such as Roberta Guaspari-Tzavaras and her musical program, the question changes. How can we afford not to?

POWER BUILDER

JIM NEWMAN
Retired Engineer

THE POWER OF LOVE can change a person's life forever. Jim Newman watched his wife slowly die in a Texas nursing home. Although she was in a coma, he spent hours at her bedside every day. During that time, Jim became acquainted with another resident of the nursing home—a boy with cerebral palsy named Michael Harris.

After Mrs. Newman died, Jim continued to visit the young boy. It was obvious to everyone in the nursing home that when Jim arrived, the child responded with great joy. "It means a lot to children to have somebody to talk to them," Jim explained. "They want attention and love."

Michael was a ward of the Texas courts, and he was eventually moved to a children's facility in another part of the state. After much soul-searching, Jim closed up his house and moved to the town where Michael lived.

To Michael's immense delight, Jim visits him every day, and after Michael's classes, Jim takes him for rides in his wheelchair. At the end of each day, Jim tucks Michael in bed. "I kiss him good-night and tell him I'll be back the next day," Jim says. "I tell him that I love him, and that God loves him too."

Tuesday
Week

30

POWER QUOTE

When we love each other, we worship our Creator.

SCRIPTURE

John 13:35

If you love each other, everyone will know that you are my disciples.

POINTS TO PONDER

It is easy for us to love bright and beautiful children. And we are strongly attracted to good-looking adult companions who stimulate our minds and inspire us. We are instinctively drawn to the beautiful, the successful, the glamorous. But when we are able to love the unlovely, we are beginning to understand God's love for us. As we embrace those who have little to offer us in return, we catch a glimpse of the unconditional love that has been extended to us. The ability to look past others' faults and see their needs is a spiritual gift, not a natural ability.

MARGARET PICKFORD

Professional Comforter

POWER BUILDER

POWER QUOTE

Your hands become the hands of God when you allow Him to love others through you.

SCRIPTURE

1 John 4:18

A real love for others will chase those worries away.

Human touch has a powerful ability to calm and comfort. A California ophthalmologist has added what he considers a significant new advancement to routine eye surgery. He has asked Margaret Pickford to hold his patients' hands during their operations.

In the eye surgery, a local anesthetic is used, so patients are conscious. This procedure can be very frightening because they can't see and are not supposed to either move or talk. Having a hand to hold relaxes them. It also lowers their blood pressure and heart rate.

"Some people," Margaret explains, "particularly men, don't want the support at first. But they usually end up squeezing so tightly I think my hand's going to come off at the wrist! Doctors may be experts in their fields, but they haven't had the surgery. That's where I have the expertise."

Margaret, a retired schoolteacher, has had cataract surgery. And she has held the hands of about two thousand patients. The doctor says he rarely operates on anyone without Margaret. She isn't paid for her contribution—she explains that she is doing her part to "keep medical costs down."

POINTS TO PONDER

Human touch is so important that it can be a matter of life and death to infants. Babies die unless arms embrace them and hands caress them. Our busy, high-tech world sometimes removes opportunities for tenderness and nonsexual affection, and we have to make an extra effort to demonstrate our caring. Although we are to turn to God with our needs, God has not chosen to be physically present in the world at this time. And when we need to experience the love of God "with skin on," we have to rely on each other to provide the warmth, gentleness, and nurturing human beings so desperately need.

POWER BUILDER

BARBARA LONGWORTH
Gardening Advocate

Barbara Longworth's New Orleans neighborhood, like many others, is old and gracious, but marred by graffiti and threatened by drugs and crime. One day, Barbara noticed a boy and a girl aimlessly ripping flowers off their stems and throwing them on the ground. She asked them to stop, but day after day they repeated the destructive action.

"Do you know how long it takes a flower to grow?" she finally asked them. "Have you ever planted a garden?" The children shook their heads.

Barbara bought two plants and presented them to the boy and girl, and they planted them in her yard. Every day they came by to tend the little plants. She let them understand that it was their garden. Before long, an array of color replaced the weeds that had surrounded her home. There were irises, gardenias, periwinkle, and Mexican heather. Once their garden at Barbara's was flourishing, the children went down the street and planted another one for a man with cancer "so he would have something to look at from his front porch."

Sometimes Barbara finds donated cuttings or fertilizer or a pack of seeds beside her door. "A garden—that's my way of combating crime and drugs," Barbara Longworth says.

Thursday
Week

30

POWER QUOTE

Stop and smell the roses—then stop a moment longer and marvel over the amazing process of their growth.

SCRIPTURE

Proverbs 31:20

She helps the poor and the needy.

POINTS TO PONDER

Cultivating soil, planting seeds, watering, weeding, and pruning plants are remarkably healing activities. Scripture is rich in metaphors that speak of gardens and fields, sowing and reaping. When Barbara Longworth chose to love her troubled neighborhood children, she provided them with more than a second chance. She put them in touch with life itself—the mystery of seeds that die and live again. The miracle of growth. The importance of seasons. Most of all, she gave them the gift of accomplishment—beauty in exchange for hard work, a lesson they desperately needed to learn.

KIMBERLEY MARSHALL
AND DAVID CRENSHAW

Newlyweds

POWER BUILDER

Love can mend a broken heart
and bring healing to a broken
body.

Song of Songs 8:6

The passion of love bursting

into flame is more powerful

than death.

KIMBERLEY MARSHALL AND DAVID Crenshaw had one thing in common when they met at Presbyterian Hospital in Dallas—both had cystic fibrosis and had survived far longer than anyone expected. Kimberley was sixteen; David was eighteen.

David thought Kim was beautiful, and he wanted to know her better. Eventually, his persistent pursuit paid off, and when they were twenty-three and twenty-one, they got married. The love that had grown between them seemed to be more powerful than any of their difficulties. Even though their health was continuously at risk, the newlyweds were happier than they had ever been in their lives.

When Kim was hospitalized, David slept on a cot in her room. If she wanted candy, he rushed out and bought it for her. To the amazement of everyone, Kim got well enough to go home. Then David began to struggle for his life. Determined to enjoy what seemed to be their last years together, he insisted that they take a vacation, so they went to the beach.

Not long after they returned, David was admitted to the hospital, Kim at his side. He died shortly afterward, on October 21. Less than twenty-four hours after his funeral, Kim became ill. She died on November 11. The same powerful love that had given them life had brought them together in death.

Friday
Week

30

POINTS TO PONDER

When we talk about love, we speak of a mystery. We can identify its qualities, but we have a harder time explaining how love begins and what keeps it strong and alive. Scripture describes it as "flames of fire" (Song 8:6 NKJV), so supernatural is its power. The healing ability of love, the caring it provides, and the joy it brings to life aren't limited to romance. Human love of all kinds, expressed through gestures of compassion, concern, and caring, provides rare medicine. Those who give love and those who receive love are equally blessed by its touch.

HOW HAS ANOTHER PERSON'S love and caring made a difference in your life?

_____

_____

Can you recall a time when your touch has brought health and help to someone else?

_____

_____

Weekend
Week

30

Lord,

Your love is the source of all other loves

because You love unconditionally

and Your love endures forever.

Teach me to love others

as You love them.

And when my need

gets in the way of caring for others,

love through me.

Touch them with tenderness

in spite of my limitations.

**POWER
BUILDER**

MARVIS FRAZIER
Heavyweight Boxer

POWER QUOTE

When we allow our personal power to get in God's way, He may choose to overpower us.

SCRIPTURE

Romans 5:3–5

Suffering helps us to endure. And endurance builds character, which gives us a hope that will never disappoint us.

MARVIS FRAZIER, SON OF heavyweight boxing champion Joe Frazier, learned some valuable lessons from his father. Joe told him, "Son, in this boxing ring, you can get your brains shook, your money took, and your name written in the undertaker's book." Not only is this information true about boxing, but it relates to everyday life.

Marvis writes that he never knew what his father was saying until he faced some of life's realities on his own: "Being the son of the former heavyweight champion of the world and a top contender myself, I was exposed to many of Satan's workers. You name them, I met them: drug dealers, drug addicts, pimps, hookers, gamblers and even murderers. I met those people through the boxing game. The boxing game is a rough business both inside and outside the ring. . . .

"I remember back in the 1980's right before the Olympic Trials in Atlanta, Georgia, I allowed the enemy to fill my head with foolish pride. I thought that I was Superman. . . . I was so high on Marvis and how great a boxer he was that I had forgotten who the real champion is—Christ."

Marvis lost the match he so firmly believed he could win. And the loss sent him directly back to church, Bible studies, and prayer. He writes, "The Lord had definitely humbled me. I had fought for the heavyweight championship of the world. I didn't win that honor. God, as He did with Moses, allowed me to see the promised land, but didn't allow me to cross over."

POINTS TO PONDER

As focused as we may be on our physical bodies—including our needs, wants, and wishes—God is far more concerned with the inner self. He is working to remake our spirits, to restore our souls, and to create in us a godly character. He sometimes removes from us the power we think we have in order to fill us with His supernatural power.

POWER BUILDER

TOM SIROTNAK

Football Player

Wᴴᴱɴ TOM SIROTNAK GAVE his life to Jesus Christ, he wanted just one thing in return—to play football for the University of Southern California. "God," he said, "if You'll get me on this football team, I'll be Your witness."

God answered Tom's prayer, allowing him to become the first defensive lineman to walk on to the USC team in twenty-five years. Tom enjoyed the benefits of playing on a championship team, including plenty of partying and sexual immorality. "God kept His end of the bargain," Tom recounts. "Meanwhile, I was a disgrace."

Tom repented and failed and repented several times. Then he heard former professional football player Rosey Grier speak about completely surrendering his life to the Lord. After hearing the same message twice, Tom gave the Lord his way of life once and for all.

When Tom Sirotnak's football days at USC came to an end, his days of serving the Lord really began. He continues to use his powerful physique to draw attention to his message: "Placing 425 pounds on a bar, I bench pressed it nine times. People gathered around, marveling. I said, 'If you think that's strong, wait until you hear about Jesus, who bore the sin of the world on His back. That's the strongest man I've ever seen!'"

POWER QUOTE

Spiritual power reverses the equation: the weaker we become, the stronger He makes us.

SCRIPTURE

Philippians 3:13–14

I forget what is behind, and I struggle for what is ahead. I run toward the goal, so that I can win the prize . . . that God offers because of what Christ Jesus has done.

POINTS TO PONDER

What kind of personal power do we really want? Are we seeking a way to control others, to get our way, and to create security for ourselves? That kind of empowerment is promoted by our consumer-minded culture. The kind of power God offers, however, is far different. We know that Christ's greatness arose from His humility, and His power came from His Father. If that is the power we want, we find it by dying to ourselves and following Him.

ART MONK
Professional Football Player

POWER QUOTE

There is a deep, inner void in every person, and only God's Spirit can fill it.

SCRIPTURE

Isaiah 26:3

The LORD gives perfect peace to those whose faith is firm.

ART MONK HAS THREE Super Bowl rings to represent his achievements. But no one has ever heard him brag about his accomplishments, either on or off the playing field. Private and thoughtful, Art is far more comfortable with his family than surrounded by wildly enthusiastic fans. He gives few interviews. Art's reputation for silence has almost become legendary. He says, "I do two important things in my life. I play football and I spend time with my family. Most everything else is a distraction."

However, even his chosen distance from football's madness couldn't protect him from inner struggles. Dissatisfied in the late 1980s, Art hid his personal turmoil from the world: "I just wasn't happy with the way my life was going. I was reaching for things to make me feel good—cars, houses, money. But something was missing."

Noticing the peace of mind that surrounded teammates who attended a regular Bible study, Art asked to join them. Soon thereafter, the peace of God began to warm his heart. He says, "All those things I'd learned in my early years came flooding back. My parents were right, I thought. This is what I need. It makes a big difference in my life."

Wednesday
Week

31

POINTS TO PONDER

Having right priorities doesn't guarantee peace of mind. Like Art Monk, we can prevent some confusion by keeping our lives in order, yet we may still have a pervasive emptiness that speaks of spiritual need. A relationship with God is the only antidote for personal emptiness. We need an infusion of God's power, and we need His companionship as we hold to His promise never to leave us.

POWER BUILDER

GEORGE HERMAN "BABE" RUTH

Professional Baseball Player

Georg**GEORGE HERMAN "BABE" RUTH** was a powerful slugger, probably the best-known player of the 1920s and early 1930s. He teamed up with Lou Gehrig to form the heart of the 1927 Yankees, a team still viewed by some baseball experts as the best in the history of the game.

Nicknamed the "Sultan of Swat," Ruth led the league in home runs a record twelve times. His lifetime batting average was .342. He was elected to the Baseball Hall of Fame in 1936 as one of the first five charter members.

Although Babe Ruth is still remembered as an invincible hero, his personal life was not befitting a great role model—his hard drinking and other wild exploits were legendary. As Ruth's career waned, he became more aware of his spiritual and moral weaknesses. He said, "I guess I was so anxious to enjoy life to the fullest that I forgot the rules—or ignored them."

Later in life he wrote, "While I drifted away from the church, I did have my own 'altar,' a big window of my New York apartment overlooking the city lights. Often I would kneel before that window and say my prayers. I would feel quite humble then. I'd ask God to help me not make such a big fool of myself and pray that I'd measure up to what He expected of me."

The strength of God sustained Ruth in his final years. In 1948, he died a repentant and forgiven man who had found peace, forgiveness, and comfort in God.

Thursday
Week

31

POINTS TO PONDER

We rub shoulders with powerful, prestigious men and women every day. We feel the impact of their decisions. We watch them as they exert control in many areas of life. If we're wise, before we envy their clout, we'll ask ourselves whether they have the kind of inner power that will sustain them through all of life. For that matter, do we?

POWER QUOTE

God wants to be our source of strength, not only in public, but in private, where our personal weaknesses are carefully hidden.

SCRIPTURE

Psalm 50:15

Pray to me in time of trouble. I will rescue you, and you will honor me.

JOHN BLUE
Professional Hockey Player

POWER QUOTE

The thing we want the most can become our greatest source of misery until we release its power to God.

SCRIPTURE

Psalm 40:5

You, LORD God, have done many wonderful things, and you have planned marvelous things for us. . . . I would never be able to tell all you have done.

JOHN BLUE OF THE Boston Bruins learned about the power of relinquishment after several successful years in hockey. Three years after the joy of making the U.S. national team at the Olympics, his world fell apart when he was told, "You're not a good goalie. We don't want you. . . . You really ought to retire and forget hockey."

Filled with despair, John finally turned to God and released his uncertain future. He prayed, "Lord, it's in Your hands. If You want me to serve You in the minor leagues, that's where I'm going to serve You."

He later wrote, "That decision marked my turnaround. I realized it didn't matter as much where I was as who I was: His servant. I felt a release from the pressure that dogged me everywhere I played. . . . Whatever happened, I knew it was in the Lord's hands and He had me where He wanted me. That allowed me to go out and play the game. I love hockey and feel God's given me a gift for it."

Not many months later, John Blue was playing in the famed Boston Garden. His success has continued since he handed over the controls of his life to God: "It took so long to get here that it helps me keep perspective. To be arrogant or cocky when I didn't have any control over the outcome would be foolish. . . . I know the source of my strength and blessings."

Friday
Week

31

POINTS TO PONDER

God has good plans for our lives, and His will may be the same as ours. But when we get overly committed to our own agenda for the future, we become tense and fearful, and our emotions don't allow us to perform at our best. By relinquishing ourselves to the will of God, we accomplish two things at once. First, we give up our willfulness, so He is free to guide us in a different direction if He wants to. Second, we allow ourselves to relax, be in top form, and enjoy ourselves.

Have you had power struggles along your professional path? How were they resolved? Take a moment and write your thoughts about the struggles.

_____

_____

What would you do differently if the same situation arose today?

_____

_____

Lord,

sometimes I want things so much

that they become gods to me.

They consume my thoughts,

affect my emotions,

and eventually drive me away from You,

especially if I think You aren't giving me

what I want.

Forgive my idolatry, Lord,

and teach me to say, "Thy will be done,"

and to mean it wholeheartedly.

POWER BUILDER

POWER QUOTE

God's thoughts are beyond ours, and His purposes are inscrutable.

SCRIPTURE

Psalm 139:9–10

Suppose I had wings like the dawning day and flew across the ocean. Even then your powerful arm would guide and protect me.

DINO ANDREADIS DREAMED ALL his life of being a movie star. He made his way to Hollywood from Montreal, and he pounded on doors, trying to get a part in the film or television industry.

Just as his agent was beginning to find opportunities for Dino, the Immigration and Naturalization Service informed him that, as a Canadian, he could not work without an American green card. There were two alternatives—pay $5,000 for a green card or marry an American.

Short on cash, Dino began a search of nightclubs, and he found a beautiful young woman who was willing to marry him. Energized, he rushed home to make plans. On the bus, a man slipped a printed message into his hand: Jesus Christ is coming soon! Suddenly confused, Dino got off at the next bus stop—the wrong one. There stood David, the man who had given him the tract, who took the opportunity to share the gospel with Dino.

The next morning, a woman came to Dino's door. She was a friend of David's. "I felt compelled to pray for you all night," she explained. "Whatever it is you're about to do, don't do it!" She left.

Dino called off the marriage. He asked Christ into his life, a decision that led him from acting to evangelism; from LA to Montreal; from a false marriage to his true love.

Monday
Week

32

POINTS TO PONDER

God's sudden, seemingly uninvited intervention into people's lives is a divine mystery. To us, it may seem too early, or it may seem too late. But from His eternal perspective, His timing is perfect.

POWER BUILDER

BEN CARSON

Neurosurgeon

Bᴇɴ CARSON BELIEVED GOD wanted him to be a doctor. It was an unlikely dream. He lived in the ghetto with his mother, a single parent. Ben was getting terrible grades. But his eyesight was to blame. Once he got glasses, his grades improved. By high-school graduation, Ben had earned a scholarship to Yale.

His first semester at Yale was sobering. The day before his chemistry final, Ben knew that he was on the verge of flunking out. He crammed for the test until he could no longer focus his eyes. As he crawled into bed, exhausted with his last-ditch efforts to rescue his grade, Ben wearily prayed for a miracle.

As he slept, Ben dreamed of a shadowy figure who began writing chemistry problems on a blackboard. In the dream, Ben memorized every problem and solution. When he awoke, he recorded them. In class, the chemistry exams were distributed. Ben was stunned. Page after page mirrored exactly what he had dreamed, and of course, he knew all the answers.

After graduating from Yale, Ben Carson went on to become a world-acclaimed neurosurgeon. His gifted hands have saved the lives of several children, including Siamese twins he separated.

Tuesday
Week

32

POINTS TO PONDER

Just as God intervenes unexpectedly in some circumstances, on other occasions He steps into the picture after we have begged, struggled, and given up. God doesn't help us because we have done our best, because we have been good, or because we have donated to His favorite charity. God intervenes because He loves us and because He knows we cannot make it without Him.

POWER QUOTE

Just when you think there is nothing God can do, He does the impossible.

SCRIPTURE

Lamentations 3:22–23

The Lᴏʀᴅ's kindness never fails! If he had not been merciful, we would have been destroyed. The Lᴏʀᴅ can always be trusted to show mercy each morning.

MARGARET POWERS
Poet

POWER BUILDER

PAUL POWERS WAS LYING in intensive care. He was in physical pain, unable to pray, and hopeless when a nurse asked if she could read to him the beloved poem "Footprints." The poem describes a person walking on a beach, seeing one set of footprints in the sand. When he asks God why He left him, God replies that He carried him.

The words of that poem were more meaningful to Paul than that nurse could have ever imagined. Paul's wife had written the poem.

Twenty-six years earlier, Paul and Margaret Powers had walked along a secluded beach and talked about the power of God's loving care—how He would carry His children through hard times. Margaret had gone home and written the words, which she excitedly presented to Paul.

Years later, while the Powerses were moving, six cartons containing Margaret's poetry disappeared from the moving van. It wasn't long before Margaret began seeing "Footprints" on plaques and cards, cups and key chains, always with the signature "Author Unknown." She eventually struggled through the theft of her masterpiece and gave its ministry to God—without her name on it.

The poem "Footprints" was returned to its original recipient—Paul Powers—just when he needed it most.

POWER QUOTE

Most miracles seem so impossible we never think to ask for them.

SCRIPTURE

Isaiah 40:1–2

Our God has said: . . . "Give them comfort. Speak kindly."

POINTS TO PONDER

When we go to God with our requests, we often tell Him what would best improve our lot and ask Him to provide it—as quickly as possible. Sometimes He gives us what we have asked for; sometimes He doesn't. But when we are so broken that we have no idea what to request, He does His most amazing work. He reaches into His eternal riches and brings out the very thing we need the most—something we couldn't have imagined.

POWER
BUILDER

VIKTOR FRANKL

Philosopher

VIKTOR FRANKL, AUTHOR OF *Man's Search for Meaning*, experienced the terrors of the Nazi Holocaust with his family. His father died of starvation in the Terracia camp; his mother went into the gas chamber at Auschwitz.

Not long before being sent to Auschwitz, Viktor received an immigration visa from the United States. His parents were thrilled at the prospect of seeing their son escape the threat of death and able to further his promising career in philosophy and psychotherapy.

But Viktor struggled with a troubling question: Should he leave his parents behind in Gestapo-controlled Austria? Where was his responsibility? Viktor entered St. Stephen's Cathedral to listen to the organ and think. Unable to find an answer, he told himself, "Viktor, you need a hint from heaven."

When he arrived home, his father showed him a piece of marble he had found in the debris of a bombed-out synagogue. "I brought it home because it is holy," he told his son.

It was a piece of the two tablets on which the Ten Commandments had been engraved. A closer look revealed one Hebrew letter, which indicated the commandment the fragment had represented: honor your father and mother. Viktor Frankl stayed in Austria, survived Auschwitz, and has since inspired millions with his books and wisdom.

POWER QUOTE

God's wisdom is available for the asking—we only have to be willing to receive it.

SCRIPTURE

Jeremiah 33:3

Ask me, and I will tell you things that you don't know and can't find out.

POINTS TO PONDER

Asking God for guidance involves one very challenging issue—we have to be willing to take His advice. God is quite prepared to clearly answer our requests for wisdom. The problem lies with us. Do we really want to know what He thinks?

DIANE KOMP

Pediatric Oncologist

POWER
QUOTE

We live by faith, not by sight; but from time to time, we catch a glimpse of God's invisible world.

SCRIPTURE

Matthew 18:10–11

Don't be cruel to any of these little ones! I promise you that their angels are always with my Father in heaven.

DR. DIANE KOMP BEGAN her career as an agnostic. Gradually, she changed her mind, in part because of her experiences with dying children.

Dr. Komp recounts the story of seven-year-old Anna: "Before she died, she mustered the final energy to sit up in her hospital bed and say, 'The angels—they're so beautiful! Mommy can you see them? Do you hear their singing? I've never heard such beautiful singing!' Then she lay back on her pillow and died."

Nine-year-old Donny climbed onto his grandmother's lap just before he died and said, "Grandma, I'm going to be with Jesus soon," even though no one had told him he was dying.

Mary Beth had a dream of Jesus and her grandfather telling her of her impending death and encouraging her not to be afraid; Mary Beth recognized her grandfather from family photographs. He died before she was born.

Dr. Komp concludes, "I've come to trust God for the continuing care of my patients. When God is so palpably present in those crisis moments, how can I say that I'm disappointed?"

POINTS TO PONDER

We live in a very practical, visual world where seeing is believing. And in matters of personal belief, we may try to apply our objectivity to spiritual concerns. How can we prove something we have accepted by faith? We can't. But now and then, God gives us a glimpse of something beyond our human view. We hear or see or catch a vision of another world. In doing so, our faith is strengthened; our doubts are assuaged. God's love becomes more personal, more practical, and more perceptible than it has ever been before.

REFLECT ON THE TIMES when God has intervened in your life. What did He do? How did His action affect your faith? Did you think of it as a miracle?

_____

_____

_____

_____

_____

Weekend
Week

32

Lord,

You have told me to walk by faith,

to believe in Your Word,

and to seek inner growth, not outward signs.

But when my trust is weak,

show me something beyond myself.

Help me catch sight of heaven, Lord;

show me the angels that guard me,

the home You have prepared for me.

Let me touch the face of Jesus.

Whatever it takes to make me strong,

whether it is sight or blind faith,

give me what I need,

according to Your perfect will.

POWER BUILDER

PETER OCHS

Former CEO, Fieldstone Foundation

POWER QUOTE

We can never outgive the One who gave His life for ours.

SCRIPTURE

2 Corinthians 9:6

A few seeds make a small harvest, but a lot of seeds make a big harvest.

A SIXTH-GENERATION BUILDER of homes, Peter Ochs built more than quality residences in southern California. He built a reputation for himself as a man who walked his Christian walk as well as talked about it.

Peter continued his interest in building until his fiftieth birthday. He established neighborhoods. His foundation supported humanitarian and fine arts projects. He taught his fellow Christians principles of godly stewardship and faithfulness.

Then at fifty, Peter began to build something new. He was a multimillionaire, and his land development business was thriving. But Peter had made a decision years before, and he was as good as his word.

Peter resigned his position as CEO of Fieldstone Foundation, relinquishing his responsibilities to his partner. He and his wife packed their bags and left California for an intensive training session, preparing them for their new career—as missionaries.

Exchanging his powerful executive position for a life of service, Peter Ochs spoke of the reflective life he hoped to gain in his new life. "The contemplative life in the 20th century is a lost art," he said. "Do I know how to do that? No. Is it scary? Yes. But we're going to try."

Monday

W e e k

33

POINTS TO PONDER

God is generous with us—giving us health, friends, and family and meeting our needs. His generosity inspires us to give back to Him something of ourselves. But what? We can tithe money; we can do volunteer work; we can donate food and clothing to needy persons. Is that enough? Peter Ochs and his wife felt that they could give nothing short of their lives to God. That is the least any of us can give—whether in full-time service or in full-time submission to His will.

POWER BUILDER

JOHN EDWARD JONES
Attorney

JOHN EDWARD JONES COULDN'T be anything but the best. He was determined to be a successful attorney, and he often said, "God helps those who help themselves," not realizing he was quoting Ben Franklin instead of the Bible.

After graduating from law school, John served as a military judge during the Vietnam War. Once he was settled into his own general law practice in Florida, he continued to be success driven.

But having power and knowing how to use it are two different things. Even after John gave himself to Christ, he followed old patterns and merely attached Christian labels to them.

Tuesday
Week

33

Fear of failure drove John to take on a heavy case load. Then the sudden deaths of several attorneys in their forties shocked him into a new awareness. They had worked hard to achieve their goals, and they had died in the process.

John Jones began to pray for a new way of life. He spent more time with his family. Then he began to work toward reconciliation in divorce cases. Today, he has seen hundreds of couples reconciled in their marriages. He says, "As I surrender my goals to Him daily, He gives me the privilege of being on the scene when He performs miracles."

POWER QUOTE

The more power we take for ourselves, the less of ourselves we have to offer God.

SCRIPTURE

2 Corinthians 9:12

What you are doing is much more than a service that supplies God's people with what they need. It is something that will make many others thank God.

POINTS TO PONDER

Career success appears to remove us from vulnerability and gives us a sense of control over our circumstances. The truth is, as we pursue success, we are often feeding our pride. God wants to be God. All power belongs to Him; all provisions emanate from Him; all glory returns to Him. As we submit to His authority, our grasping for success weakens, and we give back to Him the power and authority we tried to take for ourselves.

POWER BUILDER

BUDDY COX

Country Santa

WHEN A SCHOOL PRINCIPAL asked Buddy Cox to buy one of his elementary school students a pair of shoes, Buddy noticed that the little girl was carrying a rag doll that looked as if she had found it in a trash can. "I got it for Christmas," she proudly explained.

Buddy bought the child shoes and the biggest doll he could find. Since then, Buddy has come to be known as the Country Santa in a five-county area of northwestern South Carolina. He and his friends have provided Christmas presents to 1,700 needy youngsters every year.

Buddy enlists the help of students who give their time, preschoolers who donate pennies, and adults who assist with the collection and distribution. Local mail addressed to Santa Claus is delivered to Buddy's mailbox. The project requires a thirty-square-foot building outside his house to store the donated gifts.

Buddy was raised by a single mother who struggled to support him and his two sisters: "I realize what my mother sacrificed to have a few things under the tree." Reflecting on his efforts as Country Santa, he smiles and says, "We're not able to change the world, but we're able to show someone cares."

Wednesday

Week

33

POINTS TO PONDER

As Christians, although we are called to give of ourselves, we may not always know just what to offer. Then an occasion arises, as it did for Buddy Cox, where we have no choice but to get involved. Buddy's heart left him no alternative—he saw a need and knew he had to fill it. It's worth noting that Buddy Cox didn't try to do it all by himself. He organized, promoted, and motivated others to participate. He gave more than money—he gave time, energy, and love. We, too, can offer ourselves.

POWER BUILDER

FRANK GOODWIN

Dockmaster, Boston Yacht Haven

Frank Goodwin bakes delicious macaroons for fine dining rooms in the Boston area. And he has done so since 1949 when he first began to use profits from his "macaroonary" to fund private educations for nine elementary and high-school children from needy homes. "I don't know how some of these kids live," he says. "They are in toxic environments, toxic to their development as human beings."

A private school education is a reach for kids who come out of poverty. The headmaster at the prestigious St. Albans School in Washington, D.C., describes one student sent to him by Frank: "On paper, the youngster was a risk. But Goodwin's gentle persistence eventually persuaded the admissions office to take a chance on the boy, whom Goodwin called 'a priceless gift.'" Despite the challenging academic standards of the school, the boy's grades rose from D's and F's to A's and B's. He is now majoring in political science at Tulane University.

Frank Goodwin feels compelled to provide for these children with his cookie-baking business: "A few years in a prep school won't solve all their problems, but like the buttresses on a cathedral, it will give them the strength to deal with them."

Thursday

Week

33

SCRIPTURE

Psalm 37:25–26

Good people . . . gladly give and lend, and their children turn out good.

POINTS TO PONDER

God is original in His assignments. He places in our hearts ideas that only He can bring about. Then He inspires the ways and means through which He wants the job done. If God is the initiator of a project, it will probably seem impossible at the outset, and we may think we have gone overboard with our ingenuity. But with His help, the idea suddenly makes sense as He brings along people and resources, seemingly out of nowhere, to make it all work out. His word of inspiration, as with any other word He speaks, cannot fail to accomplish His purpose. We have to trust and obey.

JOHN JORDAN
Volunteer Firefighter

When we give God everything we have, we have given Him all He needs to get the job done.

Proverbs 11:25

Generosity will be rewarded: Give a cup of water, and you will receive a cup of water in return.

JOHN JORDAN MAKES IT his business to be on the spot every time a fire breaks out in the town where he lives—Sarajevo. Although he is a Rhode Island native, John has led a volunteer fire-fighting program in that war-torn city since late 1992.

A construction worker and ex-marine, John says, "Sometimes you just have to do something bigger than yourself." Since starting the fire-fighting program in Sarajevo, John has arranged delivery of three hundred fire-resistant suits, two fire trucks, a pickup truck, a water cannon, and diesel fuel. He has also organized a group of volunteers from Rhode Island, Maryland, New York, Virginia, and Florida who have helped extinguish more than one thousand fires.

Why would an American get involved in another country's ongoing tragedy? "I was at home watching the news about how these guys in T-shirts and jeans with no protection were fighting fires in the middle of sniper and mortar attacks," John Jordan explains. He promptly purchased a plane ticket and got involved. "It's like coming on a car accident. You either stop and help or you drive by. I stopped."

Friday
Week

33

POINTS TO PONDER

It is exciting and inspiring to see people doing things we couldn't imagine doing. When we discover a hero like John Jordan, working overseas for the benefit of people to whom he has no obligation, we shake our heads in wonder. And yet some of the things we do for others may be amazing to some people. As we make the most of our talents, God often uses the things we do in our everyday lives as powerful ministry tools. We offer Him our ordinary lives; He accepts our humble capabilities, blesses them, and multiplies them. Later on, we find that we have done exceptional things, and we didn't even notice we were doing them.

AS YOU REFLECT ON the generosity of others, have you thought about giving something back to God? Is there something you would like to do for Him? What is it?

_____

_____

_____

_____

Weekend

Week

33

Lord,

You have been so good to me,

and the more I think about

Your amazing generosity,

the more I realize that

I haven't been generous in return.

Lord, forgive my selfishness:

my jealous protection of my time,

my caution about my emotions, and

my hoarding of money.

Teach me to be like You—

lavish in Your gifts,

selfless in Your giving.

Thank You for all You have done;

help me to give more and take less.

POWER BUILDER

When we are remade in the image of Christ, His integrity becomes part of our character.

Psalm 25:21 NKJV

Let integrity and uprightness preserve me, for I wait for You.

WHEN BILL LEAR LEARNED that two Lear aircraft had crashed under mysterious circumstances, he was devastated. He had developed the airplane to offer business travelers a fast, economical alternative to the airlines. At that time, fifty-five Lear Jets were privately owned, and Bill sent word to all of the jet owners to ground their planes until he and his team could determine what had caused the two crashes.

Bill, a Christian, learned early in life that God expects courage and honesty of His children. The thought that more lives might be lost was far more significant to him than the adverse publicity that the grounding of all Lear Jets might generate in the media.

As he researched the ill-fated flights of the two planes, the possibility of a specific technical problem began to emerge. Using his own plane, Bill personally experimented to re-create the same problem. He nearly lost control of the jet in the process, but he found that a defect in the plane's mechanism did exist. All fifty-five planes were fitted with a new part, eliminating the danger.

Bill spent two years rebuilding the business. Lear Jets were soon soaring again, carrying thousands of businesspeople safely to their destinations. Bill Lear protected the lives of his customers while he counted on God to protect the reputation of his corporation. He has never regretted his decision.

POINTS TO PONDER

Is integrity a human character trait, or is it a God-given virtue? In the life of the Christian, it is both—a combination of our own best behavior and the work of God's Spirit in our lives. Righteous people who come to Christ know that our best still doesn't qualify us for eternal life. The work of the Holy Spirit strengthens and sanctifies our personal integrity.

POWER BUILDER

CLAUD FOSTER

Inventor

W HEN THE GREAT DEPRESSION hit Cleveland, Ohio, Claud Foster was grieved by his parents' debt. Yearning to help, fourteen-year-old Claud planted four acres of potatoes. He leaned on his pitchfork and spoke to heaven, "I can plant potatoes, but I can't make them grow. It's up to You, Lord."

That spring, the potatoes flourished, and the family's finances were reversed. From that day on, Claud knew that he needed God to be his partner—the Power behind his efforts.

As years went by, Claud tinkered with machinery, and he made a respectable living with his efforts. Then he invested $1,500 in a small manufacturing company to make "Gabriel's Horn." Not many years later, the Gabriel Company was exceptionally profitable.

When he reached an age where he wanted to sell his business, although its estimated worth was $10 million, Claud agreed to sell it for $4 million. He wanted to be sure stockholders in the firm that purchased it would not be cheated.

Claud had a party for his friends, many of whom had worked long and hard on charitable projects. At his party, Claud gave away every dime of his profits to those charities. Since his powerful partnership with God was still in effect, Claud knew he would be well provided for as long as he lived, so why not share the wealth?

Tuesday
Week
34

POWER QUOTE

Having integrity is another way of demonstrating that we love our neighbors as we love ourselves.

SCRIPTURE

Proverbs 13:6

Live right, and you are safe! But sin will destroy you.

POINTS TO PONDER

It is unusual to see a man take a loss to assure himself that his customer is guaranteed a profit. It is even more rare to see him give away his fortune in the later years of his life. Personal integrity is a cousin to generosity. By its very nature, integrity desires fair treatment for all and sees that justice is done. Generosity goes a step farther, giving beyond the limitations imposed by obligation, sharing with those qualified only by their need.

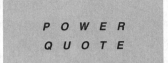

PETER GRACE
Former CEO, W. R. Grace and Co.

POWER BUILDER

POWER QUOTE

Integrity means people can trust
us the way we can trust God.

SCRIPTURE

Proverbs 14:8

Wise people have enough sense
to find their way.

Peter Grace was president, CEO, and chairman of W. R.
Grace and Co., one of America's largest industrial firms. A staunch
Christian, Grace believed in priorities: God, family, and then business.

Grace wrote, "The third priority—business—is a terribly important
one. When I became president of Grace in 1945, we had thousands of
employees who had been with the company for years. They were all depen-
dent on something that was going to completely disappear—the Latin
America Grace line. . . . That was a massive preoccupation with me. . . .

"We were responsible for between twenty and thirty thousand people.
Multiply that by four, to include their families, and that is almost one
hundred thousand people directly affected by any major error you might
make. . . . When you are a business man, it is very hard to avoid inadver-
tently hurting many people because of some oversight on your part.
Consequently, that third priority affects the first two because it is so all
encompassing.

"God will help you. I sincerely believe that if you are faithful to
God's injunction, He will help you along the way. I believe that when a
company is dedicated to Christian principles, and then carries them out,
the Lord will help them."

POINTS TO PONDER

Peter Grace was right, God's special blessings will be granted to those of us
who are faithful to our consciences. But there is a greater benefit. When
we demonstrate integrity, we see its impact on the lives of others. We see
them cared for properly, and we set an example for them with our upright
behavior. Integrity means we have done our best to treat others the way
we want to be treated.

POWER BUILDER

A YOUNG AND GIFTED film producer in Hollywood owns four media companies and has eight feature films in development. The young man, a Christian, has committed himself to making films with "redemptive, wholesome, biblical values."

The first of the producer's eight films was shopped around town, and it picked up a $6 million investment from a major studio. (Ironically, the young producer rejected $12 million for the film because he mistrusted the buyer's values.) With the studio involved, the producer began to develop the film. The studio executives viewed the quickly emerging story. They frowned in disapproval and said, "It definitely needs a harder edge." The execs threatened to withdraw their funding if changes weren't made in the script. The young producer, committed to principles, refused to spice up the story to satisfy their demands. The studio executives demanded their money back. The producer agreed.

When asked about the prudence of his decision, the young producer smiled. "You can't buy principles," he explained. "Not even for six million dollars!"

Every person has a price. The Son of God paid our price on the cross.

Proverbs 14:26

If you respect the LORD, you and your children have a strong fortress.

POINTS TO PONDER

Jesus asked, "What will it profit a man if he gains the whole world, and loses his own soul?" (Mark 8:36 NKJV). In our highly competitive, consumer-driven society, at times our very souls are placed on the bargaining table. Will we sell our integrity to make sure our families are cared for? Will we act dishonestly to move forward in a strategic corporation? It all comes down to faith in the One who paid the ultimate price for our souls. We cannot sell out—we belong to Him.

E. MARIE BOTHE AND
EDITH M. GRIPTON

Founders, Wetherill Associates, Inc.

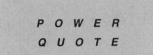

POWER BUILDER

POWER QUOTE

Finding the balance between money, personal mission, and the real meaning of life is the challenge of a lifetime.

SCRIPTURE

Proverbs 14:14

You harvest what you plant,

whether good or bad.

WOULD REASONABLE PEOPLE START a company to prove that honesty is a viable basis for doing business? It seems to be a far-fetched idea. But that very principle motivated E. Marie Bothe and Edith M. Gripton to found a corporation—Wetherill Associates, Inc. (WAI). It rebuilds and distributes replacement parts for cars. The firm is based on the ethical teachings of Richard W. Wetherill. The women wanted to prove in a practical experiment what Wetherill taught: "Right action leads to right results. Wrong action leads to wrong results."

Employees were taught basic skills, but their primary instructions had to do with matters of ethics and integrity. Salespeople were told never to pressure customers. They were not to discredit competitors or use negative sales tactics. Most important, under no conditions were they to lie. The underlying concept of WAI was that honesty pays. But does it?

In 1994, profits at WAI were more than $12 million on sales of $114 million, and the company is debt free. Founders Bothe and Gripton not only proved their point: they made themselves a small fortune in the process.

Friday
W e e k

34

POINTS TO PONDER

No one is immune to the temptations of greed, consumerism, and materialism. Jesus stated, "You cannot be the slave of two masters! You will like one more than the other or be more loyal to one than the other. You cannot serve both God and money" (Matt. 6:24). Are we willing to set aside our profiteering to seek the kingdom first, even if we're deeply involved in business? How far can we go with Jesus' teaching before it robs us of revenue? As believers, we must consider and answer these questions.

CAN YOU RECALL A time when you were torn between profit and integrity? Write your thoughts about the situation and what you learned from it.

_____

_____

_____

_____

_____

Lord,

I know You are at work in my heart,

changing me into a person of better character,

higher values, and greater love.

Thank You for what You are doing,

and help me to do my part in the process.

I struggle between integrity and personal gain,

between honesty and profit.

Deal with me, Lord,

and forgive me. Teach me Your ways.

POWER BUILDER

CONNIE SELLECCA
Actress

POWER QUOTE

Preparations for successful living are just as important as success itself.

SCRIPTURE

Psalm 142:7

Rescue me from this prison, so I can praise your name.

CONNIE SELLECCA IS REMEMBERED for her appearances in such TV shows as *Greatest American Hero, Hotel,* and *P.S. I Love You.* But some of her most memorable experiences took place before either her successful roles or her marriage to handsome television host John Tesh.

Connie describes the struggle that made her success so meaningful: "I was devastated by the break-up of my first marriage. Within a year of my divorce my father died, and that was also really, really hard.

"My son Gib was four when we separated and only five when his grandfather died. So even though it was a very painful time for me, I also had to recognize how difficult it was for a child to lose so much, and I had to put his needs before mine at times.

"Even though those times were terrible, I thank God for them now. . . . I became a different person because of the pain. I remember a friend's words during those times: 'Be faithful. God has a plan for you that is greater than you could ever imagine.' I had a hard time believing those words then, but that's exactly what's happened. . . .

"This is the best time of my life and I thank God that He knew better than me. He knew what I needed. Today I have great friends, great fellowship. I have a wonderful husband and great kids. It was all worth it to get to this point."

POINTS TO PONDER

God allows us to be without the things we want for a season so they will mean more to us when He finally provides them. The lean times of our lives are the times of the greatest growth—when we are hungry and needy and have no one but God on whom to rely. Suffering prepares us for the times when we will be happy, successful, and filled with gratitude. Our God sometimes allows us to be hungry so He can fill us with the bread of heaven.

POWER BUILDER

MIKE KLAUSMAN

President, CBS/Studio Center

MIKE KLAUSMAN IS WELL aware that Hollywood wields incredible influence over the lives of people around the world. As a Christian, Mike is in a unique and somewhat surprising position.

Mike describes the way God's power, through him, makes an impact on international television: "I attribute whatever success people think I have to hard work, dedication and loyalty to my bosses. I've had a lot of 'breaks' along the way. I've never sat with anybody to interview for a job. In all the job moves and promotions, somebody has come and asked me to move up. It's always been God at the right time and at the right place. These breaks have all come because God intended them to be. God's got His plan.

"People know where I stand. I don't make any excuses about or hide my testimony. I walk this lot and pray for the people here. I tell them we are blessed because God blesses us. I try to live the way I feel Jesus would live. You can't help but have people recognize that you are different than people in the world. . . . I don't believe in beating someone to death with the Gospel. I want people to see something in my life that Jesus has given. If what they see is good, then they will want it. They'll ask about it. Then I can tell them."

Tuesday
Week

35

SCRIPTURE

1 Peter 3:15–16

Always be ready to give an answer when someone asks you about your hope. Give a kind and respectful answer.

POINTS TO PONDER

If we see a professional position as an end in itself, we will have to work very hard to maintain our status, competing aggressively and jealously guarding our turf. But if we see a professional position as a place from which we can shine as a light to the world, we can entrust that position entirely to God. He will keep us where He wants us; He will move us when He wants to. When we give Him responsibility for our future, we have no need to fear the political gains and losses that are unavoidable in places of power. We belong to Him—He will place us, protect us, and provide for us.

POWER BUILDER

POWER QUOTE

God wants you to shine—He has called His people to light up the world.

SCRIPTURE

Mark 6:50

Don't worry! I am Jesus. Don't be afraid.

BEN VEREEN WAS WALKING along a darkened stretch of Pacific Coast Highway in Malibu, California, when a car struck him. He was critically injured, and the prognosis was grim. He was in a coma, barely breathing. The tracheotomy that had saved his life left a hole in his windpipe, threatening his ability to sing. And his right leg was severely fractured, posing a peril to his future as a dancer.

Miraculously, less than a year after the accident, Ben was back on a Broadway stage, performing the physically demanding lead in *Jelly's Last Jam.*

Ben attributes his exceptionally quick and complete healing to God. After the doctors had done all they could do, he could only seek God's help for the rest.

He says, "It's like when Peter stepped out of the boat—he was fine while he kept his eyes on Jesus. But then he started looking around at the waves. . . . When you take steps in the right direction, you start to look around and say, 'Am I really doing this?' Then you start to doubt, if you don't keep your eyes on the One who is bringing the change."

Wednesday
Week

35

POINTS TO PONDER

God's people are precious to Him, no matter what kind of work we do. His plans include high-level visibility for some and quiet, prayerful invisibility for others. He places us everywhere, at every level of success, in every stratum of society. And just as He keeps the voice of Ben Vereen singing and his legs dancing, He also protects the strong arms of the laborer and the organizational skills of the secretary. Earthly fame is of no concern to God—His idea of glory is washing feet and offering a cup of cold water. He asks only that we serve Him, and not ourselves, seeking His approval, not the applause of men and women.

POWER BUILDER

ROSEY GRIER
Former Professional Football Player

Thursday
Week
35

Power was familiar to Rosey Grier. He had been one of the "Fearsome Foursome," professional football's most intimidating defensive line. He was also a television actor, film star, and author. And he helped wrestle the gun away from Sirhan Sirhan, who shot Robert F. Kennedy.

But after his football career ended, Rosey could find no satisfaction. He worked long hours among inner-city youths and with older citizens. Yet his life seemed to have no purpose, and a divorce made him wonder whether he wanted to keep living.

Weeping in his house, alone and despondent, he began to recite the Lord's Prayer. While he was repeating the words, a friend came through the front door unexpectedly. "God sent me!" he smiled.

"Who?"

"God. You need to read the Bible."

Rosey asked his friend to leave.

A few days later, he was on an airplane when the flight attendant told him about a preacher she enjoyed. When Rosey got home, he watched the man, who was talking about everlasting life.

The following Sunday, Rosey went to church. He invited God into his life through Jesus Christ. His depression vanished. His aimlessness was transformed into purpose. The power of God—the one power Rosey Grier had never encountered before—had come into his life.

POWER QUOTE

No amount of applause, acclaim, or accomplishment can meet our need for a relationship with God and peace of mind.

SCRIPTURE

Romans 15:13

May the power of the Holy Spirit fill you with hope.

POINTS TO PONDER

The power and glory the world offers are fleeting things. No matter how busy or famous or beloved an individual is, his emptiness returns when the spotlights grow dim. In the case of a successful, popular man such as Rosey Grier, it seems impossible that anything would be lacking from his life. But the void was vast, made worse by the momentary highs his career provided. Only God can fill that void in any life—that's why He placed it there in the first place.

STEVEN CURTIS
CHAPMAN

Gospel Singer

POWER BUILDER

POWER QUOTE

Crowd pleasing may reap temporary rewards, but it cannot bear eternal fruit.

SCRIPTURE

Psalm 33:1

You are the LORD's people. Obey him and celebrate! He deserves your praise.

STEVEN CURTIS CHAPMAN GREW up in Paducah, Kentucky. He was surrounded by music—his father owned a music store and occasionally performed in Nashville. And although Chapman enjoyed some rock bands, he was far more attracted by the early Jesus bands of the 1970s because of their powerful message. By the 1990s, Chapman's albums were making an impact.

He says, "The last thing I want to do is give a perception that I've got it all figured out and if you just do it like me, all your problems would be over. I think Christian music can do a real disservice if we're not real careful to explore the valleys, because in reality that's where a majority of the lessons are learned anyway.

"But at the same time, there's so much music that just asks questions that leave you feeling almost hopeless. . . . And I feel like, with my music, I would be leaving business unfinished if I didn't at least offer some sense of hope. . . .

"The thing I count myself most fortunate to get to do is know that the message I write my music about is—I believe with all my heart—a timeless one that will have an eternal impact on a few people whose lives have been changed the way mine was, as a result of gospel music."

Friday
Week

35

POINTS TO PONDER

We may be drawn toward popular styles, toward modern messages, toward contemporary images. But the statements we make as Christians are more than superficial forms of attraction—we represent Jesus Christ on earth. With that in mind, we find ourselves taking a second look at what we're saying, what we're promising, and what kind of people we're claiming to be. Perfect? Certainly not. But we do have the truth of Christ, and He has challenged us to communicate it to the world. That awareness makes a huge difference in the way we present ourselves.

WHAT COMES TO YOUR mind when you reflect on the rewards of fame and fortune? Write your thoughts as you compare spiritual life with personal success.

_____

_____

_____

_____

_____

Weekend
Week

35

Lord,

You have given Your people wonderful opportunities;

You have placed them in extraordinary places

and allowed them remarkable success.

I want the best You have for me.

That may mean fame and position,

or that may mean a life of quiet service.

Place me where You want me, Lord,

because doing Your will

offers the only lasting satisfaction on earth.

Wherever You put me, Lord,

let me shine for You,

and make me a blessing to others.

WRESTLING COACH
Christian Motivator

Anger activates our human pride; a loving response to conflict allows God's powerful love to work through us.

SCRIPTURE

Romans 12:21

Don't let evil defeat you, but defeat evil with good.

DR. DAVID ALLEN, CHIEF psychiatrist with Minirth Meier New Life Clinic in Washington, D.C., tells of a distinguished wrestling coach who changed his style of coaching when his personal relationship with God began.

Originally, the coach taught each wrestler to approach his adversary with the thought, *Kill him! Just kill him!* The men on his team would rush onto the mat, their minds bent on destruction. They often won with overpowering expertise and energy.

However, when they didn't win, the wrestlers were emotionally distressed. The coach noted that by using anger as a motivator, he was causing his team to view life in a negative way.

When he came to know Christ, he quickly grasped the significance of love. He gained a new respect for his team as his spiritual transformation progressed, and he began to reach out to them in encouragement, in positive support, and in belief in their ability. The men responded warmly and enthusiastically to their coach's love and respect by wrestling more successfully than ever.

Better yet, the men developed self-acceptance. Whether they won or lost, they were confident in their skills and appreciative of wrestling as a sport. They went home at peace with themselves and their opponents, no matter what the outcome.

Monday
Week

36

POINTS TO PONDER

Our human nature operates on an eye-for-an-eye basis, and we feel strongest and most invincible when we are fighting mad. Afterward, however, we often feel exhausted and depressed, regretful of both words and actions. When we operate under God's authority, we are taught to gain power through love, not through anger.

POWER BUILDER

MILTON HERSHEY
Founder, Hershey Corp.

Tuesday
Week
36

THE BOY ARRIVED AT Hershey Industrial School scared and penniless. His parents, suffering in the Great Depression, were unable to support him. They sent him to the famous boys' home founded by Milton Hershey, the man behind the success of Hershey's chocolate.

William Dearden was deeply grateful to Mr. Hershey for the free care and education. In his young mind, he imagined his benefactor being ten feet tall, with a booming voice and a powerful appearance. Instead, William discovered that he was gentle, soft-spoken, and genuinely concerned about "his" boys.

William graduated from a university and started to make a name for himself in business. One day he got a call from his athletics coach at Hershey's school, inviting him to become director of student placement there. He took the job and ended up being president of Hershey's multinational corporation.

Remembering the man who gave him a chance at life, William Dearden wrote of "a similarity between my first false impressions of Mr. Hershey and the concept some people have of God. What we don't realize at first is that the main attribute of the mighty Creator isn't power or authority or awesomeness at all—it's love. That's the good news. That's what Christianity is trying to say to all of us."

POWER QUOTE

Love is the mightiest weapon in God's arsenal, capable of destroying hatred and overcoming evil.

SCRIPTURE

Ephesians 5:1–2

Do as God does. After all, you are his dear children. Let love be your guide.

POINTS TO PONDER

We rarely equate love with power because it seems like such a gentle aspect of our lives. And yet love is the most transformative force on earth. The Bible goes so far as to say that God is love. Love changes our attitude, transforms our self-image, provides for our needs, and cares for us in our darkest hours. Like God Himself, love never fails, never forgets, and never dies—love is eternal.

ARTHUR LANGLIE

Politician

How would your life change if you made every decision based on true love?

SCRIPTURE

Ephesians 4:15–16

Love should always make us tell the truth. Then we will grow in every way and be more like Christ, the head of the body.

ARTHUR LANGLIE WAS MAYOR of Seattle for two terms and governor of Washington for three terms. National leaders of his political party asked him to run for the United States Senate. Arthur felt his gifts were not in that area but were more geared toward administrative posts.

However, Arthur had faithfully attended a Bible study, and he had become more concerned about the subject of Christian love. He had come to see the spiritual dangers involved in self-protection, self-aggrandizement, and self-attainment. And he consequently believed that all his career decisions must be based on love, not self.

He and his wife discussed the possibility of a Senate post. Although neither wanted that position for him, they agreed in prayer that the loving decision would be for him to run for the sake of those whom he would serve. He worked diligently toward election. And he was defeated. Yet Arthur was exhilarated. He had obeyed his commitment to love; God had kept His commitment to guide him.

Not long thereafter, Arthur Langlie became board chairman of the McCall Corporation. "Only human beings have the free will to accept or reject God's will," he said. And in Arthur's obedience to love, God's power led him into a new realm of success and service.

Wednesday
Week

36

POINTS TO PONDER

Selfish people talk about love because it serves their purposes. True love doesn't talk about loving; it simply loves. Selfish love uses; true love gives without concern for repayment. Selfish love offers flattery; true love paints an honest portrait of the loved one. Selfish love is jealous; true love is open and generous. Selfish love feeds itself; true love nurtures all it touches. Selfish love is human nature; true love is supernatural.

POWER BUILDER

I N 1956, A TRAGIC EVENT in the Ecuadoran jungle galvanized the world. Five young American missionaries were speared to death while working to befriend the Auca Indian tribe. At first it seemed that the young men's lives were tragically wasted. But the story wasn't over.

New Christian leaders arose and recounted how the killings had inspired them to give their lives to Christian service. Pastor Chuck Swindoll. Lecturer Josh McDowell. Youth with a Mission director Don Stephens.

But there was more. Both Rachel Saint and Elisabeth Elliot, wives of the murdered missionaries, went to live among the Aucas. They made the courageous decision to carry on their husbands' vision and to share the love of Christ with the murderers. The very men who had killed the Americans eventually received Christ into their lives. And they told an interesting story.

While the bodies of the missionaries still lay on the ground, the killers heard singing. They glanced at the bodies, assuring themselves that their victims were dead. Then they looked up. Above the trees, they saw bright lights gleaming in the sky. Those men came to understand the power of God's love. They saw and heard evidence of His watchfulness over the death of His saints.

Thursday
Week

36

POWER QUOTE

The love of God is revealed through our love for each other. The more we love, the more people believe in Him.

SCRIPTURE

Philippians 3:10

All I want is to know Christ and the power that raised him to life. I want to suffer and die as he did.

POINTS TO PONDER

How important to God are the lives of His children? We sometimes feel detached from Him. When times are difficult, we wonder whether He sees our pain. When we are lonely, we long to reach out and touch Him. Does He really care? When we hear the miraculous story of angels singing above the martyrs, we catch a sense of the value of their lives—and of ours. He sees. He understands. And He loves us forever.

POWER BUILDER

TOM SKINNER
Evangelist

TOM SKINNER, A PASTOR'S son and a brilliant high-school student, was the leader of the Harlem Lords, a powerful and deadly gang. One night, Tom found himself listening to a poorly educated radio preacher talking about Jesus Christ. By the end of the broadcast, Tom had repented his former life and asked God to forgive his sins through Christ. He knew all too well that he would have to stop his gang activities.

Tom prayed and prayed for help as he prepared to go to a gang meeting. Just days before, he had personally broken the legs and arms of two young men who had tried to leave the Lords. He stood up in front of the group, and he began to tell them about his conversion experience. There wasn't a sound in the room. Angry eyes glared at him. He walked out the door, afraid to look back.

Later on, he ran into one of the gang members. He told Tom that he had tried to jump up and stab him. Others in the room had a similar urge. The puzzled boy said, "We wanted to kill you. But not one of us could move out of our seats."

Tom Skinner always said that the power of God's love was greater than the power of violence and death. From that experience, he went on to lead his first convert to Christ. In his next thirty years as an evangelist to African-Americans, there would be thousands more.

POINTS TO PONDER

How can we face the angry, violent world with a message of love? The Bible teaches that perfect love casts out fear. That means allowing God's love to fill us. God's love is far more than an emotion. It is a spiritual power, able to heal people who are sick and bring new life to people who are spiritually dead. God's love is also a principle, teaching us to behave in a loving manner, no matter how we feel. Love empowers us to do the works of God in spite of our all-too-human weaknesses.

D ESCRIBE THE WAY GOD'S love has most powerfully affected your life. What changes has it made in you? How has it affected others in your life?

_____

_____

_____

_____

Weekend
Week

36

Lord,

thank You for Your mighty love

and for the way it has touched my life.

Thank You for empowering me,

enabling me to do things

I never thought I could do.

You have allowed me to serve You,

equipping me with Your Spirit,

and filling me with Your love.

Help me to act in love,

speak in love,

walk in love, and pray in love.

Keep my emotions under the power of love,

and make my thoughts loving ones.

I want to serve You, Lord.

JOSH MCDOWELL
Writer and Speaker

WHEN JOSH MCDOWELL WAS a young man, he learned an important lesson about getting ahead in the world: *where there's a will, there's a way.* With that in mind, he set a goal to become the governor of Michigan.

One day Josh talked to a young Christian student. She explained that she was involved with a person—Jesus Christ—not a religious system. But Josh was skeptical, particularly about the story of the Resurrection.

Josh learned that 119 separate incidents had to be thrown out for Christianity to be refuted. He became convinced of the truth about Jesus Christ, and he chose to follow Him.

Josh began to preach, teach, and debate. At the invitation of Bill Bright, he moved to Arrowhead Springs Conference Center to manage Campus Crusade for Christ's summer staff training. But with no opportunities to preach or teach, Josh was troubled. He was even more distressed when an epidemic of dysentery occurred, and he had to clean latrines. Then the realization dawned on him: "If Jesus can wash their feet, why can't I scrub their floors and clean their toilets?"

He went on to become one of Christianity's most powerful representatives of truth both as a speaker and a writer. From that day on, Josh McDowell added four words to his credo. Where there's a will, there's a way *if it's God's will.*

POWER QUOTE

We don't have to close our minds when we open our hearts to Jesus.

SCRIPTURE

Psalm 26:2–3

Test my thoughts and find out what I am like. . . . I am always faithful to you.

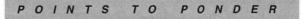

POINTS TO PONDER

Some people may be tempted to ignore the intellectual integrity of their beliefs by clinging to blind faith: God said it; I believe it; that settles it. However, thoughtful researchers such as Josh McDowell and others have pursued the proofs of the faith. When we take the time to study and learn, we find that Christianity is a thinking person's faith, intellectually sound and rich in reason and logic.

POWER BUILDER

CHARLES MALIK

Statesman

THE HUMAN SPIRIT, CONVERTED to faith through Christ, is a source of great power in the world. But Charles Malik believed that a well-disciplined Christian mind was of equal importance. His vision was to restore intellectual integrity to the evangelical Christian culture.

Impeccably educated, Charles served as the president of the United Nations General Assembly, the UN Security Council, and the UN Commission on Human Rights, among other leadership roles. And yet his highest allegiance was not to any human organization, but to Jesus Christ.

Charles was deeply troubled by the anti-intellectualism he perceived in the evangelical church, and he appealed to Christians around the world that just as souls must be won by the gospel, minds must be saved by the same good news. He believed that truth would hold up under any scrutiny, and he complained that few evangelical scholars were standing up to secular scholars on their own terms.

His commitment to education carried him beyond the United Nations into service as a professor, as the vice president of the United Bible Societies, and finally as president of the World Council of Christian Education. "Save the universities," he repeatedly said, "and you will save the world." For him, the strategic power of the well-educated Christian mind was an essential weapon in spiritual battle.

POWER QUOTE

God has placed within each of us the crown of creation—the human mind.

SCRIPTURE

Romans 12:2

Don't be like the people of this world, but let God change the way you think.

POINTS TO PONDER

The human brain is one of God's most awe-inspiring creations. It tests the scientist's skill with its complexity, and it mocks the researcher who tries to explain its complicated relationship to the mind, the emotions, and the physical body. Just as we owe God thanks for His handiwork in the brain, we owe Him the respect shown when we develop our minds, acting as good stewards of the brain's vast storehouse of riches.

POWER BUILDER

SANFORD MCDONNELL

Chairman Emeritus, McDonnell Douglas Corp.

POWER QUOTE

God wants to complete a good work in us, not give us a good rest.

SCRIPTURE

James 1:5

If any of you need wisdom, you should ask God, and it will be given to you. God is generous and won't correct you for asking.

AS AN ENGINEER, SANFORD McDonnell wanted to understand everything about Christianity before he chose to believe, but a friend helped him see that if he waited until he had all the answers, he would never take the first step. He chose to take the step, then to seek understanding along the way. "You don't have to understand television technology to tune in your favorite show," he explains.

Since his decision to follow Christ, McDonnell has been through some traumatic times, particularly after some DC-10 crashes that resulted in the loss of many lives. He remarks about how he fits his faith with his career: "Something I feel very strongly about is a saying I once heard: 'Pray as if it all depended upon God but act as if it all depended on you.' God gave us the wherewithal to carry out His work. He wants us to utilize our God-given talents.

"Le Tourneau, in his book *Success Without Compromise*, gave an example and asked a question. If God gave a sailor a compass, would it be more godly to be in a frenzy of prayer and ask God to tell him where to go or to use the compass? Obviously, he should use the compass. . . . You pray to God for help and then trust that He is going to let you know how to use your God-given talent to find a solution. That is the way I integrate my Christian beliefs in my career."

Wednesday
Week

37

POINTS TO PONDER

Faith requires us continuously to seek, to knock, and to ask for guidance. It challenges us to get out of our chairs and do the works of God. And it encourages us to persistently search for the answers to our deepest questions about God and His relationship with us. Yes, there are times when we can only stand and wait. But in those idle times, we are still active in prayer. And they are times of restfulness because since we have done all we can do to get the job done—the rest is up to Him.

POWER BUILDER

BOB MOSES

Organizer, Algebra Project, Inc.

WHEN BOB MOSES WAS a young boy, he lived in a Harlem housing project. After two hours of struggling to complete an algebra assignment, he suddenly saw the answer. He told himself, "I never thought I could, but I did it!" The self-esteem that he experienced after solving that nearly impossible equation formed the foundation for a project that he initiated years later.

Concerned that his daughter wasn't learning algebra properly, he decided to teach her himself. After consulting her math teacher, Bob agreed to teach three other advanced students along with her. He curtailed his studies at Harvard and devoted himself to the Algebra Project.

In every class Bob innovated new and creative ways to teach his algebraic lessons. Some of the most unlikely students in the Boston area experienced the same "I did it!" excitement that he had known as a boy.

In 1990, Bob organized the nonprofit Algebra Project, Inc., so he could initiate pilot programs in other inner cities. Finally, he was able to open the doors to the Algebra Project in the Mississippi Delta. "Our mission is to give young people the tool of mathematics and a chance at the good life," he says. "That chance is not meant just for the few, but for everyone."

Thursday
Week
37

POWER QUOTE

Intellectual growth demonstrates good stewardship of the mind, and we should pursue it in an attitude of worship, honoring the Creator.

SCRIPTURE

1 Peter 1:13

Be alert and think straight.

POINTS TO PONDER

Why would God care whether children learn algebra? What purpose does intellectual pursuit serve in the spiritual realm? At the beginning of time, God gave people authority over His creation, and that creation includes the human mind. Each person is a steward of the mind and is expected to develop it, educate it, and honor its gifts, whatever they are. Our self-esteem improves as we learn because we intuitively know that we are becoming the best we can be—and that is clearly God's will for our lives.

OS GUINNESS
Writer and Lecturer

POWER
QUOTE

Faith in God does not
compromise our intellectual
integrity—it does not require
blind faith.

BORN IN CHINA, OS Guinness received his D.Phil. degree from Oxford University, and he has written and lectured on religion and public life. He maintains that anti-intellectualism among American evangelicals is both a scandal and a sin. It is a scandal because it obstructs people of earnest thought from taking Christianity seriously and, therefore, from coming to Christ. It is a sin because it does not satisfy the commandment requiring God's people to "love the Lord your God with all your . . . mind."

Os writes, "We evangelicals need to examine our anti-intellectualism, confess its pervasiveness, repent of its wrongness and seek God's restoration to live up to our name—truly being people of the gospel who love God not only with our hearts, soul and strength, but also with our minds. . . . Thus, if we take the commands of Jesus seriously, we cannot dismiss the charge of anti-intellectualism as elitism or intellectual snobbery. As God has given us minds, we can measure obedience by whether we are loving Him with those minds, and disobedience by whether we are not."

Friday
Week
37

SCRIPTURE

Matthew 22:37

Love the Lord your God with

all your heart, soul, and mind.

POINTS TO PONDER

Our world is focused on scientific inquiry and information, and we may find it difficult to express our beliefs about matters of faith. But those who believe in humanism, nontheistic evolution, or other modern doctrines have less authoritative sources for their belief systems than Christians do. And the impact of their godless philosophies on our world is tragic. We worship a real God, and His instructions for living establish love, truth, and justice on the earth. We can defend our beliefs both intellectually and practically.

W HAT ARE YOUR THOUGHTS about the relationship between the intellect and the spirit? Reflect and record your ideas.

_____

_____

_____

_____

_____

Weekend
Week

37

Lord,

I thank You for the human mind

and its amazing ability

to understand the rest of Your creation.

Make me a wise steward of my mind,

and show me the areas that You would have me develop.

I thank You that I have known You by faith,

but I pray that You will help me learn

the facts behind the faith,

the objective truth that undergirds the trust.

Make me a person of intellectual integrity

and of childlike confidence in You.

POWER BUILDER

JOHN DE BUTTS
Former Chairman, AT&T

People are the most valuable commodity in the marketplace.

SCRIPTURE

Proverbs 1:5

If you are already wise, you will become even wiser. And if you are smart, you will learn to understand.

JOHN DE BUTTS OFFERED an interesting response when asked, "What is the most important thing you've learned in business?" In answering, John referred to a time when he was the general manager of a smaller company. He tried to cash a check at the cashier's office, but the teller couldn't identify him or recognize his signature. She made him wait while she found an assistant manager to approve the check. John learned a harsh lesson—his employees didn't know who he was. He said, "I'm convinced that an open door policy is important not only in business but in every area of living."

John learned early in his career from his own supervisors how valuable he felt when he was noticed and listened to, and he knew his boss was there whenever he needed help. He carried that awareness and the concern that his employees be acquainted with him to the top of the corporate giant, AT&T. But he also applied that principle in another way.

John De Butts stated, "You have to keep the door open in your spiritual life, too. Open to the still, small voice of conscience. Open to the codes of conduct like the Ten Commandments and the Golden Rule. Open to the mysterious whisper that can be divine guidance."

Monday
Week

38

POINTS TO PONDER

Some truths are not exclusively Christian, yet confirm Christian truth. One of them is that all people are important and deserve to be heard and respected. Of course, this is a variation of the teaching that we are to love our neighbor as ourselves. When applied to business, this principle inspires a sense of equality and encourages all employees to do their best.

POWER BUILDER

SAM MOORE

CEO, Thomas Nelson, Inc.

SAM MOORE CAME TO America from Lebanon with $600 in his pocket and a dream of being a physician. To pay his way through medical school, he took a part-time job selling Bibles. He was a quiet young man, and his English vocabulary wasn't strong. But by the end of the summer Sam had saved $2,535. His uncanny ability to earn and manage money has fascinated observers. He describes his seven keys to success:

"The Bible says, 'Except the LORD build the house, they labour in vain that build it' (Ps. 127:1 KJV).

"The first key to my success is very simple—faith. My faith comes from the Lord.

"Second I ask, 'Is there a need?' I find a need, then we fill it.

"Third, 'Will it help people?' We are in the business of helping people.

"Fourth, I have the desire to accomplish what God has given me the faith for.

"Fifth is discipline. People who don't discipline themselves will fail.

"Sixth is consistency. We must stay committed to a project day in and day out, whether we lose today or win tomorrow; in the long run we will win.

"Seventh, one must have a heart for God, to say, 'I love You, Lord, and I want to serve You.' If we put Him first in our lives, He will bring us the desires of our hearts."

POINTS TO PONDER

The basic skills necessary for wise business practices are foundational to success. But faith means people are treated more humanely; it means money is handled more responsibly; and it means that success is not entirely up to the expertise of management and the hard work of employees. Success is the final blessing God bestows on an enterprise that has been, by faith, dedicated to Him.

POWER QUOTE

Partnership with God reduces stress, increases wisdom, requires integrity, and promises positive results.

SCRIPTURE

Psalm 127:1

Without the help of the LORD it is useless to build a home.

IGNATIUS LOYOLA
Founder, the Jesuits

POWER BUILDER

POWER QUOTE

Management accountability is the first step toward corporate integrity.

SCRIPTURE

James 3:13

Are any of you wise or sensible? Then show it by living right and by being humble and wise in everything you do.

IN THE EARLY SIXTEENTH century, Ignatius Loyola was a Spanish nobleman dedicated to military heroism and honor. During a conflict between the French and the Spanish, a cannonball pulverized one of his legs and severely injured the other.

Both his legs required extensive reconstruction. The brutal efforts of the doctors left both limbs nearly impossible to walk on. As Loyola lay in his family's castle recuperating from two nearly fatal operations, he asked for some books. He had always enjoyed "worldly books of fiction and knight errantry."

Only two books could be found at the Loyola castle. One was about the life of Christ; the other was about the lives of the saints. At first, Loyola was continuously distracted by daydreams about a woman he longed to court. But eventually, the battle for his imagination was swayed by his unwelcome reading materials. Instead of imagining himself as a mighty warrior, he began to understand a different kind of power: "Suppose that I should do what St. Francis did, what St. Dominic did?"

By the time he was able to travel, instead of pursuing the woman of his dreams, he felt "a powerful urge to be serving our Lord." After years of biblical study, in 1534, he established the Society of Jesus, also known as the Jesuits. This highly educated order of priests is still actively at work in schools and seminaries.

POINTS TO PONDER

Any organization reflects the character and personality of its founder—his or her original vision is reproduced in the actions of those who implement it. When godly principles are evident in the initial mission, godliness finds its way throughout the company. As leadership changes, the original vision is often at risk. To maintain it, a corporate decision must be made to honor the founder's original objectives and to allow them to be reflected throughout the organization.

POWER BUILDER

DONALD SEIBERT

Former Chairman of the Board, J. C. Penney

Donald SEIBERT WANTED TO make his fortune playing big band music. But he lost his summer job at a resort when a series of storms ruined the tourist trade, and the band he had been performing with fell apart. "You've got to look out for number one," one of the musicians remarked.

Don and his wife knew the man was right. But the Person they thought of as number one was God. They would trust Him, honor Him, and not walk out on the lease they had signed with their landlord. Don did odd jobs and eventually paid all his past due rent—just as the lease was up.

Then he found a job selling shoes at J. C. Penney. Don's capability in retail soon landed him a promotion. And another. Then store manager. He continued to play his music for pleasure and extra income, but he was on his way up the corporate ladder. His final destination at J. C. Penney was chairman of the board, a position from which he retired in 1984. When he left, he was still praying and seeking God as the source of power and direction in his life. "I knew," he explained, "that so long as I looked out for the *real* Number One, I'd be doing it right."

Thursday

Week

38

POWER QUOTE

Pleasing God is our number one priority in business.

SCRIPTURE

James 4:10

Be humble in the Lord's presence, and he will honor you.

POINTS TO PONDER

Looking out for number one is a way of life for many men and women in business. They set goals, seek personal power, learn to dress for success, and plan strategies to get ahead—no matter what it costs them or others. Those of us who believe in God's guidance and personal involvement include Him in our plans, seeking His will, not ours. We ask for His power and add concern for others to our list of priorities. We may succeed in business if it is His will. But we will certainly succeed in our desire to know God—He will be with us, no matter where He leads us.

POWER BUILDER

DAVID SCHWARTZ
Founder, Rent-A-Wreck

DAVID SCHWARTZ NEVER INTENDED to get in the used car business. But David bought a car from a friend, then sold it for a $200 profit. It was so easy, he tried it again. Before long he was a university graduate with a small used car business. David believed in the power of truth. If a car needed work, he told the customer about it up front, and he priced it accordingly.

One day a woman asked him to rent her a used car. He explained that he wasn't insured for that sort of transaction. She said, "Well, then sell it to me for three months, and I'll bring it back when I'm finished with it." He agreed, and the woman brought the car back as promised. Then he had an idea: Why not rent used cars to budget-minded customers?

David applied the same values he had always followed in business—truth, integrity, and sincerity—and Rent-A-Wreck used car rental service was launched. By the time his Rent-A-Wreck franchises had spread like wildfire across the United States, he was making plenty of profit. He says, "I believe that, in any enterprise if you make money your god, then the business will never be really successful because you're never satisfied. But if you enjoy filling needs and making people happy, there's no end to your success."

Friday
Week

38

POINTS TO PONDER

Whatever we choose as a motivator in business can easily reach godlike status. If we are power hungry and crave control, our quest for power will start to influence our decisions, values, and behavior. The same is true of prestige and money. We cannot leave spiritual values outside our places of business. If God motivates other aspects of our lives, He and His agenda should also be the driving force behind our professional efforts.

T AKE A MOMENT TO list the five most important principles you apply to your professional life.

_____

_____

What is your single most important motivation in your career?

_____

Weekend
Week

38

Lord,

You know how much time I spend working,

and You know my need for financial security.

Sometimes I get so busy trying to earn my paycheck

that I forget You are my Provider,

and I forget about Your way of doing things.

Forgive me, Lord,

for getting caught up in the system.

I want to honor You in every aspect of my life.

Make me more conscious of Your presence,

and teach me to pray instead of panic

when things go wrong.

Most of all, continue to guide me.

I'm so grateful, Lord, that You love me.

Set my mind on Your kingdom,

not on building one of my own.

MILTON LEVINE
Toy Maker

MILTON LEVINE HAD BRAINSTORMS that were usually exciting, but their results were short-lived. People bought his toys for their children for a year or so, and then the interest fizzled. He couldn't seem to find the right product to keep the money coming in consistently.

In childhood, heroes like King David, Jonah, and Moses had always fascinated him. And he loved to read the proverbs of Solomon. One proverb had taught him the power of hard work: "You lazy people can learn by watching an anthill" (Prov. 6:6).

On a summer afternoon, Milton was enjoying a barbecue with his family, but his mind was wrestling with possibilities. "God, give me direction," he prayed. Absently, he watched an ant carry a crumb across the pavement. All at once he remembered his childhood fascination with dirt and ants in glass jars. He wondered whether children would be attracted to the astonishing organization and ingenuity of ants. That afternoon, Milton Levine had an idea for ant farms. Thirty-six years later, more than 13 million of Uncle Milton's Ant Farms—and 200 million ants—had been sold to children all over America.

Monday
Week

39

POINTS TO PONDER

Where our creative power leaves off, God's begins. The One who created every life form, designed every molecule, originated color and light, and set all things in motion is certainly capable of giving us good ideas when we ask for them. He initiates ideas that reflect His principles and character—there is nothing cheap or compromised about God's projects. God's ideas often make use of our immediate circumstances. Once they come to mind, we may ask ourselves, "Why didn't I think of that before?"

POWER BUILDER

EDITH SCHAEFFER
Writer and Speaker

Hᴇʀ WORLD-RENOWNED HUSBAND prepared and preached intellectually challenging messages and wrote books that molded evangelical Christianity for decades. But Edith Schaeffer had a powerful ministry of her own.

Edith's parents were missionaries to China, working with Hudson Taylor's China Inland Mission. Born in Wenchow, she relocated in the U.S. with her parents in 1919. A good education and a strong faith were the pillars of young Edith's upbringing. And those priorities were reflected in her choice of a mate—Francis Schaeffer's intelligence and Christian commitment instantly attracted her to him.

The couple settled in Europe in 1948. Francis established Bible classes and eventually founded L'Abri, an intellectual Christian community in Switzerland. There Edith's quiet, loving concern for young people touched countless lives. There was never a hippie too tattered, never a youngster too addicted to drugs, never a rebel too angry not to merit her compassion and words of wisdom.

As years went by, Edith's books became best-sellers, and her name became well known. But personal love empowered Edith Schaeffer, first of all in dealing with her husband, family, and friends. That same personal love was the seed that flourished into her fruitful worldwide ministry.

Tuesday
Week

39

POWER QUOTE

Bloom where you are planted is a principle for godly living.

SCRIPTURE

Proverbs 31:10 NKJV

Who can find a virtuous wife? For her worth is far above rubies.

POINTS TO PONDER

When we choose to serve God, we need to start serving within the small circle of friends and loved ones close to us. Be faithful in a few things, the Lord promised His listeners, and God will reward you with greater responsibilities. We need to start with the immediate and love faithfully there. Then God will move us into larger fields of service if He wants to.

THOMAS BARNARDO

Inner-City Missionary

Wednesday
Week
39

A YOUNG IRISHMAN NAMED Thomas Barnardo came to know Christ. He longed to go to China and work with Hudson Taylor's newly founded China Inland Mission.

A medical student, young Thomas left Ireland to work in London, preparing himself for his overseas mission. But Thomas never made it overseas. In the London slums, he encountered dozens of homeless children, and he knew he had to do something about their plight.

Thomas was able to raise funds and find housing for the children. He took in as many as possible, always reluctant to turn anyone away. One young boy, however, was rejected by a facility, and before a place could be located for him, he was found dead of malnutrition in a London street. From that point, Thomas declared a slogan for his work: "No destitute child ever refused admission."

Thomas Barnardo, like many visionaries, had blind spots. He was chastised for calling himself Dr. Barnardo when he hadn't completed medical school. But by the end of his life, he was maintaining the largest children's hospital in London. He had rejected the prestige of working as an overseas missionary and had changed the lives of countless children right in his own backyard.

POINTS TO PONDER

The world is filled with needs, and God has called His people to be caregivers. When we are filled with God's power, He places within us His own heart for hurting people and stirs us up to respond to some specific area of deprivation. When you are troubled by a situation, ask God what He wants you to do about it. You may be troubled because He is calling upon you to take action—you may be the very person He has chosen to make the difference.

RICHARD NEILL
Dentist

O NE MORNING DR. RICHARD Neill took his daughter to an ophthalmologist, and what he saw on the TV in the doctor's waiting room changed his life forever. As he watched—along with twenty small children—Phil Donahue interviewed a woman who identified herself as a "sex priestess."

Dr. Neill was enraged. He snapped off the television. In the days and weeks that followed, he entered a new role. He single-handedly took on the battle to get Phil Donahue's show off the local Dallas television affiliate. Two years later, he succeeded.

In the process, Dr. Neill battled with cynical journalists. He learned about writing letters to sponsors of television broadcasts—not just a few letters, but thousands of them. He appeared on national television, sometimes depicted as a fanatical fundamentalist, and sometimes as a caring father and professional man. He saw himself as David confronting a massive, monolithic Goliath—Phil Donahue's show and its corporate sponsors.

Dr. Neill says, "Looking back, I see a battle that was far more spiritual than intellectual, political or emotional. Many times, as I came to the end of my rope in other areas, I had to rely completely on my faith. I was certainly not the most qualified person to launch a campaign against exploitational television. But because I was available, the Lord used me."

Thursday
Week
39

When we invite God to help with an impossible task, He gets the job done better than we could possibly imagine.

1 Corinthians 1:27

[God] chose the weak things of this world to put the powerful to shame.

POINTS TO PONDER

A sense of personal inadequacy always weakens us. When enormous challenges seem to overwhelm us, we feel vulnerable and helpless. But God delights in choosing seemingly unqualified people to accomplish wonderful things.

What qualifies people for tasks beyond our natural abilities? In a word, *humility*. When we acknowledge that we are powerless, we immediately turn to God for help.

POWER BUILDER

HENRIETTA MEARS
Teacher and Publisher

POWER QUOTE

Our best accomplishments may be the results of our worst disappointments.

SCRIPTURE

Ecclesiastes 9:10

Work hard at whatever you do.

Aᶠᵀᴱᴿ GRADUATING FROM COLLEGE, Henrietta Mears was engaged to a young man who did not share her Christian faith. In a struggle between her heart and her spirit, she eventually chose to sever the relationship. Around the same time, doctors told her that her deteriorating eyesight would make it impossible for her to serve in the overseas missionary position she desired.

Henrietta soon accepted the position of director of Christian education at the First Presbyterian Church in Hollywood, California. She reached thousands of young lives with her excellent teaching, including Bill Bright, Dr. Richard Halverson, and Dr. Paul Carlson.

Henrietta wasn't satisfied with the Sunday school curriculum she was given to teach, so she wrote and published her own, founding Gospel Light Publications. She founded the Hollywood Christian Group, which ministered to entertainers. She saw a need for a quality Christian retreat area in southern California, so she established Forest Home. She co-founded the National Sunday School Association, and she founded Gospel Literature International.

Henrietta Mears submitted her plans to God. He adjusted them, blessed them, and caused the fruits of her labors to grow all around the world.

POINTS TO PONDER

Life in an imperfect world brings its share of setbacks. But for those who persevere, nothing is wasted. God's plans for our lives may not prevent disappointments, but He turns them into opportunities for greater blessing and more effective service than we could possibly imagine. He calls us into action where we are, just the way we are, and He turns our disappointing detours into remarkable surprises.

D O YOU FEEL THAT your immediate circumstances are getting in the way of service to God? Reflect on some ways you could better serve Him right now in your present situation. What more could you be doing? Are you overlooking a ministry opportunity?

_____

_____

_____

_____

Weekend

Week

39

Lord,

I have dreams and goals,

and as You know, I sometimes slip into

an "if only" state of mind.

When my dreams are put on hold

and my goals get lost in disappointments,

I sometimes feel unable to get past

my present circumstances.

Lord, show me the opportunities around me.

Forgive my dissatisfaction and my impatience.

Make me a blessing today,

right here, right now.

POWER BUILDER

GENE THOMAS
Launch Director, NASA

POWER QUOTE

As the darkness in our souls diminishes, hope dawns, bringing the promise of wonderful new beginnings.

SCRIPTURE

Psalm 18:28

You, the LORD God, . . . turn darkness to light.

IN 1986, THE WORLD looked on breathlessly as mighty rockets majestically lifted the *Challenger* off the launchpad. "It's a go!" an exuberant voice announced. Suddenly, the *Challenger* burst into flames and fell into the ocean.

Frozen in his chair was launch director Gene Thomas. Gene's career seemed to be reduced to ashes as the *Challenger* burned. However, within minutes, his phone rang. It was his son. "Dad," he said, "God told me to tell you He is still in control."

Gene writes, "I awoke the next morning with the hope that the whole disaster had been a bad dream, but reality quickly set in. I made my way to work, where I remember giving a short speech about getting some answers and pressing on with the shuttle program. In my own heart, I had already lost a lot of spirit, and I had to swallow hard to keep the words 'I quit!' from escaping my throat."

Weeks turned to months, and still Gene relived the tragedy, trying to make sense of it. He prayed. He struggled. Gradually, he visualized a successful liftoff.

Because of the love of family and friends and a God-given hope for the future, Gene Thomas was able to go on. Through his refusal to give up came new priorities in NASA safety and new successes in space.

POINTS TO PONDER

The biggest successes in life begin with glorious dreams. Reaching for the stars may send us into orbits we never dreamed possible. But suppose failure causes our dreams to shatter. Then what?

When we take our broken dreams to God, He begins a restorative work within our inner selves as well as with our losses. He looks beyond the present, reaches into the future, and does whatever it takes to make everything work out for the best according to His purposes.

POWER BUILDER

ARNOLD STURTEVANT

Banker

Tuesday

Week

40

THE LITTLE TOWN OF Livermore Falls, Maine, was crumbling away, and businesspeople were leaving for bigger communities with better opportunities. Arnold Sturtevant was a third-generation banker, whose grandfather had helped the townspeople through the Great Depression.

What could Arnold do? He and his wife prayed one night that God would give them direction to save their town.

Instead of leveling the large, poorly maintained bank building, Arnold decided to remodel. It was an expensive decision, but he thought others would follow suit. When they didn't, he organized a nonprofit development company, which applied for federal aid and began to rebuild Livermore Falls.

By the time the work was nearly done, the federal government refused to loan the money. A local pastor encouraged a discouraged Arnold. "Open your mind to new ideas, and He'll tell you."

Arnold's bank had extended all the money it could afford. But he contacted nearby institutions and worked out a finance plan with them that cost less than the federal plan. Livermore Falls was rebuilt, and the economy quickly turned around. The townspeople rediscovered a sense of community.

Arnold said, "He who said He came, not to destroy the past but to build on it, directed our townspeople so that our love of home and community . . . formed the basis for tomorrow's roots."

POINTS TO PONDER

Some people don't know how to give up. They don't seem to understand what it means to quit. Most of us could learn a great deal from them. Commitment doesn't mean we feel good about the way things are going; it means we are going to persist until we get the job done.

POWER QUOTE

Commitment isn't an emotion—it's a necessary principle for meeting goals.

SCRIPTURE

Nehemiah 2:20

We are servants of the God who rules from heaven, and he will make our work succeed. So we will start rebuilding.

GERMAN SILVA

Marathon Runner

Quitting is easy—living with yourself afterward is the hard part.

SCRIPTURE

Proverbs 17:17 NKJV

A friend loves at all times, and a brother is born for adversity.

WHEN GERMAN SILVA RAN off the course during the New York City Marathon, he didn't know he had taken a wrong turn until he saw the surprised faces among the crowd. He made a quick U-turn, but by then he had lost forty yards and fifteen seconds of precious time. He had only half a mile to go in the 26.2-mile race.

Benjamin Paredes, his training partner and friend, was also running. He was quite sure that Silva would try to make up for the lost time. Paredes began to work harder, too.

Meanwhile Silva knew he would have to virtually sprint to make up the lost time. Did he have the reserve energy to invest in the extra effort? He realized that the struggle might break him. "I had to take the chance," he said.

With 220 yards to go, Silva passed Paredes. As Silva flew by, Paredes patted his friend on the back. "Take it! You deserve it," he gasped. Later he said, "He went off course and came all the way back. He had more fight than me."

The two had trained together for years, investing their lives in marathon training. "Too much work had been done," Silva said. "I had to fight. The most difficult part was behind me."

Wednesday
Week
40

POINTS TO PONDER

We can view life as a marathon. Most of us have wandered off course more than once. What do we do to get back into the race? Refocus, make up our minds we're going to continue, and try twice as hard to make up for lost time. As Silva's story demonstrates, it takes an act of the will to keep trying—and a tremendous amount of courage and energy. If we give up, we've wasted all our hard work. As Silva said, the most difficult part is behind us.

POWER BUILDER

BILL BOWERMAN

Track Shoe Designer

Thursday

Week

40

THE RUNNERS AT THE University of Oregon were plagued with pulled muscles and shinsplints. And the track coach knew exactly what caused the problem—inferior shoes. Bill Bowerman was determined to solve the problem. He decided to design a lightweight shoe that would provide support, stability, and traction.

After countless redrafts and improvements, Bill presented his idea to a sporting goods company. "We already have good shoes," the company responded. He tried another and another. No one was interested.

One day he was teaching his track team some principles he had learned from the apostle Paul. "'They which run in a race run all, but one receiveth the prize' [1 Cor. 9:24 KJV]. Winning is important, but it's not everything," he explained to his team. "Losing can be a real beginning." Driving home, he realized that he had been talking to himself about the shoes. Inspired by Paul's faith, he decided to persevere.

With the help of a local cobbler, Bill constructed his first pair of shoes. One of his best runners tried them out and wouldn't give them back. Bill knew immediately that his design was a winner. A friend of Bill's convinced some Japanese businessmen to produce the shoes. At Bill's kitchen table, where the first two shoes were painstakingly made, a new company was born. Bill Bowerman named it after the Greek goddess of victory: NIKE.

POWER QUOTE

God works best when we come to the end of ourselves.

SCRIPTURE

James 1:4

You must learn to endure everything, so that you will be completely mature and not lacking in anything.

POINTS TO PONDER

Problem solving requires patience, persistence, and a passion for the solution. Persistence is a key godly principle, and patience is a godly virtue. When we are impassioned about our calling, we try, fail, and try again. We may want to quit, but we can't. At the very moment when we think we can't go on, God steps in and gives us the strength and ingenuity to solve the problem and put the solution to work. He always honors our perseverance.

GEORGE VERWER
Founder, Operation Mobilization

POWER QUOTE

Giving up is an emotional reaction; persistence is a behavioral principle.

SCRIPTURE

Revelation 2:19

I know everything about you, including your love, your faith, your service, and how you have endured. I know that you are doing more now than you have ever done before.

GEORGE VERWER KNOWS THAT there is power in persistence. As a student, he was part owner of a Christian bookstore in Mexico. He wanted to preach the gospel on Mexican radio, even though religious broadcasting was illegal.

After months of prayer, George visited a Mexican radio station. He said, "I want to advertise the Bible on your station, and explain what's in it so people will be more interested." The station manager agreed.

In his "advertisements," George read from Scripture and explained its meaning while promoting the bookstore. The fifteen-minute program was on the radio for several years.

That same powerful persistence served George well years later when Operation Mobilization's ship, the *Logos*, was lost off the coast of South America. What was Operation Mobilization's response? A new ship was launched in 1990—the *Logos II*.

Not all George's battles were external. Bouts of depression and occasional explosions of temper caused him to stumble, and they required renewed faith in God's relentless forgiveness and sanctification. George rejoices that God not only works *through* him, but *in* him. The power of persistence—both God's and George Verwer's—have done great things toward reaching the world with the gospel.

POINTS TO PONDER

When we obey our calling as a divine assignment, we have no choice but to be persistent, no matter how difficult the task. The proper response to God's calling is a lifetime commitment, and that commitment will eventually require tenacity. The key to fighting discouragement is to remember that God is responsible for the results of our efforts. We are to obey, offer Him our best efforts, and continue to move forward. And as His Word promises, if we refuse to allow our negative emotions to sabotage our efforts, we will be richly rewarded.

THINK ABOUT YOUR PERSONAL reactions to adversity. Does persistence come easily to you, or do you give up easily? Write your thoughts about persistence and patience in your life.

_____

_____

_____

_____

Weekend

Week

40

Lord,

I have to admit that at times I'm a quitter.

I have given up on relationships,

projects, and ideas

that required more energy than I could muster.

I long to finish what I've started.

Teach me tenacity

that relies on You for motivation,

that calls upon You for strength,

that counts on You for good results.

You are the Author and Finisher of my faith;

teach me to follow Your example of faithfulness.

POWER
BUILDER

POWER QUOTE

Conversion means turning from false hopes to the reality of God's love.

SCRIPTURE

Romans 3:23–24

All of us have sinned and fallen short of God's glory. But God treats us much better than we deserve, and because of Christ Jesus, he freely accepts us.

As A PLAYER WITH the Atlanta Falcons, Greg Brezina seemed to have everything he could want. But nothing made him happy. To fight off his continuous frustration, he started drinking heavily. After two and a half years of dealing with his bad habits, his wife, Connie, threatened to leave him.

The Falcons went to play the LA Rams on the West Coast, and Greg was invited to an NFL chapel service. He hoped that God would "bless [his] playing on the field." Instead, he found answers about playing the game of life.

Greg listened skeptically as a weight lifter spoke about having a personal relationship with Jesus Christ. Unwilling to admit he was a sinner in front of the other football players, he returned to his room.

Greg prayed: "God, if You're out there, if Jesus Christ is who He's supposed to be, come into my life and show me that my sins are forgiven."

As he read the Bible, he received an inner power that changed his desires and his behavior, from the inside out. After twenty-two years of football, Greg Brezina retired and founded a Christian retreat center. He says, "In the game of life, as in football, when you realize it is the fourth down, don't punt. Go for the goal. Stake everything on God and His Word. My life with Jesus is more exciting and fulfilling than playing in the Pro Bowl."

POINTS TO PONDER

Dreams can be wonderful motivators. But they often deceive us with their promises. When anything less than God promises us joy, peace, and fulfillment, we are hearing an empty promise. Like Greg, some of us have to hold the ashes of our burned-out dreams in our hands before we are ready to turn to reality. Fortunately, reality is solid ground. God's promises are never broken, and they are lifetime commitments, assuring us of His best blessings.

CHARLES COLSON

Founder, Prison Fellowship

CHARLES COLSON KNOWS ALL about power—both personal and political. He was a senior aide to President Richard Nixon. He wrote, "I entered government believing that public office was a trust, a duty. Gradually, imperceptibly, I began to view it as a holy crusade; the future of the republic, or so I rationalized, depended upon the president's continuation in office. But whether I acknowledged it or not, equally important was the fact that my own power depended on it."

That misplaced vision led Colson to the end of his political successes in the kingdom of this world. He began a different journey, led by another King. In the throes of the Watergate crisis, Colson gave his life to Jesus Christ. Colson's subsequent time in prison brought him into a life of service to those whose lives have been shattered.

Colson founded Prison Fellowship in 1976. He channeled his world-class management skills into work that reaches into the souls of the most powerless men and women. One writer remarked, "Colson's life in government prepared him to deal with people in power; prison enabled him to share the suffering of people without power."

Prison Fellowship continues to thrive, to expand and to teach faithfulness to people who need it.

POWER QUOTE

Subjecting our personal power to the laws of God can save us from being blindly corrupted by our own egos.

SCRIPTURE

John 8:32

You will know the truth, and the truth will set you free.

POINTS TO PONDER

The rules seem to shift as human power becomes more and more unlimited, and men and women operate above the law, making their own rules. If we are careful to acknowledge God's authority over our lives on a daily basis, we can avoid the dangers of playing God ourselves. We need to be reminded that the ultimate outcome of self-worship is shattered dreams and broken promises.

A B R A H A M   L I N C O L N
U.S. President

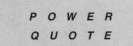

P O W E R
B U I L D E R

P O W E R   Q U O T E

Positive values are the by-products of a life that has been spiritually transformed by God's power.

S C R I P T U R E

John 3:16

Everyone who has faith in him will have eternal live.

A BRAHAM LINCOLN WAS A man of high moral character. He is often cited as the personification of American values and righteous causes.

In most of his years as president, Lincoln did not have a personal faith in Jesus Christ. Although he believed in biblical ethics, he weathered his many political and personal battles in the strength of his own iron will.

Then came the loss of his favorite son, Willie. At the boy's deathbed, Willie's nurse told the grieving father about Jesus Christ and His promise of eternal life to anyone who would believe in Him. Lincoln listened but did not respond. Days later, as he surveyed the grim battlefield at Gettysburg, he came face-to-face with his own mortality. He wrote, "When I buried my son—the severest trial of my life—I was not a Christian. But when I went to Gettysburg, and saw the graves of thousands of our soldiers, I then and there consecrated myself to Christ."

Not many months later, Abraham Lincoln was abruptly ushered into his own eternal home, felled by John Wilkes Booth's bullet. Although he lived an apparently godly life and defended the faith, Lincoln discovered that without a personal relationship with Jesus Christ, he could not face death: his son's, his soldiers', or his own.

P O I N T S   T O   P O N D E R

We hear much about values—family values and personal ethics. These things are particularly dear to us because they seem to be vanishing from our world. We long to instill in our children the foundational principles that will help them avert tragedy. But without the power of God living through us, none of us are able to live a righteous life.

POWER BUILDER

CARYL MATRISCIANA
Writer and Lecturer

CARYL MATRISCIANA WAS A free-spirited young artist in the 1960s. After several disappointing relationships, she realized that she could not love as generously and wholeheartedly as she wanted. In her emotional pain, she wandered the Chicago streets, trying to sort out her thoughts. She found herself drawn into a church. She began to pray, "Oh God! I want to know how to love."

She writes, "Having nothing more to say, I looked up. For the first time I noticed an enormous wooden cross hanging down from the high, domelike ceiling. It seemed to be reaching down to me. . . . My heart melted as I thought of the mutilation and hurt that the Person on the cross went through. *I wish I had that kind of attitude*, I thought, *that kind of sacrificial love.*"

Several weeks later, Caryl was invited to meet some new friends at a gathering that turned out to be a Bible study. After the lesson, the teacher spoke with her a while, then asked, "Do you believe that Jesus Christ is the Son of God and that He died for your sins on the cross?"

"I considered his question with deep contemplation. Vividly I recalled the giant wooden cross that I had prayed under just a few weeks ago. . . . I remembered my prayer begging God to teach me what love was all about," she writes.

At last, Caryl found the love she wanted. She received Jesus Christ into her heart by faith. Her life was never to be the same again.

POINTS TO PONDER

Apart from the cross of Jesus Christ, there can be no relationship between human beings and God. By sending His Son, God built a bridge between God and men and women. Jesus said, "Without Me, no one can go to the Father." He died, taking upon Himself the sins that separate us from God. If we ask Him to forgive us and to put His new life in us, we have access to the Father.

POWER QUOTE

A relationship with God is Jesus Christ's free gift to the world—we have only to accept it, and it is ours.

SCRIPTURE

Galatians 6:14

I will never brag about anything except the cross of our Lord Jesus Christ.

RABINDRANATH MAHARAJ

Brahmin

POWER BUILDER

POWER QUOTE

Anything that occupies our minds, weakens our faith, or influences our emotions can become a false god in our lives.

SCRIPTURE

Ephesians 6:12

We are not fighting against humans. We are fighting against forces and authorities and against rulers of darkness and powers in the spiritual world.

RABINDRANATH MAHARAJ WAS RAISED to be a god. He was born of Indian parents in the Brahmin caste, and he was expected to become the local guru, as his father had been.

Something nagged at Rabi, even in childhood. He had a vague awareness of some other God, Someone greater than himself and the gods he worshiped. He knew deep inside that he was a sinner. And his Hindu scriptures provided nothing for him but "sowing and reaping."

One day he was worshiping Mother Nature and all the universe. All at once a poisonous snake slithered toward him. Rabi cried out to the Hindu gods—one after another. Still the snake moved toward him. Then he remembered that when he was very small, his mother had once told him about a God of protection: "If you ever need help, call out the name Jesus." Terrified, Rabi cried, "Jesus! Help me." The snake immediately went away.

That incident was followed by another—a young woman confronted Rabi: "God loves you. Jesus Christ died for your sins and wants to come into your heart."

Once Rabi received Christ, he felt a "great weight of dark things go out of me. All my idols came off the altar. . . . I had served my false gods with my whole being. I knew that I must give nothing less than my best to Jesus Christ."

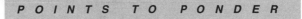

POINTS TO PONDER

In the Western world, we are rarely drawn to the gods Rabi worshiped. Our chosen idols are more likely such seductive deities as money, power, relationships outside marriage, illegal drugs, and alcohol. Some of these gods offer us pleasure, others are gods of fear and bondage. But they are all counterfeits, and when we need protection, they are powerless to help us. Only the true God—the One who transformed Rabi's life—can love us, protect us, and guide us.

W HAT WERE THE CIRCUMSTANCES when you came to know the Lord? Take a moment to write your story on the lines below and to reflect upon the changes God's presence has made in your life.

_____

_____

_____

_____

Weekend
Week

41

Lord,

thank You for coming into my life,

for changing me from the inside out.

Thank You for taking my broken dreams,

my foolish pride,

my false gods,

and exchanging them for a new life in Christ.

Thank You for sending Your Son

to die on the cross for my sins,

for raising Him up, victorious over death,

and for allowing His death to take the place of mine.

Continue to remake me, Lord.

Transform me into a Christlike person

with a renewed mind and a passion for You

and Your work.

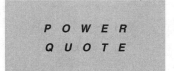

GLEN CAMPBELL

Entertainer

POWER BUILDER

SCRIPTURE

Ephesians 2:8–9

You were saved by faith in God. . . . This is God's gift to you, and not anything you have done on your own. It isn't something you have earned, so there is nothing you can brag about.

WHEN GLEN CAMPBELL SANG about God during the 1970s, he sang from a sincere heart that longed to be in touch with his Creator. But Glen was serving two other gods in those days—alcohol and cocaine.

Glen's background was Christian, and when he was sober, he was a true gentleman. His marriage to Kimberly Woollen in 1982 gave him hope, but there seemed to be no cure for his addictions.

Kimberly devoted herself to prayer for Glen. But as months went by, her faith seemed unrewarded. Little by little she understood that God alone could change Glen.

Not long after their son Cal was born, Glen spent an evening with some friends using cocaine. When he got home, Kim was ready to leave him. Glen fell to his knees and pleaded with God for forgiveness and help. He had prayed the same prayer many times before, but that time God answered—the power of cocaine was broken.

Alcohol continued to be a problem. And prayer remained Kimberly's only defense. One morning sick and exhausted, Glen pleaded with God for help. He laid everything at the cross—his life, his sin, his despair— and turned to Christ, the Higher Power. Again the Lord answered. Another addiction was broken. A new life had begun.

POINTS TO PONDER

We aren't aware of our need for a Power beyond ourselves until we are confronted by our own powerlessness. The helpless feeling we experience when we fail again and again drives us away from our self-confidence and forces us to seek other help. Those who seek the Higher Power—God— eventually are confronted with His Son, who brings us to God. Through Him, access to God's power is immediate.

POWER BUILDER

ORVILLE YATES

Lineman, Ohio Power Co.

Tuesday
Week

42

ORVILLE YATES WAS CALLED out to troubleshoot some downed lines after a storm. While he and another lineman were inspecting the damage, a live wire dropped and struck Orville on the right hip. It left him hanging upside down by one leg, completely paralyzed.

He later wrote, "Suspended there between heaven and earth, my body burned and torn by the power of all those volts—I called out to an even Higher Power." His heart began to beat again, his lungs to breathe. A rescue crew lowered him to the ground and untangled him.

The doctor at the hospital said, "He won't live very long." The diagnosis appeared to be right. But people were praying. While the medical community agreed, "We'll give him about twenty-four hours," Christians were asking for more.

One surgery followed another. One-third of his right hip was removed. Reconstruction of his hands began. Despite pessimistic predictions, Orville regained the ability to walk and the use of all his fingers.

He later wrote, "God saved my voice so I could sing and minister for Him; my legs for following in His footsteps; my eyes for reading His word; my ears for hearing His voice . . . and my hands, what's left of them, to reach out to others. Wherever I go, I sing praises to the Lord Jesus Christ, who alone is the Higher Power."

POWER QUOTE

We can depend on the same Power that created the universe. Why would we want to rely on ourselves?

SCRIPTURE

Romans 4:20–21 NKJV

[He] was strengthened in faith, giving glory to God, and being fully convinced that what He had promised He was also able to perform.

POINTS TO PONDER

The power of God provides more than a source of strength when we are weak. When we consider what God's power really is, we see that He is the source of life itself. Scripture tells us that the Power that raised Jesus from the dead can flow through our physical bodies. He makes His power available to us through prayer and through dependence upon Him. He came so we could have life—His life—in us.

POWER BUILDER

WENDELL TYLER
Professional Football Player

POWER QUOTE

God's power would be unavailable to us if it weren't for Christ's cross and His empty tomb.

SCRIPTURE

Psalm 147:5

Our LORD is great and powerful! He understands everything.

WENDELL TYLER WAS DRAFTED by the LA Rams. But his use of drugs and alcohol nearly cost him his life as well as his career.

After drinking too much at a dance, he was in a major collision. The team doctors said that he had only a 10 percent chance of playing football again. Filled with bitterness and rage, Wendell remembered all the "fanatics" in LA who would yell out, "Jesus loves you! Jesus can heal you!"

Wendell asked for a Bible. He opened it to the book of Romans and read about Paul's struggle to live a godly life. Wendell prayed, "God, that's just like me. Every time I try to stop drinking or chasing women, the very thing I'm trying to avoid just comes up and grabs me. I need You to come into my life and change me. Jesus, please change me."

Not only did God heal him, but He helped him become an even greater football player. The following season, Wendell gained more than a thousand yards and tied the Rams' record for touchdowns. And after each score, Wendell knelt and thanked God. "I was happy to do it. After all, Jesus died on the cross. He died for our sins. He died for my marriage to be healed. He died for me to be delivered from drugs. The power to overcome all obstacles was given to us right there on the cross and we can receive that power."

POINTS TO PONDER

Now and then we are wise to reflect upon Christ's cross. We get so caught up in the activities of our lives—even Christian activities—that we forget about the sacrificial death that made it all possible. The Higher Power we talk about broke the power of sin and death—He did it by becoming sin and by dying. Then when that work was completed, He shattered death's permanence by coming back—alive. Jesus died so we can live. Shouldn't we live for Him?

POWER BUILDER

RICHARD FARRELL
Christian Writer

THE FIRST TIME RICHARD Farrell tried to get an article published in a newspaper, his story, "The Evil Eye of Crack" was published in the *Boston Globe*. Richard wasn't exactly a successful journalist, but he knew more than his share about the evils of drugs. As an affluent real estate executive, he had once followed a regular daily schedule. He drove away from his lovely home and held an important meeting with his drug dealer. By the time his habit caught up with him, he was being investigated for connections with organized crime and drug smuggling.

After Richard had been through several unsuccessful detox attempts, an orderly at a hospital said something unexpected to him. "I know a man that can help you—Jesus Christ." Moved to tears by the man's words, Richard drove to see a Christian he knew, and he accepted Christ, who helped him break his habit.

Richard returned to school to become a lawyer. But his journalism teacher said, "You have a talent which is probably natural and is one of the best I've seen in my twenty years of teaching." Next came the *Boston Globe* article, and with it new dreams for a future lived in company with the "man that can help you."

"Now faith is the key to my life," Richard Farrell explains. "I could fill the pages of several books with God's miracles in my life."

POWER QUOTE

Independence from God is the root of all sins.

SCRIPTURE

2 Timothy 1:7

God's Spirit doesn't make cowards out of us. The Spirit gives us power, love, and self-control.

POINTS TO PONDER

How does God manage to give us strength to overcome our weaknesses? As long as we're hanging on to the idea, "I just need to try a little harder," we are headed for a fall. We have to come to Him in utter helplessness, knowing once and for all that we can't make it without Him. Then, and only then, is He free to come into us with His supernatural power.

POWER BUILDER

FRANKLIN D. HOUSER
Attorney

FOR MOST OF HIS life, Franklin D. Houser was a firm believer in humanism. He treasured the poem "Invictus" by William Earnest Henley, which declares in part, "I am the master of my fate. I am the captain of my soul."

For a time, Franklin seemed to be a very capable captain. His income soared as he achieved success in the courtroom. Yet he was beginning to see that he had sacrificed his family on the altar of his success, and his success was no longer satisfying.

Increasing depression dogged Franklin. Grieved by his pain, his wife told him, "You need God."

One night while staying in a hotel, he picked up a Bible. He began to read from Romans 1: "Professing to be wise, they became fools, and changed the glory of the incorruptible God into an image made like corruptible man" (vv. 22–23 NKJV).

Franklin Houser wrote, "I understood what these words meant. They were for me. Professing to be wise and following the design of the world, I had become a fool. That was me." A few weeks later a Christian led him in a simple prayer. He received Christ as his Savior and relinquished the control of his life to the power of God.

SCRIPTURE

Psalm 14:1

Only a fool would say, "There is no God!"

POINTS TO PONDER

In both the Old Testament and the New Testament God plainly states that people who deny His existence are fools. Some people are quick to say that they believe in Him, but they function as practical agnostics, acting as if they believe He does not exist until they have a need. Then in desperation, they plead with Him for help. This, too, is foolishness. We need to rely on God for everything. Otherwise, we are trusting in our own strength and subtly playing God ourselves.

D O YOU FEEL POWERLESS in some areas and strong in others? Write your thoughts about your personal power and your feelings of powerlessness. When do you ask God for help?

_____

_____

_____

_____

_____

Weekend
Week

42

Lord,

I know my weaknesses,

I know I have made many mistakes in the past,

and I want You to know

that I can't make it without You.

Please have mercy on me,

and with Your great power,

help me live my life in peace and hope,

knowing You are there to catch me when I fall.

POWER BUILDER

EDWARD THOMPSON
New York Magistrate

POWER QUOTE

Sins and shortcomings occur more frequently when we are living for ourselves and are not loving God.

SCRIPTURE

Psalm 111:10

Respect and obey the LORD! This is the first step to wisdom and good sense.

E DWARD THOMPSON HELD A firm belief that God could change lives more powerfully than any judicial system. He liked to tell the story of fifty-four-year-old Mary, who appeared before him with fifty-three previous convictions for drunk and disorderly conduct. She had been jailed six times. But this time the circumstances were different. For one thing, she was in love with an older gentleman. For another, her son was on his way back from World War II, and she was eagerly awaiting his arrival.

Judge Thompson decided to put Mary on probation with a few conditions. He insisted that she go to church regularly and pray for God to change her. He said, "Try going to church—loving God—and see if it doesn't help you find a new self-respect and happiness."

Would Mary really be changed, or would she appear again in front of his bench, disheveled and disoriented? Judge Thompson rather anxiously checked with Mary's probation officer week by week. Yes, she was attending church services. And she was getting involved in the church's social life.

When Judge Thompson returned from an out-of-town assignment, he was informed, "Mary was back." His heart sank.

A court officer told him, "She came to see you—to thank you and tell you good-bye. She's getting married to that elderly gentleman, and her probation officer has given her permission to move to California. She's a changed woman."

Monday
Week

43

POINTS TO PONDER

When we are forced to confront our shortcomings and to find out why we fail, we usually come to one conclusion—we have not lived God's way. Whether our lives are as out of control as Mary's, or we are unable to keep our commitments to ourselves and others, the reason is usually that we aren't loving God and we aren't putting Him first in our lives.

POWER BUILDER

Tuesday
Week
43

S TUDENTS AT WINGFIELD HIGH School in Jackson, Mississippi asked their principal, Dr. Bishop Knox, for permission to say a prayer every morning over the school's PA system. Since the state allowed prayer at public school graduation ceremonies, Knox couldn't see any difference between student-initiated, nonsectarian commencement prayers and daily prayers by student volunteers. The students voted 490 to 96 in favor of the prayers.

The student body president read the first prayer: "Almighty God, we ask that You bless our parents, teachers, and country throughout the day. In Your name we pray. Amen." The following day the prayer was read again, and Knox was suspended. Two weeks later, he was fired. However, students walked out of classes. Families marched on the state capital. The governor eventually signed a bill allowing student-initiated prayer in the Mississippi public schools.

Finally, after lengthy debate that reached the Supreme Court, Knox was allowed to complete the school year as Wingfield's principal. The student body president says of him, "Dr. Knox never preached to us about prayer or religion, but he was always there for us. It isn't fair that his job was in danger because of what the students wanted. We admire him for fighting for what we believe in."

POWER QUOTE

We should not sacrifice principles to the natural fear of confrontation.

SCRIPTURE

Psalm 138:3

When I asked for your help, you answered my prayer and gave me courage.

POINTS TO PONDER

Most of us do our best to avoid confrontation. We are to seek peace and to be peacemakers. But some situations require direct confrontation—circumstances where truth is being smothered, where justice is being denied, where individual rights are being deprived. If we have been given power, we have also been given an obligation to confront. Like Dr. Knox, we needn't be trying to promote our own agendas. When we defend a principle, we set ourselves aside and fight for the good of the community.

TAKASHI NAGASE

Writer

TAKASHI NAGASE WAS A noncommissioned interpreter for the Japanese army during World War II when he first saw a British soldier named Eric Lomax. Nagase had been called in to interrogate Lomax. Lomax was already encased in splints and bandages, and Nagase was horrified to see him brutally tortured during the questioning.

After the war, Lomax was filled with physical pain and bitterness toward the Japanese, and the face that always came into his mind when he thought of his torturers was that of Nagase. Although Nagase had not inflicted the wounds, his voice and face always accompanied the brutality. Lomax was consumed with hatred.

Meanwhile, Nagase was tormented by the memory of Lomax and his ordeal. Had he survived? As years passed, Nagase become more determined to find out. He wrote a book called *Crosses and Tigers,* in which he described the torture of Lomax and his own deep remorse. The story, condensed into magazine form, fell into Lomax's hands.

After an enormous struggle, Lomax met Nagase. The two men wept, forgave, and became friends. Later Lomax said, "What I have discovered is the healing power of forgiveness. With that gift, I now can get on with my life."

POWER QUOTE

Fear of confrontation is a relationship killer.

SCRIPTURE

Jeremiah 15:19 NIV

If you repent, I will restore you.

POINTS TO PONDER

As time passes, grudges intensify, and we build up scenarios in our minds that take on lives of their own. The desire to get the past behind us is a powerful motivator, but fear of confrontation can rob us of the reconciliation we long for. We have to understand that confronting fear is easier than living with fear. Then we are able to take the first steps, which are always the hardest ones.

GEORGE MACDONALD

Writer and Lecturer

Georg**E MACDONALD WROTE MORE** than thirty-five books during the latter half of the nineteenth century, and C. S. Lewis regarded him "as my master." As courageous and gentle as he was gifted, MacDonald met both spiritual and physical challenges with loving resistance.

As a young pastor, MacDonald taught that doctrine was not as important as practice, and that love was more important than legalism. His stand against Calvinism caused him to lose his church. He supported himself for the rest of his life as an itinerant writer, lecturer, and preacher.

MacDonald, a devoted husband and eventually the father of eleven, had tuberculosis, which also took the lives of four of his children. Illness made his writing and his travels doubly difficult. Nevertheless, he faced his hardships without self-pity. In fact, his work is best known because of his overpowering sense of God's grace and love.

MacDonald's loving spirit overcame poverty, disapproval, and illness, while his powerful writings influenced generations of Christian thinkers. C. S. Lewis wrote of him, "I know hardly any other writer who seems to be closer, or more continually close, to the Spirit of Christ Himself."

POWER QUOTE

Confronting dishonesty demonstrates our love for people who need to know the truth.

SCRIPTURE

1 Peter 4:8

Most important of all, you must sincerely love each other, because love wipes away many sins.

POINTS TO PONDER

We somehow have the idea that a loving person never confronts anyone about anything. Jesus was not afraid to confront. His encounters with the Pharisees are peppered with harsh words and accusations. When He heard their hypocrisy, He addressed it directly without apology. When He saw religion practiced without love or mercy, He powerfully and publicly denounced it. And when the devil himself tempted Him, He used the most powerful weapon available—the Scriptures—and confronted Satan's lies one by one.

POWER BUILDER

SIMEON III
King of Bulgaria

Choosing righteousness may cost you everything but your conscience. How much is your conscience worth?

SCRIPTURE

1 Peter 5:10

You will suffer for a while, but God will make you complete, steady, strong, and firm.

WHEN HITLER SOUGHT SUPPORT from Bulgaria in 1943, King Simeon III refused to send Bulgarian troops to the eastern front. More dramatically, he rejected orders to send Bulgaria's fifty thousand Jews to Germany. Two weeks after taking a hard line on these issues, King Simeon III mysteriously died, and the cause of his death remains unknown.

Bulgaria fell to the Soviet occupation, and King Simeon III's son was forced to flee the country. He eventually settled in Spain. After 1,300 years of monarchy, Bulgaria had become a Soviet satellite.

Simeon III's son was honored for his father's heroism by a Jewish group in America, and during the presentation he recalled his father's determination to defy Hitler and the family's subsequent plight: "Quite honestly, had I not had my faith, with all the diversities and difficulties, I don't think I would have ever felt secure or had hope. After so many years, things have changed in Bulgaria. We lived long enough to see democracy returning gradually." Although he and his family lost everything because of his father's confrontation with Hitler, the family's reputation for solidarity with the Jews is still remembered half a century later.

POINTS TO PONDER

Sometimes a necessary confrontation may cost us everything. What was gained by King Simeon's refusal to cooperate with Hitler? Primarily, Jewish lives were saved. But a deeper principle was at work—the human truth that dying for a righteous cause is far better than living in moral compromise. Rarely do we face such life-and-death concerns. More often, we are concerned with our jobs, our material goods, or our relations in the community. How tragic to preserve those things and lose our self-respect!

A RE YOU A CONFRONTATIONAL person, or does the thought of confrontation terrify you? Make a list of situations in your life right now that might benefit from a confrontation, then write your reasons for not facing up to the conflict.

_____

_____

_____

_____

Weekend
Week
43

Lord,

You came to earth and lived in human form

to teach us how to live.

And as we read the story of Your life,

we see how fearless You were,

how little You cared about the opinions of people.

You stood up for needy people,

defended sinners who had failed,

and faced off with the most powerful

religious leaders of Your time.

I know it wasn't easy, Lord.

It cost You Your life.

Help me learn to follow You,

both in peacemaking and in confrontation.

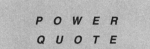

POWER BUILDER

JAMES HUDSON TAYLOR

Missionary

POWER QUOTE

God has committed Himself to our care. He wants us to commit ourselves to trusting Him.

SCRIPTURE

Philippians 4:19

God will take care of all your needs with the wonderful blessings that come from Christ Jesus!

JAMES HUDSON TAYLOR WAS a young boy when he came to Christ, and he decided to serve Him in China as a medical missionary. To prepare, he worked for his uncle, who was a doctor in the slums of England. The uncle often forgot to pay his nephew. Hudson determined that it would be a valuable exercise in trusting God to refuse to ask for the money. Instead, he decided he would pray and let God provide.

On one occasion, he gave his last coin to a beggar, praying that God would restore it to him. The next day, when he opened his mail, he discovered a pair of kid gloves with a coin hidden inside.

When Hudson arrived in China and began his half century of labor there, one of his most challenging circumstances was financial. The mission board rarely sent him money. He remembered, however, his earlier experiences in England. He prayed, and his needs were met.

In 1865, Hudson founded the China Inland Mission, which was to become one of the primary evangelistic outreaches in Asia. A tenet was that without solicitation, funds would be supplied through prayer. The power of faith was Hudson Taylor's financial secret. "Depend upon it," he said. "God's work, done in God's way, will never lack for supplies."

Monday

Week

44

POINTS TO PONDER

Letting go of our financial concerns may seem irresponsible and imprudent. Yet one of Jesus' best-remembered teachings involved the lilies and the sparrows, their lack of money sense, and God's total care for them. Has God changed, expecting more of us than He did of Jesus' disciples? Can we let go of our fears and really believe He will take care of us?

GORDON OGDEN

Christian Father

GORDON OGDEN SERVES IN Christian ministry in the Baton Rouge area. But a struggle with what he describes as "the love of money" has brought him to a new awareness of God's provision.

Gordon had just prayed with his daughter Lauren, asking God to provide for her tuition to Tulane Medical School when bankruptcy hit the company that paid his $90,000 annual income. "Did you hear my prayer, Lord?" he protested. "What's the deal? We asked for more money, not less. And particularly not NO MONEY!"

Gordon later wrote, "This circumstance seemed insurmountable. I had five children in college and a sixth who was a senior in high school. . . . I had to face up to the mistakes I had made, including past borrowing to handle my children's requests. I sought the counsel of an elder in our church and he asked me a sobering question, 'Which one of your children is going to repay these loans when you're not able to?'"

As God's hand began to meet each child's need, Gordon came to see that God is far more capable of caring for us than we are. All of his children were able to secure jobs and loans—learning to pay their own way in life and to take responsibility for their futures. All but one of them completed a college education. He wrote, "God's greatest blessing was the removal of my large income."

Tuesday
Week

44

POINTS TO PONDER

God always teaches us to work hard and to be responsible. He doesn't treat all of His children the same way. He provides more for some of us than for others. The lesson isn't about having or not having. It is about our ability to give and receive from each other—about knowing when to provide and when to allow others to grow in their own faith, work, and financial responsibility.

POWER QUOTE

God is fair with all His children, but His ways of meeting our financial needs are as unique as we are.

SCRIPTURE

Philippians 4:6

Don't worry about anything, but pray about everything. With thankful hearts offer up your prayers and requests to God.

POWER BUILDER

POWER QUOTE

God provides whatever we need. He considers whatever we want, giving us what is best and denying us what is not.

SCRIPTURE

Isaiah 7:10

Ask me for proof that my promise will come true. Ask for something to happen deep in the world of the dead or high in the heavens above.

A. O. FISH HAD LONG dreamed of being an airline pilot. When he was a child, his father's death, followed by a beloved uncle's, had caused him to turn away from God in bitterness. But his dream of piloting was so intense it made him want to pray. He struggled between his lost faith and his dream. He decided to start with a small request.

He recounts his experience: "My wife, Charlotte, had lost her job as a tax consultant after April 15 and every Tuesday I drove her to the employment office where I usually had to park several blocks away.

"'Okay,' I said, directing my words heavenward, 'I'm asking You for an empty parking space right in front of the employment office.'. . .

"When we arrived, my hair stood on end as a car backed out of the exact space I had designated in prayer. We erupted in a fit of laughter. . . .

"As I waited for Charlotte to return, I realized I wasn't alone. A sharp awareness of Him filled the car, the same presence I'd felt as a child when I just knew He was there. I was still a long way from daily, carefree confidence, but had finally taken a big step in that direction."

POINTS TO PONDER

When God promises to meet our needs, He is talking about more than money. He is committed to us as whole people—physically, emotionally, and spiritually. He will provide whatever we need. And when we need a touch from Him, an assurance that He is near and that He has not forgotten us, He responds in love and faithfulness. He provides for us because He is our heavenly Father, and He wants to take care of His children. For the same reason, He disciplines us by not giving us everything we want. He is wise and generous and loving, aware of our needs even before we ask.

POWER BUILDER

President and Chairman of the Board,
Svenhard's Swedish Bakery

Ronny Svenhard is the grandson of a Swedish baker. His father was a Christian businessman who believed that his calling was to serve God through his business.

Svenhard's Swedish Bakery is one of the best-known bakeries on the West Coast, with products available in nearly every supermarket chain. Ronny was once asked, in an interview, what has empowered his company's multimillion-dollar success story.

He said, "Giving monetarily has been the thing that has carried us through. I believe in that, since we dedicated the business to the Lord and it exists for the furtherance of the kingdom of God. . . .

"On a purely secular basis, I believe quality, service, and value have been our three cornerstones. But the true cornerstone of our business has been building it on God's Word, because its foundation was its dedication to the Lord's work.

"I believe in giving yourself out of a crisis. It sounds almost foolish, but God has a bigger shovel than you do and He always shovels back more than you can give out. I've said, 'Lord, I'm going to give this amount in spite of the fact that we are tremendously short on funds.'

"I've seen Him return that amount multiplied many times over. This has happened over and over and over again."

Thursday
Week
44

POINTS TO PONDER

God wants us to be generous with others for several reasons. First of all, He wants us to remember that He is our source of provision, and when we give money away, He simply restores it. Second, He wants us to care for each other, putting our love to work in practical ways. Third, He wants us to be free from an attachment to money—if we have a hard time letting it go, He wants us to work twice as hard doing so until it ceases to control us.

POWER QUOTE

God isn't interested in money; He is interested in our hearts being totally His and our minds being set on heavenly treasures.

SCRIPTURE

John 6:11

Jesus took the bread in his hands and gave thanks to God. Then he passed the bread to the people . . . until everyone had plenty to eat.

ROBERT BROWN

Public Relations Executive

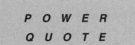

POWER BUILDER

POWER QUOTE

When we give to others, they see God's hand in the giving, and they thank Him as well as us.

SCRIPTURE

James 2:17

Faith that doesn't lead us to do good deeds is all alone and dead!

As A YOUNG AFRICAN-AMERICAN child in North Carolina, Robert Brown learned the secret to his future success from his grandmother, who raised him and his brother. He watched his grandmother share their meager provisions with a beggar, and he asked her why she was giving away the family's food when they were so poor.

"Life is all about serving and giving," she explained. "There's nothing else in life that's as great as that."

She prayed daily for her grandsons, "May they understand that if you have enough courage, that if you have enough faith in God, and that if you're willing to sacrifice and work hard enough, you can do anything."

Armed with both courage and faith, Bob quit his law enforcement job in 1960 and started a public relations firm, although everyone advised him not to. Later, their advice seemed valid when he was four months late on his car payment.

A few days later he received a call from a huge public relations firm—a call that changed the course of his business and his life. Today, he is not only a successful man, but he is a well-known philanthropist, guided by the principles he learned as a child: faith, generosity, and hard work.

POINTS TO PONDER

Is there a relationship between our generosity with others and God's generosity with us? It may not be as simple as a financial transaction where we pay into some heavenly account and expect a return with interest. More likely, when we are generous with others, God sees that we aren't clinging to our money. It doesn't own us. We are able to give it up, let it go, and feel gratified that we have blessed somebody else. We aren't giving to get; we are giving because we enjoy giving. That's when He feels free to give us more; He knows He can trust us with it.

T AKE A FEW MOMENTS to reflect and record your true feelings about money, financial concerns, and God's provision. What has He done for you financially? What have you done for His kingdom? What are your thoughts about generosity?

_____

_____

_____

_____

Weekend
Week

44

Lord,

money is such a difficult subject for me.

I can't seem to find my balance,

trusting in Your provision

and resting in Your care without worrying.

Teach me Your perspective about money,

about food, shelter, and clothing.

Help me learn to lean on You

without failing to be responsible.

You are my provider, Lord.

Help me to trust in You and You alone.

CHUCK BUCK

President and CEO, Buck Knife Corp.

POWER QUOTE

Pain is a spiritual crucible, purifying us for an eternal relationship with a holy God.

BUCK KNIVES HAVE BEEN called the best sporting knives in the world. Manufactured in southern California, Buck's knives, pocketknives, fillet knives, and survival knives are highly profitable, and the company has historically been owned and operated by a Christian family.

Like any successful company, Buck Knife Corp. has had its financial ups and downs. Chuck Buck commented on how struggles and crises have affected him personally: "Actually, the Christian life is really analogous to our process of making blades. The blade is put in the furnace, and it has to go through that 2,000-degree heat for forty-five minutes to an hour. It seems as though we have forgotten about it and left it to burn up.

"Then we plunge it into a 100-degree-below-zero container for three hours. After that, it's put in a tempering furnace for about one and a half to two hours at a low, steady, throbbing 800 degrees, and it really seems as though we've forgotten this little knife. Finally it comes out and sees the light of day again, but that knife has been toughened to a 58 Rockwell hardness and it's ready for anything.

"When a person gets saved, he or she thinks, 'Now I'm a Christian and everything is going to be okay.' But all of a sudden here come the temptations, here comes the persecution, and the person thinks that God has forgotten him. I've been tempered through the trials I've faced."

Monday
Week

45

SCRIPTURE

Isaiah 43:2

When you cross deep rivers, I will be with you, and you won't drown. When you walk through fire, you won't be burned.

POINTS TO PONDER

Pain forges strength into our character and teaches us about the character of God. Most of us have suffered pain and loss at one time or another. And in that season of heartache we learn our lessons, and we experience our growth. Pain is indeed the furnace of the Lord. It removes our impurities, hardens our moral fiber, and makes us more useful tools in His hand.

POWER BUILDER

RON BARTHELL

Accident Survivor

CRAWLING OUT OF HIS submerged tractor-trailer rig, Ron Barthell immediately understood that he had been miraculously spared from death. He knew the minute his truck careened off the highway and into the water that Someone was trying to get his attention. It was time for him to give up truck driving.

In the following years, laboring at night as a school janitor, Ron managed to work his way through Spokane Washington's prestigious Wentworth College, earning a bachelor's degree in religion.

Ron and his wife, Marti, wanted to pastor a church or to serve as missionaries. However, because they were in their fifties, they could find no opportunities for service. So they decided to spend their retirement years in Christian service, and they would provide their own support.

After much prayer, they focused their attention on small, careful investments, and they took Spanish classes in preparation for their new ministry. Ron had no money when he completed his college education. Yet six years later he and his wife owned a motel, four houses, and several parcels of land. Ron explains, "God put me in a watery tomb to demonstrate that I can't rely on the world's security. . . . He will provide everything I need as long as I live on this earth."

Tuesday
Week
45

POWER QUOTE

Pain never enters a person's life without God's permission. He has a reason for it, whether we like it or not.

SCRIPTURE

Isaiah 43:18–19

Forget what happened long ago! Don't think about the past. I am creating something new.

POINTS TO PONDER

Fearing for his life in a submerged vehicle was the means God used to tap one of His children on the shoulder. Pain never fails to get our attention. First of all, we pray that God will rescue us—and quickly. Then we begin to ask, Why did He allow this to happen? Finally, when we pass through the pain, we remember God's blessings—the good things for which we often forget to be thankful. Pain always turns our eyes heavenward.

POWER BUILDER

LARRY ALFORD

Aspiring Golfer

LARRY ALFORD LEARNED THAT he would be receiving a full-tuition golf scholarship to the University of Houston. "Now," he told his single mom, "you won't have to struggle to put me through college!"

But a car accident that summer seemed to change things. Larry woke up from surgery to discover that his left arm had been amputated just below the elbow. "My hand, my hand!" he screamed. "How can I ever play golf?"

A determined Larry tried to swing a club at the hospital's rehabilitation center. He moved the ball about fifty yards with his right hand, but he would never be able to compete again. Or would he?

Jay Hall, a psychologist and family friend, was an avid golfer. He began to research the possibility of a prosthetic device that could be a "golf hand." Jay designed a device and took it to a local prosthetics firm. Larry tried out the hand. The ball landed two hundred yards away, "I'm back!" he shouted. He returned to a tournament he had played in a year before and fired 77—a stroke better than his previous score.

Later on, Larry spoke to a group of children: "Don't think of your missing limb as something that makes you a lesser person. Think of it as something that can make you stronger. I would love to be the first pro golfer with a prosthetic hand. But I also know that if I don't succeed, I won't be a failure. We only fail when we don't try—when we don't dream."

POWER QUOTE

Pain has an incomparable power to transform an ordinary life into an extraordinary message of hope.

SCRIPTURE

Proverbs 13:19

It's a good feeling to get what you want.

POINTS TO PONDER

Why should such a terrible thing happen to a well-disciplined young man like Larry Alford? Perhaps someone with less to offer would not have overcome his disability and then taken his positive message to other people. Larry is a winner, and his pain has given him something powerful to say and a vital reason for saying it.

POWER BUILDER

HENRI LANDWIRTH

Hotelier

Thursday

Week

45

HENRI LANDWIRTH SPENT FIVE years in Nazi concentration camps during World War II. He felt powerless during those nightmarish years: "I had no control over my life." Later, the subject of suffering, powerless children never left Henri's consciousness. How could he use his past pain to make present lives better?

In 1986, Henri learned that a little girl had died of leukemia while her last-wish plans for a trip to Walt Disney World were still being made. He was heartsick, realizing she never saw her dream come true. Hoping to prevent similar tragedies, Henri organized the group Give Kids the World. The organization would provide travel opportunities for families with desperately ill children.

To further his vision, Henri raised $4.5 million to create a special resort for boys and girls. Today, Henri operates the Holiday Inn Kids Village in Kissimmee, Florida. It is a unique resort for children with life-threatening diseases, where a full-time staff of thirty-eight runs the resort along with about four hundred volunteers.

"We're talking about life, joy, and laughter," Henri says. "We prolong lives here. Kids come looking one way and leave looking another. I don't know of any better medicine."

POWER QUOTE

God has promised to work all things together for good if we love Him; sometimes He helps us to do it ourselves.

SCRIPTURE

Isaiah 63:9

It troubled the LORD to see them in trouble, and his angel saved them.

POINTS TO PONDER

Would Henri Landwirth have cared so deeply for children if he hadn't suffered as a child? The Nazi death camps made an indelible impression on his young mind. But rather than seething in hatred and bitterness, Henri opted to allow his pain to be the source of something wonderful. Although few of us have had to endure concentration camps, all of us have suffered in one way or another. And our past hurts leave us with a choice. We can allow our abuses to overwhelm us, or we can use them as an inspiration for good works.

JOHN YEH
Founder, Integrated Microcomputer Systems

Our suffering makes us either bitter or beautiful—the choice is ours and ours alone.

SCRIPTURE

Proverbs 10:4

Laziness leads to poverty; hard work makes you rich.

WHEN THE YEH FAMILY of eight arrived in Washington, D.C., from Asia, their youngest son John brought with him more challenges than any of his siblings—he could not hear. So he had to learn both English and sign language.

After completing his college education, John wanted to teach math, but he was unable to find a job because of his disability. He earned a master's degree in computer science and sought a different job. Still no luck. No one wanted to deal with an employee who had a hearing impairment.

By the late 1970s, John concluded that he would be able to succeed only if he started his own company. After obtaining financing from the Handicapped Assistance Loan program, he started Integrated Microcomputer Systems.

John's wife, who also cannot hear, taught people with hearing impairments while John put in long hours and took no salary. But the work paid off.

John began with two employees; he now employs more than five hundred, 6 percent of whom have a hearing impairment. In the early 1990s, the company had revenues exceeding $34 million. John Yeh still has a mission to accomplish: "I want the business world to understand that disabled people can perform well if given the opportunity."

Friday
Week
45

POINTS TO PONDER

John Yeh's personal pain carved deep compassion into his soul. He felt his own trouble acutely, and when he helped himself, John helped others with similar disabilities. When our pain carries us beyond ourselves, into the hearts and lives of other hurting people, it has accomplished its best work—it has taught us to love.

W HAT IS THE MOST painful experience you have ever endured? How did God use it in your life? How did you use it in the lives of others?

_____

_____

_____

_____

_____

Weekend
Week

45

Lord,

You have been through my hurt with me.

You remember when it happened,

who was responsible,

and how it affected my life.

Today, I bring that hurt to You.

I want You to use it to bless me,

and I want You to show me how to use it

to bless others.

My pain is meaningless only

if I refuse to allow You to sanctify it.

Thank You for touching my suffering with Your love.

Please transform it into a powerful force for good.

SCOTT F. O'GRADY
Captain, U.S. Air Force

SCOTT F. O'GRADY WAS flying a NATO mission over Bosnia when an enemy rocket slashed through his F-16 aircraft. After O'Grady pulled the ejection handle, ejected, and began his parachute descent, he saw Bosnians watching him. Once down, he ran for his life, scurrying for cover in the thin vegetation. "God protected me," he said later.

Then O'Grady's ordeal really began. He ate grass, leaves, and insects. Desperately thirsty, he prayed for rain. That night, it rained.

Meanwhile the Bosnians were searching for him, shooting into the bushes with their weapons. Not willing to give away his position, he was afraid to turn on his electronic beacon for several days. Then on the fifth day, he heard a radio call: "Basher One One." Basher was O'Grady's code name—he was in contact with a search aircraft.

An elite marine unit rescued O'Grady from his hiding place. O'Grady credited his survival to prayer and his faith: "The first thing I want to do is thank God. If it wasn't for God's love for me and my love for God, I wouldn't have gotten through it. He's the one that delivered me here, and I know that in my heart."

Monday
Week

46

POINTS TO PONDER

One of the most wonderful truths about God is that He is faithful to His people. In our everyday lives, we may not always be aware of His presence—our situation isn't desperate, and our need for Him isn't overwhelming. But in the darkest days, the most frightening nights, God becomes an almost tangible presence. No matter how terrifying our circumstances may be, He is with us, around us, and within us, encouraging, guiding, and protecting. And when the crisis is over, we, like Scott O'Grady, recognize that His power has saved us, and His love for us is the only reason we have survived and prevailed.

POWER BUILDER

JOE DELOACH

U.S. Olympic Gold Medal Winner

JOE DELOACH WAS THRILLED to welcome to his home gold-medalist track star Carl Lewis and the track coach from the University of Houston. Joe had long dreamed of being part of the track program at Houston. But the visit turned out to be a disaster. The NCAA banned Joe from attending the University of Houston. Even though Carl Lewis had never graduated from the school, the NCAA ruled that his visit to a prospective student was a recruiting violation, since the school considered him an alumnus.

Instead of competing for the university, Joe soon was running for the Houston Track Club. Instead of training with classmates, he was competing with world-class runners like Lewis and Calvin Smith. Instead of going to local meets, he was traveling overseas.

At first, Joe "remained frustrated, instead of praising the Lord for enabling me to travel. Nor did I appreciate the fact that with the prize money I won at meets, I could start building a trust fund."

Eventually, the NCAA reversed its decision, and Joe ran for the University of Houston. But in the meantime he had gained enough experience and professional discipline to compete in the Olympics. By beating his friend and fellow Christian Carl Lewis, Joe DeLoach won the Olympic gold medal for the U.S. in the 200-meter race in 1988.

Tuesday
Week

46

POWER QUOTE

The disappointments of our lives are the fertile soil from which God's best opportunities take root, grow, and bear fruit.

SCRIPTURE

Isaiah 7:4 NIV

Be careful, keep calm and don't be afraid. Do not lose heart.

POINTS TO PONDER

Because of His ability to see from beginning to end, God sometimes allows events to transpire that at first seem negative or even disastrous. But He is faithful to His promises of love, provision, and guidance. And as days and months pass, we suddenly are aware of a better plan powerfully emerging from what initially seemed a total loss. Joe DeLoach might never have won the Olympic gold medal if circumstances had unfolded according to his plan.

ETHYL WATERS
Singer and Actress

POWER QUOTE

God gives joy and blessing according to our needs, our personalities, and His wisdom as our heavenly Parent.

SCRIPTURE

Isaiah 60:5

When you see this, your faces will glow; your hearts will pound and swell with pride.

AS A CHILD, ETHYL Waters was what she later described as a "real dead-end kid." She stole, lied, and caused trouble. Eventually, her remarkable talent as a singer and actress got her off the city streets and onto the great stages of the world. But something more powerful than show business came into her life first, giving Ethyl strength.

In search of peace, she agreed to attend a Christian revival with some young friends, and she went every day for nearly a week. Most of the boys and girls in attendance "got saved." But Ethyl didn't know what to say or do. She said, "God, what am I after here? What do I want of You?" Finally, the last night of the crusade, she said, "Help me! If nothing happens, I can't come back here anymore."

At last the peace of God entered Ethyl's life. She said, "Afterward they told me that I was radiant and like one transfixed. . . . I did feel full of light and warmth."

The same power that transformed Ethyl Waters's face began a new work in her young heart. During years of success as an actress and singer, she acknowledged that God was her strength. For the rest of her life she would sing, "His eye is on the sparrow, and I know He watches me."

POINTS TO PONDER

God's faithfulness in response to our prayers is guaranteed. But He answers every prayer according to His time, plan, and purpose. Ethyl Waters was a unique girl, who would grow up to walk an unusual path. For reasons of His own, God waited until Ethyl was fully prepared to receive His blessing. Then He poured it out for all the world to see—in radiance and joy. Each of us is unique to Him, and He knows the right time, place, and process to give His best answers to our sincere prayers.

POWER BUILDER

STEVE GOSE

Oil Businessman

Ⅰ N THE EARLY 1980s, Steve Gose's income from oil and gas sales averaged more than $1 million a month, but by 1985, he was more than $200 million in debt. He had no control over the OPEC oil crisis, and he could not solve his problems technically or professionally. As he contemplated the bleak future, he prayed, "I surrender, Lord. Whatever You want me to do, I'll do it."

Steve clearly felt God leading him to stay in the oil business and to resolve his problems. Trying to start up a new drilling project in south Texas, Steve could find no investors, so he managed to launch the project with no money, an arrangement that the landowner miraculously accepted.

More amazing, by the time the landowner was due to be paid, Steve had earned far more than the $2 million investment would have made possible. Plus, a new drilling technique was developed in the process, making his companies more lucrative than he had ever imagined possible.

Steve's surrender to God brought him to unprecedented success. He later said, "God's timing and guidance were perfect. Only He could have put me in the right place at the right time."

Thursday
Week
46

POWER QUOTE

God's solutions are unlimited by time, by space, by money, or by anyone else's agenda.

SCRIPTURE

Isaiah 30:18

The LORD God is waiting to show how kind he is.

POINTS TO PONDER

When we face severe difficulties, we often find ourselves on our knees before God. We struggle, cry out, and plead for help. Then we come to the end of our resources of ideas and emotion, and we give up. At that point, when we quietly ask God to take over, He does. His mind, far more intelligent than ours, creates unimaginable solutions. His perspective, far more encompassing than ours, accommodates the future as well as the past. His power, far greater than ours, makes things happen: the right things at the right time, according to His faithfulness.

POWER BUILDER

LEE EZELL
Author and Lecturer

POWER QUOTE

The proper question is never *Why?* It is, "What would You have me do in this difficult situation?"

SCRIPTURE

Psalm 139:17

Your thoughts are far beyond my understanding, much more than I could ever imagine.

LEE EZELL BEGAN HER spiritual walk on an exceptionally rocky path. Just a short time after her conversion, a coworker raped her. Then she discovered that she was pregnant. Her world fell apart. Her family was unable to provide help for her, and she was very much alone.

Abortion was out of the question, and since she was unmarried, Lee prayerfully put the infant up for adoption. Unsure what else to ask for, she begged God to place the little girl in a Christian home. Then, she struggled to get on with her life. The questions lingered, "Why did God let it happen?" and "What happened to the baby?" But there were no answers.

Twenty years later, Lee was a successful author and lecturer, married to a man with a public career. She had built her reputation on the foundation of internally choosing joy and happiness instead of waiting for them to arrive from outside.

The phone rang one day. It was the daughter Lee had given up for adoption. The young woman had only one real motive in her efforts to contact her birth mother: "I wanted to tell you about Jesus." Lee's prayers for her baby were powerfully answered. A relationship was formed between the two families. And the answers to Lee's difficult questions were joyfully received.

POINTS TO PONDER

Although our chosen trust in a sovereign God requires us, at times, to accept the seemingly unacceptable, it can be a stretch for us to let go of the *why* question. It is an even greater stretch to begin to say, "Thank You, God. You are faithful in all things." Fortunately, now and then, God allows us to observe people like Lee and her daughter. With them, we are able to smile and say, "*Now* I understand, Lord. You always know what You are doing."

Take a few moments and recall a time when you became keenly aware of God's faithfulness in your life. Briefly describe it here.

_____

_____

What is the most important lesson you learned from that experience?

_____

_____

Weekend
Week

46

Lord,

thank You for Your faithfulness.

Sometimes I think You have forgotten me

or haven't heard me

or don't see how difficult life is.

But You have proved to me that You are powerful,

You are sovereign,

and You are faithful to me

even when, at times, I'm not faithful to You.

POWER
BUILDER

JACK LOUSMA
Astronaut

We see God in nature; we read about Him in His Word; we feel His love in the caring of others.

SCRIPTURE

Romans 1:20

God's eternal power and character cannot be seen. But from the beginning of creation, God has shown what these are like by all he has made.

JACK LOUSMA SPENT NEARLY sixty days as an astronaut circling the earth. Tremendous power rocketed him and his colleagues into space. And yet, because he is a Christian, Jack realized that when God's eternal perspective was considered, "we didn't go anywhere and we didn't spend any time doing it."

From the experience, Jack became deeply aware of two parallel views of God. On the one hand, He is the Creator and Sustainer of all the universe. On the other, He remains our personal heavenly Father. As he looked down on earth, Jack imagined that God had a wide-angle lens to look over all creation and keep it operating properly. At the same time He could also be viewing the planet through a telephoto lens that could zoom "right in on the Milky Way galaxy to this planet, to your country, your city, your home, and your heart."

Jack Lousma is well aware that no one has to travel into space to know the Creator: "Look into His Word, the Bible. See how He speaks of His creation, how He delights in it and how much He wants us to know more about it."

Monday
Week

47

POINTS TO PONDER

The Word of God is a key element in developing our faith. It tells us what God is like, how He works, and how He expects us to behave. Certainly, we may worship Him and believe in Him without reading Scripture or understanding it. But the wonder of the Bible is that it provides us with the information God wants us to have about Himself. It is His love letter, written by a heavenly Father to His beloved children.

POWER BUILDER

DOUG GILMORE
U.S. Soldier

Iₙ THE MIDST OF World War II's Battle of the Bulge, Doug Gilmore volunteered to drive a truckload of gasoline to the 82nd Airborne in Belgium. Doug drove all day and all night, picked up a couple of air force hitchhikers along the way, and started down a long, steep hill.

Glancing down, he saw a sharp right curve and a narrow bridge at the bottom of the hill. He pressed the brake pedal. It slid to the floor uselessly. He reached for the emergency brake. There wasn't one. He looked down again at the upcoming curve and bridge. The truck was bound to overturn and explode—it was packed with five-gallon cans of gas.

Not a man of faith, Doug nevertheless began to recite the only Scripture he knew: "The LORD is my shepherd; I shall not want. . . . Yea, though I walk through the valley of the shadow of death, I will fear no evil: for thou art with me" (Ps. 23:1, 4 KJV).

Terror gripped him. He was afraid to look at the speedometer, certain that he was moving at more than eighty miles an hour. Navigating the sharp curve was out of the question. All at once, Doug realized he was hurtling across the bridge and gradually coasting to a stop. He had no recollection of the turn: "To this day, I don't remember rushing through that curve. Jesus must have straightened the road out—just in time. It's . . . amazing that He preserved my life before I gave my heart to Him."

Tuesday
Week

47

POINTS TO PONDER

Scripture is not a magic charm that protects us when we repeat it; it is not a formula that guarantees we'll have anything we want. Scripture is a portrait of God and a story of His work in the world. It teaches us that we can trust Him. It encourages us when we are afraid. And when we memorize it, God brings it to mind as a way of telling us that He is with us and He is in control of our situation.

POWER QUOTE

God's Word lights our way in the darkness; it illuminates His face; it allows us to catch a glimpse of His glory.

SCRIPTURE

Psalm 16:1–2

Protect me, LORD God! I run to you for safety, and I have said, "Only you are my Lord! Every good thing I have is a gift from you."

POWER BUILDER

Wednesday
Week

47

WHEN NORMAN WILLIAMS LEFT on his vacation to Casablanca, Tangiers, Morocco, Gibraltar, and the Greek islands, his flight, which departed from Los Angeles, was to stop in the Canary Islands. Because of a terrorism incident, it was diverted to the small island of Tenerife, where it sat in the heat for several hours. To make matters worse, a heavy fog rolled in.

Other planes were grounded at the tiny airport. When a KLM 747 pilot chose to refuel at Tenerife, he added 142,000 pounds to the weight of his plane. Just as he tried to take off, he realized that the LA jumbo jet had pulled onto the runway. The KLM pilot tried to lift his airplane over the other 747, but he hit it. Jet fuel gushed through the cabin in waves. Both planes were rocked with repeated explosions, and flames engulfed the passengers.

Norman spoke a Scripture aloud as he tried to lift his 260-pound frame through a hole in the roof: "When thou walkest through the fire, thou shalt not be burned; neither shall the flame kindle upon thee" (Isa. 43:2 KJV). Somehow he hoisted himself through the ten-foot ceiling, ran across the wing, and jumped off. He shattered his foot and shredded his hand in the process. He heard two more explosions. When he looked back, his plane was gone. Only 60 of 653 people who had been on the two aircraft survived.

POINTS TO PONDER

Did the Scripture Norman Williams quoted protect him from the flames, or did God bring it to his mind to assure him that he would be protected? There is power in God's Word—supernatural power that brings its message to life when we need it most. But the power of God is at work both in His Word and in our lives. He speaks to us in many ways—through Scripture, through other people, through our own inner voice, and through our circumstances.

POWER BUILDER

JOHN HARRISON

Taster and Flavor Developer of Ice Cream

JOHN HARRISON'S TASTE BUDS have been insured for $1 million. But, with God's power, his sensitive mouth and tongue weren't touched after a near fatal traffic accident. John and his son had been riding through a high mountain pass when their car careened off the side of a mountain, plunging into a ravine. His son was barely bruised. But X-rays confirmed that John's back was broken in two places.

John had long believed in God's power to heal, and he began to pray. Friends arrived, laid hands on him, and also prayed that God would mend his back. Upon learning that a bone scan was about to be taken, John said, "Lord, I believe You want to heal me. What do You expect of me?"

In his mind came Psalm 34:19–20. John wrote, "The next morning the orthopedic surgeon came to my hospital doorway and said, 'John, you can rise up and go home, you've been healed.'"

John's employer, who was expecting him to be out of work for six months, welcomed him back in three days. God's power was dramatically evident to everyone involved. John Harrison simply credits the miracle to "Jesus—our Healer" and the power of His Word.

Thursday
Week

47

POWER QUOTE

The Word of God is honest, reliable, and irreversible: God will do what He says He will do.

SCRIPTURE

Psalm 34:19–20

The LORD's people may suffer a lot, but he will always bring them safely through. Not one of their bones will ever be broken.

POINTS TO PONDER

God's Word springs to life in our hearts when He has something to share with us. Out of nowhere, a passage will suddenly resound in our minds. Once we've heard it, a strange peace touches us, warming us with the assurance that God has spoken, and that His word will be kept. The same things happens when we are reading the Bible. A passage strikes us unexpectedly, speaking directly to some problem or circumstance. We stop, reread it, and pause to give thanks. God has spoken, and His Word will not fail to accomplish its purpose.

SAMUEL BANFO

Colonel, Ghana Army

**POWER
QUOTE**

When God's Word stirs our
hearts, it is as if He personally
whispers in our ears. We hear
His voice, and we believe.

SCRIPTURE

Psalm 91:11

God will command his angels

to protect you wherever you go.

COLONEL SAMUEL BANFO WAS sentenced to be executed. He was arrested after a successful coup d'état overthrew the government in 1979. Awaiting his time to face the firing squad, he tried to use his religion of fetishism to make himself disappear. It proved powerless, and his only remaining comfort lay with the Catholic priest, who visited him in prison.

Banfo wrote, "I called for the priest who told me about Jesus Christ. The priest ministered to every condemned man; offering the sacrament and taking personal messages that would later be delivered to each man's family. He spoke directly to me, saying, 'Do you believe that Jesus Christ can save you?'

"'Yes. . . .'

"He then opened the Bible to Psalm 91:7 and read: 'A thousand shall fall at your side and ten thousand at your right hand; but it shall not come nigh you.'

"That evening my fellow prisoners and I agreed together in prayer. During the solemn course of events, a word of prophecy was given declaring that the executions were finished.

"Three days later, the Chairman of the Armed Forces Revolutionary Council announced to the world that we would not be sent to the firing squad. It was a miracle! I knew that Jesus Christ had saved my life. Therefore I committed my life to Him."

Friday
Week

47

POINTS TO PONDER

In the very shadow of death, God's Word gave Samuel Banfo a promise of life. Was he grasping at straws when he received the words of Scripture the priest read to him? Of course, he was searching for hope. But the words were compelling. The words of Scripture carry with them the authority of God Himself. When we hear them, they are invigorated by His power. They are rich in His wisdom. They are irresistible because of His integrity.

Can you think of a time when a passage of Scripture spoke to you clearly and directly, assuring you of God's presence in your circumstances? What was the passage, and how did He use it in your life?

_____

_____

_____

_____

Weekend
Week

47

Lord,

Your Word has guided me through the darkness;

it has stayed with me in the good times.

It has always been reliable

when I have taken the time to listen.

There have been situations

when I have tried to use it

to get my way;

but it didn't work so well—

my way wasn't Your will,

and You were gracious enough to say, "No."

Thank You for teaching about Yourself,

for helping me understand myself,

and for equipping me to love others

through the pages of Your Word.

R. DAVID THOMAS
Founder, Wendy's

POWER QUOTE

Prayer is one important way we practice being in the presence of God.

SCRIPTURE

Psalm 91:14–15

I will rescue you and keep you safe. When you are in trouble, call out to me. I will answer.

WHEN R. DAVID THOMAS tried to turn around the fortunes of a restaurant chain in Columbus, Ohio, everyone thought he was crazy. Only one person seemed to have encouraging words for Thomas—Harlan Sanders, also known as the Kentucky Colonel. And the floundering restaurants owed him money. Thomas could barely keep enough of the "secret herbs and spices" for fried chicken in stock—Colonel Sanders shipped them to Thomas COD because he wasn't sure he would get paid otherwise.

Thomas was a man of prayer, and he continued to bombard heaven with requests for help. One day, he studied the menu, which took a full ten minutes to read. A revolutionary idea dawned on him: simplify! He called Harlan Sanders and announced that the restaurants would be called Colonel Sanders' Kentucky Fried Chicken Take-Homes. The turnaround was immediate. The profits were extraordinary.

Years later, Thomas was able to open his own restaurants. He prayed for another idea. God had helped him before; surely He would help him again. The idea came to him: hamburgers—in a pleasant environment. Thomas decided to name the restaurants after his daughter—the hamburger chain would be called Wendy's.

Monday
Week

48

POINTS TO PONDER

When we are searching for answers, we may buy books. We may watch videos. We may listen to tapes and radio shows. We may ask our friends for advice. We may even write to advice columns. R. David Thomas did what we should do first—he prayed. Although he had a major problem to solve, he never thought for a moment that he was on his own. God was an ever-present part of his life. When the answers came, they came in response to his prayer.

POWER BUILDER

LEON JOLSON
Concentration Camp Survivor

Whi HEN LEON JOLSON CAME to the United States after World War II, he was a refugee with less than $10 in his pocket. His devout Jewish father had operated a highly successful sewing machine distributorship in Poland, but the Nazi invasion had destroyed the family's comfortable life.

Leon brought with him two gifts from his father: he knew all about sewing machines, and he believed fervently in prayer. He and his wife borrowed enough money to settle in a tiny apartment and to purchase an inexpensive sewing machine repair tool kit. Leon traveled to the New York garment district, where he went door to door in search of work.

Meanwhile, he wrote to every sewing machine contact he could remember in Europe, asking for opportunities to assist their marketing in America. He saved his commissions, researched the American sewing market, and started distributing fine Italian machines. After locating two investors, he started his own company.

Five years after landing at Ellis Island, Leon Jolson was president and founder of a $7 million sewing machine company. He says, "If you believe in Him, you should talk to Him face to face. . . . I have always done it . . . every time I got stuck, every time it was hard, every time I was grateful. And every time I called, I was heard—and answered."

POWER QUOTE

Prayer blesses our hard work with hope; prayer blesses our efforts with faith. And with hope, faith, and hard work, anything is possible.

SCRIPTURE

Psalm 107:31

You should praise the LORD for his love and for the wonderful things he does for all of us.

POINTS TO PONDER

Hard work is certainly a primary reason for success. But hard work becomes more difficult when we have no hope. Without a reason to believe that we will succeed, our labors become exhausting, and we begin to burn out with all the effort. That is when faith and prayer become so important. When we invite God to participate in our work, we immediately feel hopeful. Our hope inspires us to work harder. And our faith assures us that God is partnering with us in our work, happy to bless it, available to prosper us.

POWER BUILDER

WALLACE JOHNSON

Founder, Holiday Inns

POWER QUOTE

God is at work in our lives for eternal purposes, but He works with us on earthly projects.

SCRIPTURE

Matthew 7:7

Ask, and you will receive.

Search, and you will find.

Knock, and the door will be opened for you.

Wednesday

Week

48

IN 1939, A BUSINESS supplies salesman named Wallace Johnson went to God in frustration. For the first time in his life, he asked God to help him find his place in the world. He admitted that he was unsuccessful, and he asked God to show him why.

Names of people began to come to mind. He started making phone calls. In the meantime, he focused his attention on Scripture. He learned that he should "ask . . . search . . . and knock" to receive. And he also concluded that he would have to become "a workman that needeth not to be ashamed" (2 Tim. 2:15 KJV). Both concepts came together to form his personal mission.

Within a year, Wallace was directed to enter the home-building industry. As he launched his new career, he began to pray about specific concerns, both small and large.

Wallace's success grew. A dozen years after he built his first house, he constructed a place where travelers could stay. He called that first building a Holiday Inn. Again, success followed. As the Holiday Inn chain of hotels crisscrossed the country, Wallace became more convinced that the power of prayer was the reason for his amazing prosperity.

Wallace Johnson firmly believed in praying for success. He wrote, "When I surrendered my life to Jesus Christ some years ago, I turned everything over to Him: money, possessions, goals, dreams, business. Any success I have achieved since is His success."

POINTS TO PONDER

God isn't concerned about success, profits, or fame when He answers our prayers. God is interested in developing a daily personal relationship with each of us. For this reason, He listens to us, answers us, and guides us in our efforts. God's partnership with us builds our faith, allows onlookers to observe His involvement in our lives, and speaks to all about His amazing friendship with His people.

POWER BUILDER

THE TROUBLED NORTH AFRICAN man entered the family garden. Despite his mother's ceaseless prayers, he was caught up in a lusty lifestyle, and he couldn't seem to break the cycle. Although he longed for a relationship with God, he was unable to stop his self-destructive behavior.

He heard the sound of children's voices chanting, "Pick it up, read it; pick it up, read it." Briefly distracted from his misery, the young man wondered what kind of game would cause the children to sing such an odd verse. All at once it occurred to him that perhaps God was sending him a message through their playful words.

He eagerly opened his Bible and began to read: "Not in rioting and drunkenness, not in chambering and wantonness, not in strife and envying. But put ye on the Lord Jesus Christ, and make not provision for the flesh, to fulfil the lusts thereof. Him that is weak in the faith receive" (Rom. 13:13—14:1 KJV).

The young man was filled with hope and yearning. He believed that God had given him a passage to assure him that divine power could and would overcome his human weakness.

He rushed into the house and told his mother, Monica—she was filled with incredible joy and wonder. Her prayers had been answered. The young man's life was transformed. Today, he is remembered as St. Augustine.

Thursday

Week

48

POWER QUOTE

In our prayers, we come to God as repentant sinners; in His response, God transforms us into saints.

SCRIPTURE

2 Corinthians 12:9

If Christ keeps giving me his power, I will gladly brag about how weak I am.

POINTS TO PONDER

When young Augustine walked through the garden, he was in prayer. And his mother, Monica, was praying, too. Both were expecting answers; both were listening for direction. When the children's words led Augustine to the Scriptures, he found what he was looking for. God met him in his need; He met Monica in her concern. And He transformed a lustful young man into one of the great fathers of the early church—all in response to prayer.

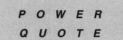
WALLY AMOS
Cookie Entrepreneur

POWER QUOTE

God never moves away from us; we move away from Him by focusing on ourselves, our problems, and our desires.

SCRIPTURE

Jeremiah 31:13

I will comfort them and turn their sorrow into happiness.

WALLY AMOS WANTED TO make a name for himself as a show business agent. He was able to get some up-and-coming acts on the road to success. People like Simon and Garfunkel. The Supremes. Actors and actresses. Finally, he made his way to Hollywood and started an agency.

But things didn't go so well for Wally. His business had some great moments, but incredible disappointments eclipsed them. The only thing that seemed to cheer Wally up was baking old-fashioned chocolate chip cookies and sharing them with his friends.

In 1974, Wally hit an all-time low. His marriage fell apart. He was financially destitute. And he was weary of the Hollywood fast track that demanded so much from him. He and his sons headed for the Grand Canyon.

As the Arizona landmark was transformed into breathtaking beauty by a sunset, Wally remembered God. He had forgotten about Him in all the hectic efforts, but the powerful display of His beauty put everything back in perspective. A new beginning seemed possible.

Days later, a friend suggested that Wally's delicious cookies deserved a store of their own. When the first Famous Amos Cookie Store opened in Hollywood, thousands of people showed up to celebrate and enjoy. Wally Amos had found his new beginning. And he had found the Power he needed to change his life around.

Friday
Week

48

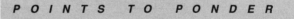

POINTS TO PONDER

How can we possibly forget about the Creator of the universe? We forget Him when we worry. We forget Him when we fantasize about success and terrify ourselves with thoughts of failure. Fortunately, God never forgets us. And in His love, He gently steers us until we reach a point where He can get our full attention. Like Wally Amos, we turn around, look into His face, and plead for His help. Of course, He helps us—He has been waiting for us to call Him.

CAN YOU THINK OF a time when God responded to your prayer in a dramatic way, giving you the kind of new beginning you so desperately needed? Take a moment to record your thoughts and to thank Him for His presence in your life.

_____

_____

_____

_____

Weekend
Week

48

Lord,

You are always with me,

even when I ignore You,

avoid You,

distract myself from thinking about You,

rebel against You,

and try to forget You because I'm doing something

You wouldn't want me to do.

Thank You for never forsaking me.

Thank You for being there when I need You most

and for reminding me of Your presence,

Your protection,

and Your love.

DARRELL WALTRIP

Stock Car Driver

NOTHING MATTERED MORE TO professional stock car driver Darrell Waltrip than winning. He didn't care what anybody thought of him. And win he did. But when his name was announced over the loudspeakers at the racetrack, the boos more than drowned out the applause. The crowds hated him.

Then a racing accident nearly cost Darrell his life. At about the same time, his wife experienced a miscarriage, and the prognosis for successful childbirth wasn't good. In her despair, she began to attend church, and she tried to get Darrell to go with her. Sometimes he did.

One day Darrell was relaxing at home. Their pastor stopped by and confronted Darrell for having a beer company as the sponsor of his racing car. Not long afterward, a woman confronted him at an autograph session: How could he endorse alcohol use so carelessly?

Darrell and his wife had been actively praying for a baby. He wondered whether he was the right kind of role model.

After praying with his wife, he made the financially risky decision to switch racing sponsors. As clear evidence of his readjusted priorities, when he won the Daytona 500 in 1989, Darrell Waltrip was a proud father. And he was voted most popular driver in the race.

POINTS TO PONDER

There is a sense of peace, of relief, even of hope when we finally say, "Okay, have it Your way, Lord. What have I got to lose?" We may have a great deal to lose in earthly terms. But by letting go of the things that control us, we are allowing God to release His power into our lives. Then we can enjoy the miracle.

POWER BUILDER

CARYLE HAMNER

Chief Petty Officer, U.S. Navy

DURING WORLD WAR II, Caryle Hamner was serving aboard a submarine, the *Halibut*, in the Aleutian Islands. The sub had been spotted by Japanese planes, which were circling overhead. The horn signaled a dive, and the ship plunged past the tested undersea depth, 350 feet, to 362 feet. The tremendous pressure on the vessel was especially unnerving to Hamner, who was not a seasoned submariner. He knew the ship couldn't stay down there forever. He was also aware that the *Halibut* had used up nearly all its torpedoes.

Shaken by his circumstances, he silently prayed, "Lord, will we make it through, or is this the end?" He walked to his locker, opened it, and took out his daily devotional book. The Scripture for that particular day was from Isaiah 43:2: "When thou passest through the waters, I will be with thee" (KJV). An accompanying poem read, in part, "When thou comest to the waters, thou shalt not go down BUT THROUGH." Hamner closed the book, stowed it in his locker, and returned to his post. He released his fears, convinced that God had answered his question.

Minutes later, the captain ordered the ship up to periscope depth. After surveying the situation, he gave orders to surface. The *Halibut* emerged into a blizzard—no plane could possibly see the sub, and there were no ships in the area. They headed back toward Midway Island, safe and sound.

POINTS TO PONDER

Once we have received God's promise about a specific situation, we are able to let it go. We may question our hearing, we may wonder if we have put words in God's mouth, but despite our doubts, releasing the circumstances is much easier because we feel He has spoken. He speaks many ways, through many voices. But His Word is truth, and when He speaks, we can safely let go, assured that we can count on Him.

POWER QUOTE

When God speaks, it is our cue to stop striving and start trusting.

SCRIPTURE

Hebrews 11:1

Faith makes us sure of what we hope for and gives us proof of what we cannot see.

CINDY ANDERSON

Christian Mother

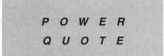

POWER BUILDER

POWER
QUOTE

In a crisis, we must look to
God's power.

WHEN ERIK ANDERSON WAS a newborn, he developed a life-threatening inflammation of the heart muscle called acute myocarditis. Nearly one-third of the children who develop the condition die.

Cindy, Erik's mom, made it through the first few days with courage and hope. The baby seemed to be doing better, and while he slept, she ventured into the hospital chapel. Just then she was given the news: "Erik went into cardiac arrest 30 minutes ago. We've been unable to resuscitate him. I'm so sorry."

Cindy and Jim Anderson were unaware of the heroic measures that were still taking place around the tiny infant. Fifteen minutes later, the doctor returned: "There's been a major change—Erik is alive. But we're not getting any neurological response."

When Jim and Cindy saw the baby, his chest was punctured and bloodied, his mouth fixed open in what looked like a scream, and his eyes unblinking and dilated. "He's worse than dead," Cindy said to herself. "He's ruined." She thought of ripping away all the life-support equipment and holding the battered baby in her arms. Instead, she wrapped her fingers around his and began to sing to him.

She said, "Suddenly I knew Erik's life was on a course unchangeable by human hands. Understanding that, on that most terrible of nights, set me free." From that moment on, Erik began to improve. His heart began to work. His mind began to function. Erik Anderson is not only alive, he is perfectly healthy.

SCRIPTURE

Isaiah 40:27

[You] say, "God pays no atten-

tion to us! He doesn't care if we

are treated unjustly." But how

can you say that?

Wednesday
Week
49

POINTS TO PONDER

In a traumatic situation, when we finally come to the end of ourselves, we speak some variation of a simple prayer: "Thy will be done." And we enter into the "peace that passes understanding." God will accomplish His will, and He will give us the strength to accept it. In that moment of release, that's all we need to know.

POWER BUILDER

MIKE GARTNER

Professional Hockey Player

MIKE GARTNER RECEIVED THE Washington Capitols Most Valuable Player Award during his rookie year in the NHL. But as his success continued, he felt unfulfilled: "Nobody had ever told me I couldn't find fulfillment in a large salary, nice home, and luxurious car. A vast void remained that I couldn't understand. Some would call it luck or circumstance, but I believe the Lord arranged for Jean Pronovost to join our team that year."

Jean ranked among the league's top twenty-five goal scorers. Not only did he teach Mike some of his skills, but he impressed him with his level-headed nature and pleasant manner. When Jean and his wife invited Mike and his roommate to a Bible study in their home, he agreed to go.

Mike comments, "Jean had already been talking to me and sharing different Scriptures while I bombarded him with questions." Finally, during a road trip, Jean asked Mike a powerful question: "Mike, if this plane went down and you died right now, would you go to heaven or hell?"

Mike says, "In the middle of that road trip, I knelt in my hotel room and said, 'Lord, if You're real, come into my life right now and change me.'" The void in Mike Gartner's life has been forever filled by the presence of Jesus.

Thursday
Week

49

POWER QUOTE

Jesus makes it possible for God's Spirit to fill us with His power and his presence.

SCRIPTURE

Acts 16:31

Have faith in the Lord Jesus and you will be saved! This is also true for everyone who lives in your home.

POINTS TO PONDER

Receiving Jesus into our lives is the most significant way we release ourselves to the power of God. Until we choose to accept His forgiveness and place ourselves under His authority, however, we are serving ourselves. The void Mike Gartner felt so acutely is present in every person. It is an emptiness that can be filled only by the presence of God. But God's presence cannot live within us unless we relinquish our rights to Him, allowing Him to be both Savior and Lord. Without letting go of the controls, we cannot escape the void.

POWER BUILDER

DOUG SUTPHEN

Chinese Missions Worker

We have the right to call ourselves God's children, and He has promised to care for His children with wisdom, love, and grace.

SCRIPTURE

Romans 15:13

I pray that God, who gives hope, will bless you with complete happiness and peace because of your faith. And may the power of the Holy Spirit fill you with hope.

Friday
Week

49

DOUG SUTPHEN (ALSO KNOWN as Brother David) has worked for many years among China's Christians, particularly those involved in the house church movement. He once talked to a man who suffered for decades in a Chinese prison, where he was placed because of his Christian faith. Although the man's body was bent and broken, and he was malnourished, Doug was amazed at his beautiful smile and radiant face. He asked the man why he was so happy after such a terrifying experience.

"God put me in school there. He showed me I needed to learn important lessons. Only then did it become possible for me to live in such an impossible situation," he said.

"How did it become possible?"

"I learned to give up my 'rights'!" the man explained.

Doug thought of the many battles for rights that took place in the Western world—human rights, civil rights, privacy rights, even animal rights.

The man continued, "The Bible doesn't guarantee that we will always live in freedom, so I learned to give up my right to freedom. I gave up my right to live with my family, too. And I gave up my right to earn my way and accumulate wealth.

"In fact, the only right I could find in the Bible was my right to be a child of God. That one I did not give up! . . . When you have died to self, you discover a freedom no man can touch."

POINTS TO PONDER

When we let go of our expectations and our "rights," we allow God to work in our lives unhindered by our resistance. He has made many wonderful promises to us in His Word. Because of His work on the cross, He has bought us as His own. We belong to Him, and in that sense, we give up our rights in exchange for an eternal relationship with Him and everlasting enjoyment of His best blessings.

Is THERE ANYTHING IN your life right now that you know you should release to God's care? Reflect on it for a moment, and record your thoughts.

_____

_____

_____

_____

_____

Weekend
Week

49

Lord,

it's hard for me to let go

of things that matter so much.

My mind says, "Yes, let God have it,"

but my heart rebels, and says, "No!"

I am afraid to lose,

and yet I know that I can't win

by trying to make things work out on my own.

I've done all I can do

to handle this myself.

Lord, please take it from me now.

Your will be done.

POWER BUILDER

GEORGE C. BOLDT
Hotel Manager

WHEN THE OLDER COUPLE arrived in the midst of a miserable storm, the small hotel's clerk began to explain that three separate conventions had filled every room. Then he stopped. "Look, I can't send a nice couple like you out in the rain at 1 o'clock in the morning," he said. "Would you be willing to sleep in my room?"

Reluctantly, the couple agreed. The next morning, the clerk said good-bye to them, and the gentleman remarked, "You're the kind of manager who should be the boss of the best hotel in the United States. Maybe someday I'll build one for you."

The clerk was mildly amused at the man's little joke, and he promptly forgot all about the incident. Several years later, along with a note reminding the clerk of the earlier circumstances, the couple extended an invitation to visit New York and included a round-trip airline ticket.

When the clerk arrived in New York, the man took him to the corner of Fifth Avenue and Thirty-Fourth Street where an elegant new building stood. "That," he said, "is the hotel I have just built for you to manage."

"You must be joking," the clerk stammered. "Who are you?"

"I am William Waldorf Astor."

The hotel was the original Waldorf-Astoria, and its first manager was former hotel clerk George C. Boldt.

POINTS TO PONDER

When we take the time and trouble to care for others, we are showing godly charity. We are also obeying God's instructions and hoping to please Him. We aren't to make a show of our charitable actions—God is the One who watches and approves of the care we provide for others. And He is the One who rewards us, often by giving us greater responsibilities, based on our faithfulness to the smallest tasks that we do for Him.

POWER BUILDER

ARTHUR DA SILVA SANTOS

French Foreign Legionnaire

Ancour DA SILVA SANTOS had served the French Foreign Legion for twenty-two years when he was assigned to work in a Rwandan refugee camp in Goma, Zaire. His mission, according to the Legion, was to relieve suffering. But the job was to assist with the burial of hundreds of bodies in mass graves.

While piling the corpses atop more corpses, Arthur thought he saw an arm move. "Stop!" he ordered the bulldozer. Working carefully, Arthur and the others uncovered a tiny emaciated body. "Thirty seconds later and the boy would have been buried alive," he said.

The child was so wasted that he was unable to stand or to drink. He was carried into the shade, and nationals shook their heads: "Just let him die . . . he's going to die anyway."

Tuesday

Week

50

But Arthur was thinking, *We got this one. He's ours—we're not going to let him go.* He found a jeep, raced to a military hospital, and pleaded for help. The boy was treated, but he was in grave condition, both physically and psychologically. Eventually, however, he rallied. He told his tragic story, which included the loss of his entire family, and he began to warm up to Arthur. One day a television reporter asked Arthur, "Why don't you adopt him?"

"Why not?" said Arthur, "I want this boy to have the same chance I did."

POWER QUOTE

When we express love and concern in the worst possible situations, God encourages us, removes our sorrow, and gives us joy.

SCRIPTURE

Isaiah 61:1

The Spirit of the LORD God has taken control of me! The LORD has chosen and sent me to tell the oppressed the good news.

POINTS TO PONDER

When we allow ourselves to be of service to others, we are doing the works of God. Burying bodies in mass graves is a nightmarish task, but it shows respect for the dead, and it prevents the spread of disease. By participating in a task that reeked of death, Arthur Da Silva Santos found to his surprise that he was given an opportunity to restore life. Our God is the God of the living, not the dead.

KEITH L. BLACK
Neurosurgeon

When we care for each another, we honor God's creation and keep His commandment to love.

SCRIPTURE

Psalm 139:14

I praise you because of the wonderful way you created me. Everything you do is marvelous!

KEITH L. BLACK HAS dedicated himself to perfecting methods of surgery that can remove brain tumors and restore physical capabilities to his patients. And his efforts have earned him the reputation for being a lifesaver and a miracle worker.

Dr. Black marveled at the mystery of consciousness: "What is this whole mind/brain phenomenon?" He struggled with that question for years but could find no answers.

Eventually, Dr. Black set aside his philosophical questions for one reason—he wanted to help people with brain tumors. In the process, he has come to appreciate the human brain. "Scientists are basically art critics, in my view. If you want to understand the artist, look at his art. When I operate and look at the structure of the brain under the microscope, what I'm looking at is God's art," he commented.

Dr. Black's ongoing fascination with the brain and his deep concern for his patients, including their quality of life, have made him nearly legendary in his role as a clutch player in the battle for life and death. Meanwhile, he works tirelessly with researchers toward the development of new therapies that may eventually provide a cure for malignant brain tumors.

Wednesday
Week
50

POINTS TO PONDER

Two things led Dr. Keith Black into his phenomenally successful career—respect for the handiwork of God and compassion for people in pain. His delight in exploring the brain has brought him great success. But his care for people who are sick is the key to his personal fulfillment as both a doctor and a human being.

POWER BUILDER

JOHN GRISHAM
Author

Thursday
Week
50

WHEN JOHN GRISHAM WAS serving in the Mississippi state legislature, he became aware of a case that was taking place in the DeSoto County courthouse. A twelve-year-old girl had been raped, and John listened to her testimony. "I felt everything in those moments," he reported. "Revulsion, total love for that child, hate for that defendant."

Inspired and troubled by the emotions the child's father must have been feeling, John wrote a novel about a father who took violent action against his daughter's rapists. The book was *A Time to Kill.* After a number of rejections, John finally located Wynwood Press, which was willing to print 5,000 copies—and that appeared to be about 4,500 too many. Frustrated with the book's meager sales, John bought up 1,000 copies and started signing and giving them away at libraries and club meetings.

Finally, the book caught on—sparked by John's commitment to its subject matter. The first signed copies of *A Time to Kill* are now collector's items. The book eventually sold 9 million copies and was on the *New York Times* best-seller list for one hundred weeks.

POWER QUOTE

When we do God's work, He enables us to succeed because He does the work through us.

SCRIPTURE

Ecclesiastes 7:8

Something completed is better than something just begun; patience is better than too much pride.

POINTS TO PONDER

What puts the passion in our hearts for a particular cause or concern? Many people of faith believe that God is the One who places the desire within us, and that He then proceeds to enable us to fulfill the desire as He works with us in the situation. One person is stirred up by a need; another is deeply troubled by a crime or an injustice. In all our various calls to action, God is available—helping us right the wrong, meet the need, fight the crime, overcome evil with good.

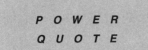

POWER BUILDER

POWER QUOTE

By reaching out to others, we personally bring God's love to a love-hungry world.

SCRIPTURE

1 Corinthians 13:13

For now there are faith, hope, and love. But of these three, the greatest is love.

TWO SISTERS-IN-LAW from the Washington, D.C., area were saddened by a news story about abandoned babies. Lynne and Patty Gartenhaus decided to do something about it.

With their husbands' support, the two women started cutting through red tape, and they initiated the process of establishing a halfway house where babies could be nurtured between birth and placement with an adoptive family. Every aspect of the task required persistence and faith.

Ultimately, their efforts paid off. A mortgage company donated a repossessed house. Civic groups raised money for furnishings and provisions. Friends, family, and neighbors provided clothing, food, furniture, and money. The house was painted blue—a few shades brighter than Patty or Lynne had expected. They commented, "That's how we got our name—'The Little Blue House.'"

The first four babies arrived from General Hospital in late 1991. "These babies had nothing—except us," the women said.

But welcoming arms were precisely what those abandoned babies needed, along with the love that caring volunteers were able to provide. The infants receive around-the-clock care and the early nurturing that is so important for healthy development. The power of love is working miracles in their young lives.

Friday

Week

50

POINTS TO PONDER

God has made it possible for men and women, boys and girls, to do the greatest work in the world—provide love—on His behalf. When homeless babies are cared for, God is loving them through those who cradle and cuddle them. When older people are visited and cheered up, God is loving them through those who share an afternoon. When prisoners are told about Christ's love, He meets them Himself, working through the volunteers who faithfully share the Word. We are God's ambassadors, and whenever we provide love to others, we do it for Him.

IS IT DIFFICULT FOR you to know what to do or when to do it in caring for others? Write your thoughts about caring for others.

_____

_____

_____

_____

_____

Lord,

You have cared for me so powerfully,

providing for my needs,

healing my wounds,

blessing me unexpectedly.

I want to love others with the love

You have shown to me.

Teach me to be caring and thoughtful, Lord.

Soften my heart

and make me more like Jesus.

POWER BUILDER

BART DAILEY
Former CEO, American Marketing Insurance Co.

POWER QUOTE

When we pray, we learn to trust God and to stop leaning on our own understanding.

SCRIPTURE

Psalm 37:10

Sinners will soon disappear, never to be found.

BART DAILEY KNEW ALL he needed to know about management—or so he thought. His businesses had grown into twelve productive and profitable Texas corporations, which dealt with petroleum production, construction, and real estate. However, several corporations were interdependent, and loss of one would severely affect another.

A new president of one company quietly began replacing board members with his own chosen individuals. Soon he had a majority of votes on the board, and new members attacked Bart in the press. Court proceedings followed. Bart was in danger of losing two corporations.

Bart prayed two hours a day, seeking help and guidance: "If You want to take these companies away from me, then it's all right . . . but if You want me to continue, then stop the court proceedings and let what is rightly mine be restored to me."

A trial began and escalated to a critical point. Meanwhile, Bart continued to pray two hours daily. During a strategic part of the trial, his attorney came to him and said, "Bart, they want to call it off!"

As quickly as the attempted takeover had begun, it was over. The new president was removed. The original board was replaced. Bart Dailey says, "Now I know that God can help us in every aspect of our lives, including our business crises . . . even to the point of stopping a hostile take-over in mid-trial."

Monday
Week

51

POINTS TO PONDER

The Bible instructs us to pray persistently, assertively, and confidently. Paul told us to pray with thanksgiving, expressing gratitude in everything. As we continue to present our reasons and plead for His intervention, we grow stronger, both in faith and in our grasp of the situation. In the meantime, He changes minds, alters circumstances, and transforms impossible problems into practical solutions—all in response to our prayers.

POWER BUILDER

RANDY CUTLP

Musician

RANDY CUTLIP DISCOVERED DRUGS as a thirteen-year-old. By the time he was eighteen, he was thoroughly addicted. Years later, he was quietly planning to commit suicide, and he had isolated himself in his house. Then an unusual experience changed the course of his life.

He said, "Suddenly I was aware of something supernatural in the room. A cloud with a white fire was moving toward me. As it moved up my feet and over my body, it felt like warm jelly. I couldn't move."

At that point, everything went black, and Randy fell into a deep sleep—the first time he had slept without the help of drugs for sixteen years. When he awoke, a still, small voice in his mind said, "Stand up." It was the first time in sixteen years he hadn't taken drugs to get out of bed.

Randy took a Bible off his shelf and began to read the passages marked in red—the words of Jesus Christ. Determined to see his life changed once and for all, he went to church where he accepted Christ into his life and was baptized.

Only then did he learn that his aunt had been praying for his salvation for twenty-four years. The power of her love and prayer had overcome Randy Cutlip's addiction and had given him a new beginning.

POWER QUOTE

Intercession touches another life with our love and God's power.

SCRIPTURE

1 Corinthians 14:15

Then what should I do? There are times when I should pray with my spirit, and times when I should pray with my mind.

POINTS TO PONDER

One reason intercessory prayer works is that God's love is the strongest power in the universe, and that love motivates our prayers. When we continue to appeal to God for someone else, pleading for His help in the other person's life for no reason except for concern and compassion, God is invited to unleash the power of His love into the situation. We don't understand how He affects the human will, except that He is persistent and He has limitless means available to reach the lost soul.

POWER BUILDER

TED ENGSTROM
Manager, World Vision

POWER
QUOTE

Human vision, enlivened by God's power, can overcome impossible odds.

SCRIPTURE

James 5:16

The prayer of an innocent person is powerful, and it can help a lot.

WHEN BOB PIERCE ASKED Ted Engstrom to apply emergency management skills to Pierce's floundering ministry, World Vision, Engstrom knew that drastic measures would have to be taken. Pierce was strong in heart, vision, and evangelism, but he was admittedly weak in practical implementation. World Vision's finances were in shambles.

Ted Engstrom had been in top management for years, but he had never encountered a challenge like that one. He was thrust into dramatic emotional ups and downs, confronted with personality clashes, and haunted by seemingly unreachable commitments at home and abroad. Worst of all, Bob Pierce became temporarily estranged from Engstrom as he restructured Pierce's humanitarian organization from the ground up.

Prayer became a way of life to the new World Vision team. From clerks to corporate executives, staff members prayed in pairs, in small clusters, and in boardrooms. From time to time, a memo would circulate "TO: All employees. We are having an all-night prayer meeting tonight. All staff members who care to join us are invited."

Months stretched into years, and gradually the emergency abated. Because of prayer, sound business practices, and hard work, debts were paid off and new growth began. Three decades later, World Vision remains one of the greatest humanitarian institutions worldwide. It stands as a monument to Bob Pierce's evangelistic vision and Ted Engstrom's management skills.

POINTS TO PONDER

Identifying a problem is the beginning of the solution. Devising a strategy is an equally important dimension. Implementing change is crucial. But in the fourth dimension of problem solving—prayer—God's power is channeled into people's plans.

BROTHER ANDREW

Founder, Open Doors

Brother ANDREW IS QUICK to say that prayer can accomplish more than believers could possibly imagine. Brother Andrew's first concern for the persecuted church came during a visit to Warsaw, Poland, in 1955. When he slipped away from his tour group, he got a glimpse of the "real" Poland. His heart broke. Soon thereafter, he was drawn to a verse that would become his source of encouragement: "Be watchful, and strengthen the things which remain" (Rev. 3:2 KJV).

Once Andrew realized that there were practically no Bibles behind the Iron Curtain, he determined that with God's help, he would put Scriptures in the hands of believers. The ministry called Open Doors began, and fasting and prayer soon became the primary weapons of Open Doors' Bible smugglers.

Once Brother Andrew was at the Romanian border. His car was loaded with illegal Bibles, and he grimly watched as the six cars in front of him were unloaded, their contents spread on the ground, and every corner of them searched. In the four hours it took him to reach the guard, Andrew prayed fervently. The armed man glanced at Andrew's papers and waved him on. Breathing grateful prayers, Andrew glanced in his rear-view mirror and saw the car behind him with the trunk open, the hood open, and the driver removed. Only the power of prayer had prevented a search that would have revealed hundred of Bibles.

Thursday

Week

51

POWER QUOTE

Prayer is an expression of our personal relationship with God and a demonstration of our reliance on Him.

SCRIPTURE

John 12:40

The Lord has blinded the eyes of the people, and he has made the people stubborn.

POINTS TO PONDER

We pray daily for our friends and family, asking for protection, peace, and prosperity in their lives. We pray for years for loved ones, asking God to intervene in their spiritual darkness. We pray urgently during crises, knowing that only God can rescue the situation. And we pray in sudden bursts of thanks or need. All these personal prayers reveal that we are aware of God's presence. We believe that He will hear us and answer.

POWER BUILDER

HERBERT HILMER
Businessman

HERBERT HILMER HAD RUN into trouble with his architectural firm. Business was slow, accounts weren't paying, and he was beginning to fear for the future. Because he was a Christian, he turned to God for help. He also asked God for a prayer partner.

The man who called him was out of work and almost without hope. He even admitted to having suicidal thoughts. The two men decided that prayer was the best hope for both of them. They located four more men who needed God's help and agreed to meet once a week, meanwhile praying for each other's needs once a day.

Every week when the six men gathered, they reported more miracles. Jobs were located; children's troubled lives were touched, marriages were mended. Everyone was elated—except for Herbert. His business continued to flounder. Why wasn't God helping him when He seemed to be blessing everyone else?

As the prayer group's success stories spread, more and more men began to attend. Soon there were four groups. Finally, others approached Herbert and asked if he would become a paid full-time director of a men's prayer movement in their city. All at once he understood—his long-hidden desire to be in full-time Christian service was being fulfilled. God had closed one door only to open another, giving him the desire of his heart.

POINTS TO PONDER

Group prayer forces us to confide our needs and desires to others, humbling us, and giving us greater clarity as we speak our concerns aloud. It forges friendships. Group prayer puts to use the promise of power available when "two of you . . . agree about something you are praying for" (Matt. 18:19). And prayer groups join us in the wonderful answers we receive, sharing our amazement, and multiplying our joy.

I F YOU ARE NOT involved in a prayer group, take a moment to list several friends you might consider praying with.

_____

_____

If you are in a group, take a moment to write down each member's name, greatest need, and pause to pray for your group right now.

_____

_____

Lord,

thank You for the people who pray for me

and for the answers I have seen to their prayers.

Thank You for hearing me when I'm afraid

and for comforting me when I tell You my troubles.

Thanks for the countless times You have intervened,

and rescued me from problems—

sometimes problems I created for myself

through disobedience to You.

Teach me to pray more consistently,

more confidently, and more courageously.

Most of all, help me to know You better

and to love You more.

STAN MICKENS
Vietnam Veteran

POWER
QUOTE

Bitterness cannot be hidden forever. Eventually, God will let us see it for what it is, then banish it from our lives.

SCRIPTURE

Colossians 3:13

Put up with each other, and forgive anyone who does you wrong, just as Christ has forgiven you.

Monday
Week

52

STAN MICKENS WAS SENT to Vietnam with thousands of other young Americans. Within five days of his arrival, he had killed innocent people. Horror surrounded him. When his best friend died, he shed no tears. With every death, his heart grew harder. He returned home bitter and nearly suicidal.

Years after the war, Stan had a vision of Jesus, during which He repeatedly asked Stan to take His hand and follow Him. Once Stan obeyed, his life began to change. Eventually, he surrendered himself to God's will, and Vietnam seemed to have happened in another lifetime.

Then came Desert Storm. Stan's close friend mentioned in passing that he thought there was biblical significance to the U.S. invasion of Iraq. Stan says, "All the brutality and insanity of Vietnam flooded back. His defense of killing threw me into a rage. Walking outside to cool off, I asked God why I had almost slugged my best friend. "

'You still have unforgiveness in your heart,' He said.

"'For who?'

"'Your country . . . Vietnam . . . others who hurt you.'

"It took six months to work through it. Yet God led me through each step and even had me praying for Saddam Hussein. It was extremely painful to forgive all those hurts. When I did, a heavy burden lifted from me."

POINTS TO PONDER

We are clever with our bitterness, hiding it from everyone—even from ourselves. Only now and then does it bubble up into our consciousness. Fortunately, God has made our spiritual growth a lifetime process. And when the time is right, He brings us face-to-face with our bitterness and forces us to pardon those who have caused it. We may even have to forgive ourselves.

POWER BUILDER

PETER MILLER

Baptist Pastor

Peter MILLER LIVED DURING the tumultuous years of the American Revolution. He was committed to Christian principles, and he tried to demonstrate them in his daily life. He had few enemies. However, Michael Wittman hated Miller wholeheartedly.

Wittman was mean-spirited, and nearly everyone in the colonial community disliked him. His ruthless behavior got him into trouble—he was accused of treason. Eventually, he was tried, found guilty, and sentenced to death.

Peter Miller, who believed in forgiveness and love above all else, was troubled by the news of Wittman's impending execution. On foot, he traveled seventy miles to Philadelphia to appeal the case to President George Washington. He wanted the president to spare Wittman's life.

Washington responded negatively. "I cannot," he said, "spare the life of your friend."

"My friend?" Miller exclaimed. "Wittman is the bitterest enemy I have!"

George Washington was amazed, and he studied Miller's face carefully. "You've walked seventy miles to save the life of your enemy?" The great president reflected for a moment: "That puts the matter in a different light. I'll grant your pardon."

POINTS TO PONDER

Even though someone hates us, we don't have to respond by hating in return. That reaction isn't appropriate. We are to love our enemies, which means setting aside our natural reactions to their words, attitudes, and actions and choosing to treat them with loving responses. We are to live by a key spiritual principle—love.

POWER QUOTE

It isn't how we feel that matters; it's what we do with the way we feel.

SCRIPTURE

Romans 12:20

If your enemies are hungry, give them something to eat. And if they are thirsty, give them something to drink. This will be the same as piling burning coals on their heads.

STEVE MARIOTTI

Founder, National Foundation for Teaching Entrepreneurship

POWER BUILDER

POWER QUOTE

Jesus forgave us, then He got involved, determined to give us abundant life.

SCRIPTURE

Matthew 5:44

Love your enemies and pray for anyone who mistreats you.

STEVE MARIOTTI WAS BADLY beaten up by a gang of New York City teenagers, all for the $10 he had. While trying to understand what had happened to him, Steve says, "I wondered why kids would do this when they could earn a lot more working legitimately."

Steve, who owned a thriving import-export company, made a decision to bless instead of curse. He set his business aside to teach entrepreneurial skills to impoverished high-school students. His first obstacle came from the schools—no one believed in his idea. Finally, a principal decided to let him try.

In 1986, Steve began the nonprofit National Foundation for Teaching Entrepreneurship (NFTE). Its eighty-hour curriculum is now taught in four New York City high schools and eleven schools in the Mideast, as well as at Columbia University, the University of Pennsylvania, and the University of Southern California.

Students who complete Steve's course gross an estimated $250,000 a year on their businesses—endeavors including hot-dog stands, cleaning and copy services, and a T-shirt company. "These kids have street smarts," Steve says, "which is no different from having business smarts. My fantasy is to teach every inner city kid how to start a company."

POINTS TO PONDER

When a situation arises that clearly indicates a need, the very fact that we have been hurt sometimes helps us provide the best solution. When we forgive, we set aside the circumstances that have wounded us and explore the reasons those circumstances took place. Once we have pardoned people who have hurt us, we may be able to solve the problems that caused them to injure us. That's what Jesus did when He forgave our sins, then began to transform us by renewing our minds.

JULIAN CARROLL
Governor of Kentucky

JULIAN CARROLL FACED SOME of the worst tragedies to strike Kentucky since the Civil War. He dealt with a horrifying fire. He worked around the clock as riots threatened to burn Louisville to the ground. When tornadoes, floods, and violent strikes nearly crippled his state, he was able to handle those crises.

But he couldn't cope with the ordeal his family faced after he left office. By law, Carroll could not run for a second term, so he chose to support a close personal friend who was a candidate for governor. Opponents mounted an all-out attack to destroy Julian Carroll's reputation in order to cripple his support.

Carroll was confronted by a grand jury hearing. He encountered unsubstantiated accusations. After five years of intensive investigation, Carroll was not charged with a single act of wrongdoing. But the experience took its toll. "Bitterness," he wrote, "crept like a repulsive, gangrenous sore."

After an encounter with Jesus, Governor Carroll realized that his bitterness was as great a sin as that of those who had attacked him. Eventually he looked his enemies in the eye, not to say, "I forgive you for what you did to me," but to explain, "I want you to forgive me for hating you."

Julian Carroll discovered the power of forgiveness.

POWER QUOTE

God is righteous—that means He always does the right thing at the right time.

SCRIPTURE

Ephesians 4:31–32

Stop being bitter and angry and mad at others. . . . Be kind and merciful, and forgive others, just as God forgave you because of Christ.

POINTS TO PONDER

When we have been hurt, we have a deep, inner hunger to get even. And when someone has hurt our loved ones, we feel even more justified in seeking revenge. We fear that "they" will get away with their wrongdoing, and that we need to give "them" what they deserve. God doesn't treat any of us the way we deserve to be treated. But He does teach His lessons well, over the course of a lifetime. If we will release the wrongdoers to His care, He will correct the problem at its source while relieving us of our burden of bitterness.

POWER BUILDER

CORRIE TEN BOOM
Author and Speaker

POWER QUOTE

When we forgive, we sign retribution rights over to God. He is then able to forgive our enemies—and us.

SCRIPTURE

Matthew 6:14

If you forgive others for the wrongs they do to you, your Father in heaven will forgive you.

THE HEROIC LIVES OF Corrie ten Boom and her Dutch family are well remembered, particularly because of the book and film *The Hiding Place*. Corrie, her sister Betsy, and her father sheltered countless Jews in their home during the Holocaust. The three were arrested by the Gestapo and sent to the Ravensbruck death camp.

Betsy and Corrie heard of their father's death not long after their imprisonment. Then Betsy died, and Corrie appeared to be headed for a similar fate. Then a paperwork "error" caused her to be set free. She enthusiastically dedicated herself to preaching the love of Christ.

In 1947, Corrie returned to Ravensbruck to speak of God's forgiveness to the German people. As a nation, she felt she had released them wholeheartedly from any personal bitterness. Yet God wanted more than that from Corrie.

There she saw the cruelest guard she had encountered at Ravensbruck. The sight of his face painfully evoked to Corrie the unspeakable brutality that had cost her father and sister their lives. Now he was asking her to forgive him. Could she?

She wrote, "It could not have been many seconds that he stood there—hand held out—but to me it seemed hours as I wrestled with the most difficult thing I ever had to do."

Finally, the power of Christ's forgiveness surged through Corrie. She extended her hand. With that agonizing gesture, Corrie ten Boon released herself from the last of Ravensbruck's control over her life. At last she was truly free.

POINTS TO PONDER

Bitterness is a powerful source of energy for many men and women. They use it to make themselves feel strong and to protect themselves from further injury. Bitterness allows them to continue to feel "in control" after a wrong has been done. Forgiveness requires us to give up that control and allow God to deal with the one who has wronged us. It allows Him to change hearts, not to pay back.

W HAT IS THE FIRST situation that comes to your mind when you think of pardoning some-one who has wronged you? Write a few lines about that situation, asking God to guide your thoughts.

_____

_____

_____

_____

_____

Weekend
Week

52

Lord,

You are so good to me,

forgiving me again and again

for things I should have stopped doing

a long time ago.

Lord, teach me to be as forgiving as You are.

Show me how to stop holding grudges,

how to overlook small wounds, and

how to release large wounds to You for healing.

You are so good to me, Lord.

Give me the power to be that good to my enemies

and to unselfishly love my friends and family.

ABOUT THE AUTHOR

Stephen Arterburn is cofounder and chairman of the Minirth Meier New Life Clinics, which has more than one hundred clinics in operation across the nation. He is currently host of the Minirth Meier New Life Clinic radio program with a listening audience of more than one million. He is a nationally known speaker and has been a regular guest on nationally syndicated television talk shows. He is the author or coauthor of eighteen books, including *Winning at Work Without Losing at Love, The Angry Man, Addicted to "Love,"* and *Faith That Hurts, Faith That Heals.* Arterburn holds degrees from Baylor University and the University of North Texas and has been awarded two honorary doctorate degrees. In 1993 he was named Socially Responsible Entrepreneur of the Year by *Inc. Magazine*, Ernst and Young, and Merrill Lynch. Arterburn and his wife, Sandy, and daughter, Madeline, live in Laguna Beach, California.

If you are interested in having Stephen Arterburn speak to your organization or at a special event, please contact:

Stephen Arterburn
P.O. Box 5009
Laguna Beach, CA 92651

714-376-0707
714-494-1272 FAX
SARTERBURN@aol.com

For assistance with personal or emotional problems, call the Minirth Meier New Life Clinics at 1-800-NEW-LIFE.

Winning at Work Without Losing at Love
Stephen Arterburn

You don't have to choose between your family and your career!

In this important book, Stephen Arterburn teaches you how to be a winner in every area of your life and achieve greater success at work and at home.

You'll learn how to:

- avoid the 7 costly mistakes that turn winners into losers
- apply the #1 guaranteed way to move up in any organization without sacrificing the important relationships in your life
- find fulfillment in any position at any salary
- develop the 11 marks of a winner
- build your career without destroying your family
- create your mission for life
- establish a foolproof foundation for success at home and at work

BOOKS BY STEPHEN ARTERBURN

Addicted to "Love" (Servant)

The Angry Man, Arterburn and David Stoop (Word)

The Complete Life Encyclopedia, Arterburn, Frank Minirth, M.D., and Paul Meier, M.D. (Thomas Nelson)

Drug-Proof Your Kids, Arterburn and Jim Burns (Focus on the Family; re-released by Gospel Light)

Faith That Hurts, Faith That Heals (originally titled *Toxic Faith*) Arterburn and Jack Felton (Thomas Nelson)

52 Simple Ways to Say "I Love You," Arterburn and Carl Dreizler (Thomas Nelson)

Gentle Eating, Arterburn, Mary Ehemann, and Vivian Lamphear, Ph.D. (Thomas Nelson)

Growing Up Addicted (Ballantine)

Hand-Me-Down Genes and Second-Hand Emotions (hardcover: Thomas Nelson; paperback as *Hand Me Down Genes*: Simon & Schuster)

How Will I Tell My Mother?, Arterburn and Jerry Arterburn (Thomas Nelson)

The Life Recovery Bible, Arterburn and David Stoop, executive editors (Tyndale)

Miracle Drugs, Arterburn, Frank Minirth, M.D., and Paul Meier, M.D. (Thomas Nelson)

The 12 Step Life Recovery Devotional, Arterburn and David Stoop (Tyndale)

When Love Is Not Enough, Arterburn and Jim Burns (hardcover: Focus on the Family; paperback as *Steering Them Straight*: Focus on the Family)

When Someone You Love Is Someone You Hate, Arterburn and David Stoop (Word)

Winning at Work Without Losing at Love (Thomas Nelson)

If you can't find one of these books in your local bookstore, you can order it through 1-800-BOOKS45.

To purchase the *Finding the Power to Win* audio and video series, phone 1-800-528-3825.